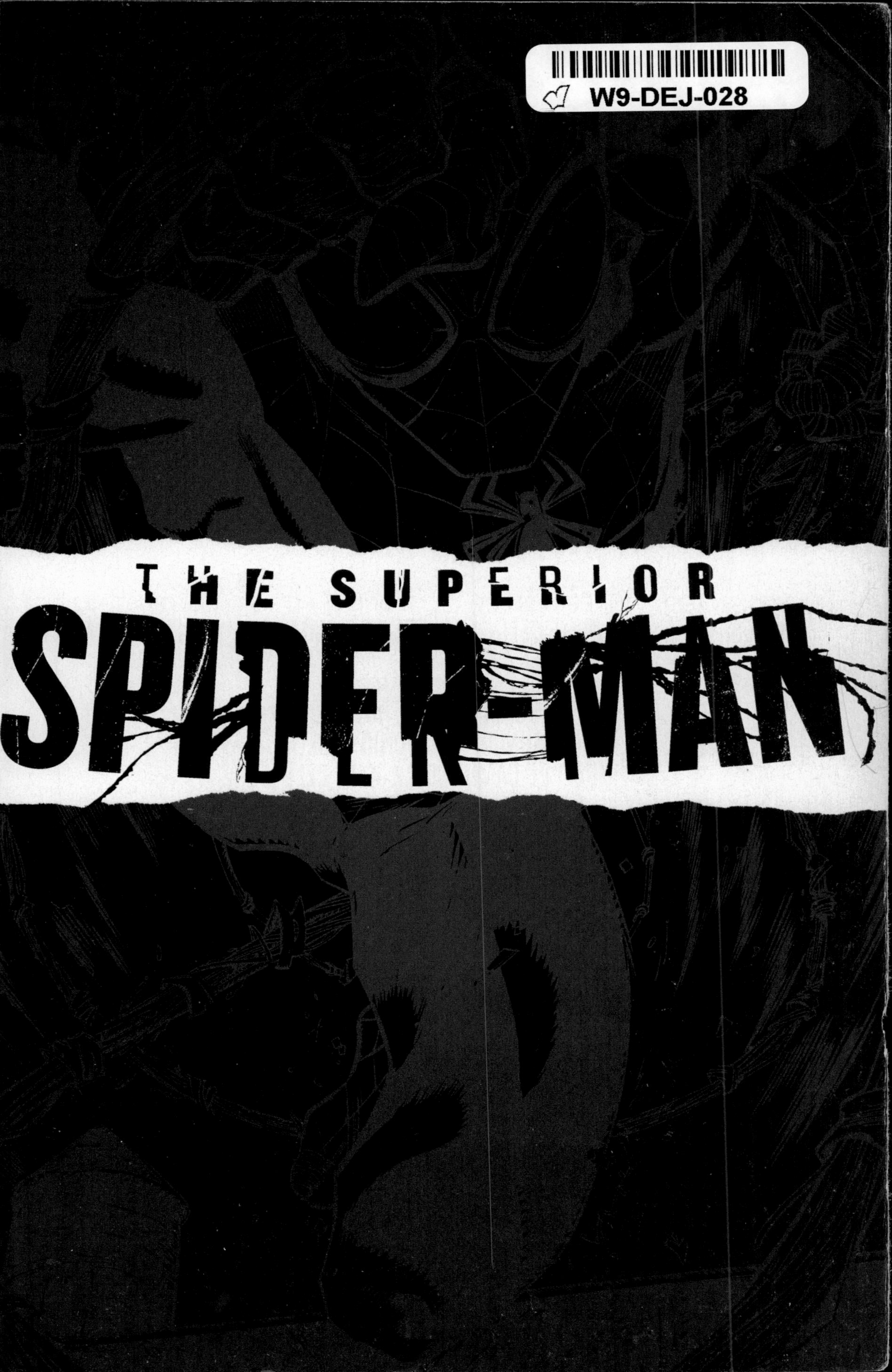
THE SUPERIOR
SPIDER-MAN

THE SUPERIOR SPIDER-MAN
NECESSARY EVIL

WRITER
DAN SLOTT

PENCILER, #17-19
RYAN STEGMAN

PENCILER, #20-21
GIUSEPPE CAMUNCOLI

INKERS, #17-19
LIVESAY

INKER, #20-21
JOHN DELL

COLORIST, #17-19
EDGAR DELGADO

COLORIST, #20-21
ANTONIO FABELA

COVER ART
RYAN STEGMAN & JASON HOWARD (#17-19),
GIUSEPPE CAMUNCOLI & ANTONIO FABELA (#20) AND
GIUSEPPE CAMUNCOLI & JOHN DELL (#21)

LETTERER
VC'S CHRIS ELIOPOULOS

ASSISTANT EDITOR
ELLIE PYLE

EDITOR
STEPHEN WACKER

Collection Editor: **Jennifer Grünwald** • Assistant Editors: **Alex Starbuck & Nelson Ribeiro** • Editor, Special Projects: **Mark D. Beazley**
Senior Editor, Special Projects: **Jeff Youngquist** • SVP of Print & Digital Publishing Sales: **David Gabriel** • Book Design: **Jeff Powell**

Editor in Chief: **Axel Alonso** • Chief Creative Officer: **Joe Quesada** • Publisher: **Dan Buckley** • Executive Producer: **Alan Fine**

SUPERIOR SPIDER-MAN VOL. 4: NECESSARY EVIL. Contains material originally published in magazine form as SUPERIOR SPIDER-MAN #17-21. First printing 2014. ISBN# 978-0-7851-8473-7. Published by MARVEL WORLDWIDE, INC., a subsidiary of MARVEL ENTERTAINMENT, LLC. OFFICE OF PUBLICATION: 135 West 50th Street, New York, NY 10020. Copyright © 2013 and 2014 Marvel Characters, Inc. All rights reserved. All characters featured in this issue and the distinctive names and likenesses thereof, and all related indicia are trademarks of Marvel Characters, Inc. No similarity between any of the names, characters, persons, and/or institutions in this magazine with those of any living or dead person or institution is intended, and any such similarity which may exist is purely coincidental. **Printed in Canada.** ALAN FINE, EVP - Office of the President, Marvel Worldwide, Inc. and EVP & CMO Marvel Characters B.V.; DAN BUCKLEY, Publisher & President - Print, Animation & Digital Divisions; JOE QUESADA, Chief Creative Officer; TOM BREVOORT, SVP of Publishing; DAVID BOGART, SVP of Operations & Procurement, Publishing; C.B. CEBULSKI, SVP of Creator & Content Development; DAVID GABRIEL, SVP of Print & Digital Publishing Sales; JIM O'KEEFE, VP of Operations & Logistics; DAN CARR, Executive Director of Publishing Technology; SUSAN CRESPI, Editorial Operations Manager; ALEX MORALES, Publishing Operations Manager; STAN LEE, Chairman Emeritus. For information regarding advertising in Marvel Comics or on Marvel.com, please contact Niza Disla, Director of Marvel Partnerships, at ndisla@marvel.com. For Marvel subscription inquiries, please call 800-217-9158. **Manufactured between 11/22/2013 and 12/30/2013 by SOLISCO PRINTERS, SCOTT, QC, CANADA.**

10 9 8 7 6 5 4 3 2 1

17

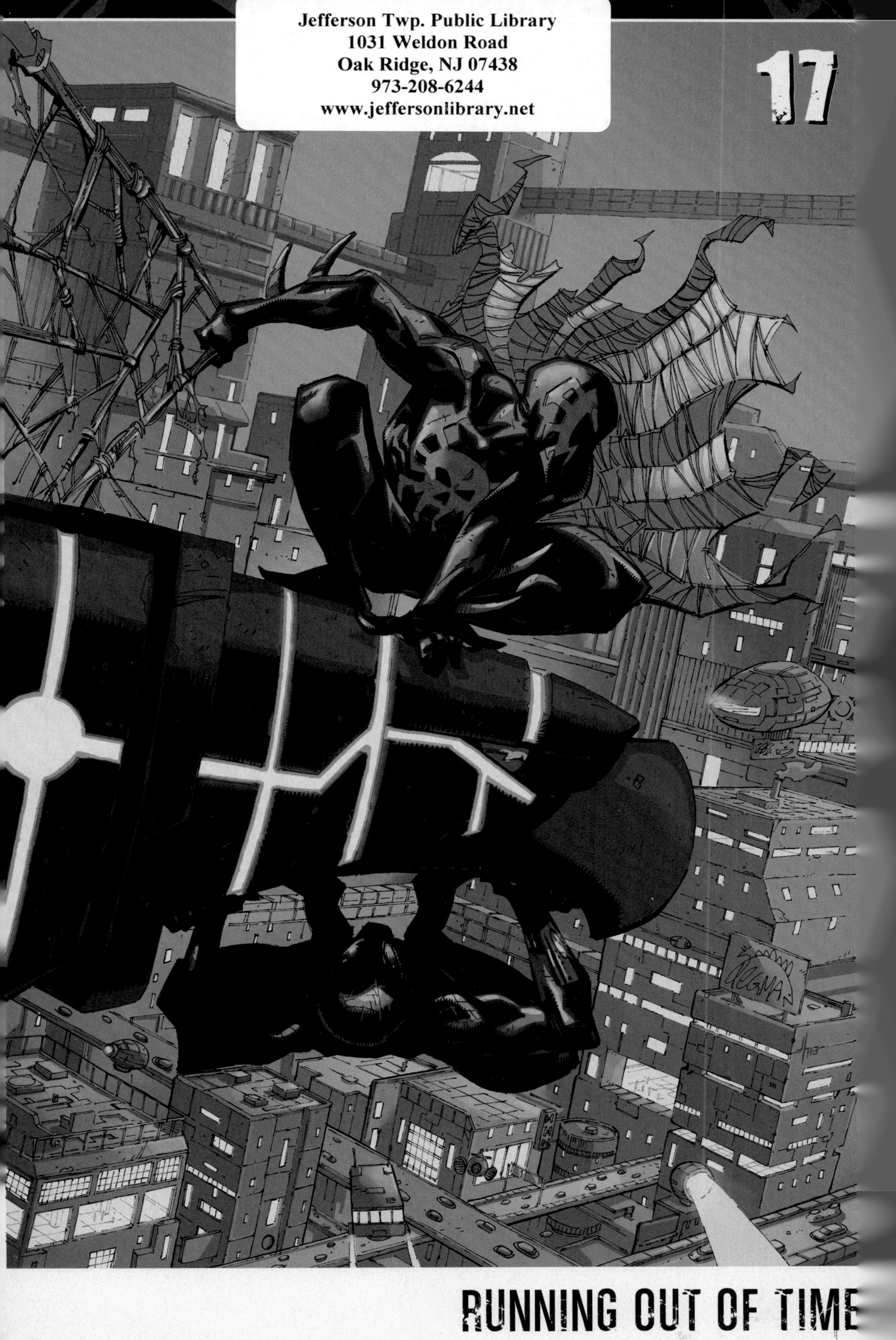

RUNNING OUT OF TIME

F★★★★ FINAL

DAILY 🎺 BUGLE ®

NEW YORK'S FINEST DAILY NEWSPAPER

SINCE 1897
★★★
$1.00 (in NY)
$1.50 (outside

INSIDE: SCARLET SPIDER PAINTS NEW YORK RED, SPIDEY AND NOVA TAKE MANHATTAN, POSSIBLE GOBLIN SIGHTI

LET'S DO THE TIME WARP AGAIN

All across the world, rifts in the space-time continuum continue to appea. These rifts are believed to be the result of The Avengers' recent tamperin with time travel. No word on when these rifts will cease. Interviews wit Horizon Labs specialists on the subject matter inside.

The Daily Bugle is deeply sorry to report that staff writer Norah Winters has been let go due to her ties to recent tragedies. Ms. Winters is an extremely gifted writer, and we wish her the best of luck in the future.

When you see this: **AR**, open up the MARVEL AR APP (available on applicable Apple ® iOS or Android ™ devices) and use your camera-enabled device to unlock extra-special exclusive features!*

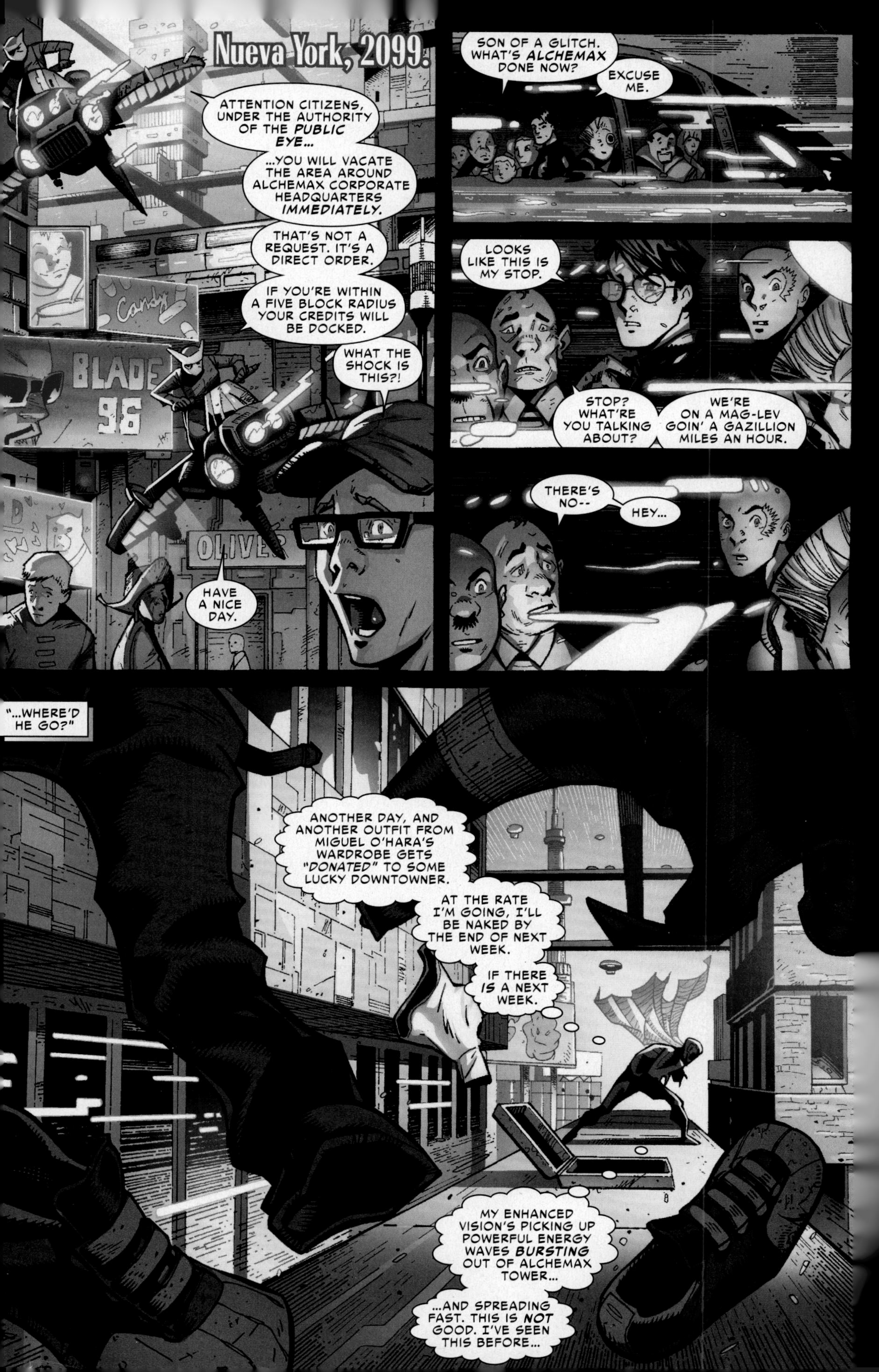
Nueva York, 2099.
ATTENTION CITIZENS, UNDER THE AUTHORITY OF THE PUBLIC EYE...
...YOU WILL VACATE THE AREA AROUND ALCHEMAX CORPORATE HEADQUARTERS IMMEDIATELY.
THAT'S NOT A REQUEST. IT'S A DIRECT ORDER.
IF YOU'RE WITHIN A FIVE BLOCK RADIUS YOUR CREDITS WILL BE DOCKED.
WHAT THE SHOCK IS THIS?!
HAVE A NICE DAY.
Candy
BLADE 96
OLIVE
SON OF A GLITCH. WHAT'S ALCHEMAX DONE NOW?
EXCUSE ME.
LOOKS LIKE THIS IS MY STOP.
STOP? WHAT'RE YOU TALKING ABOUT?
WE'RE ON A MAG-LEV GOIN' A GAZILLION MILES AN HOUR.
THERE'S NO--
HEY...
"...WHERE'D HE GO?"
ANOTHER DAY, AND ANOTHER OUTFIT FROM MIGUEL O'HARA'S WARDROBE GETS "DONATED" TO SOME LUCKY DOWNTOWNER.
AT THE RATE I'M GOING, I'LL BE NAKED BY THE END OF NEXT WEEK.
IF THERE IS A NEXT WEEK.
MY ENHANCED VISION'S PICKING UP POWERFUL ENERGY WAVES BURSTING OUT OF ALCHEMAX TOWER...
...AND SPREADING FAST. THIS IS NOT GOOD. I'VE SEEN THIS BEFORE...

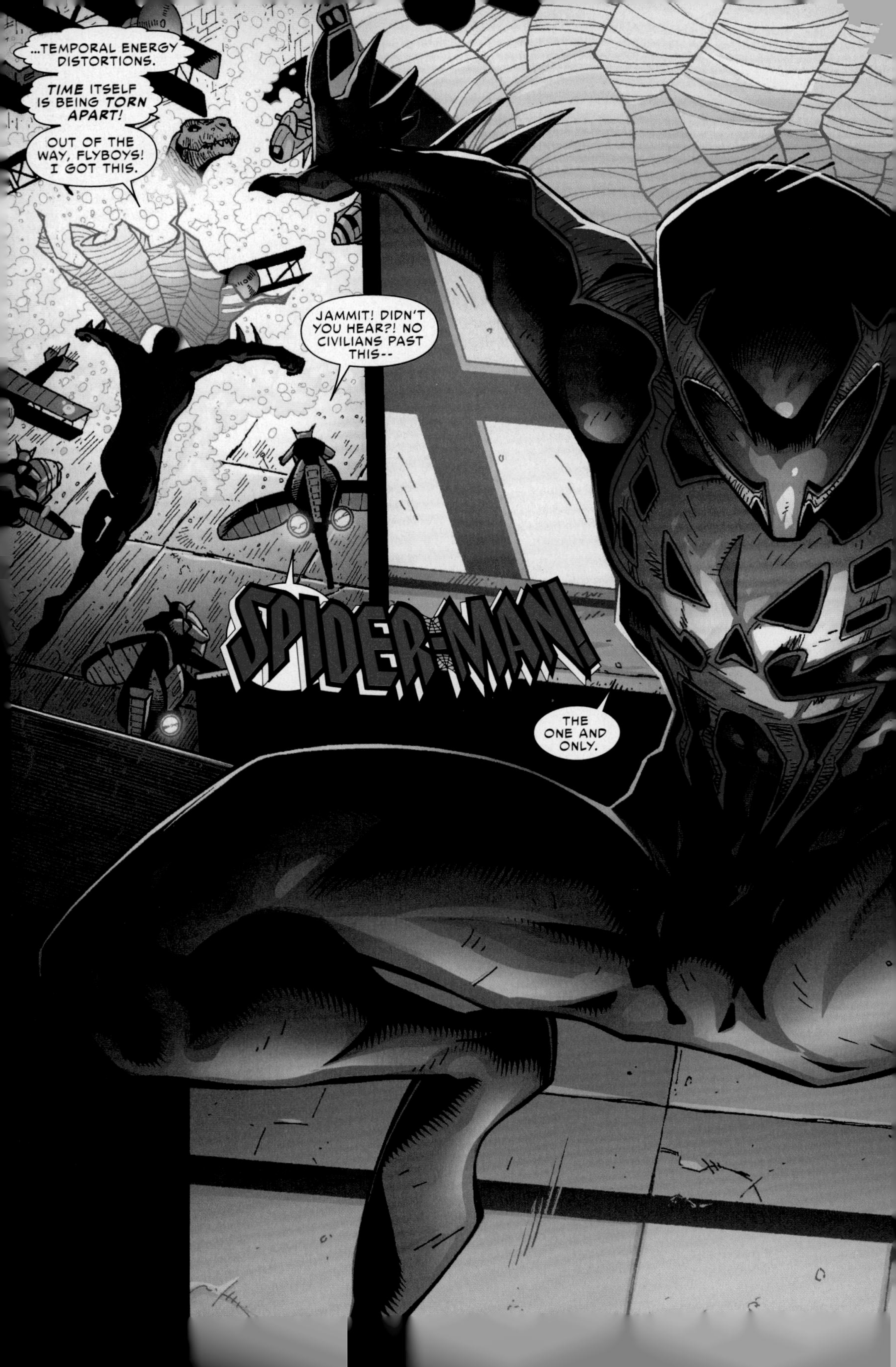
...TEMPORAL ENERGY DISTORTIONS.
TIME ITSELF IS BEING TORN APART!
OUT OF THE WAY, FLYBOYS! I GOT THIS.
JAMMIT! DIDN'T YOU HEAR?! NO CIVILIANS PAST THIS--
SPIDER-MAN!
THE ONE AND ONLY.

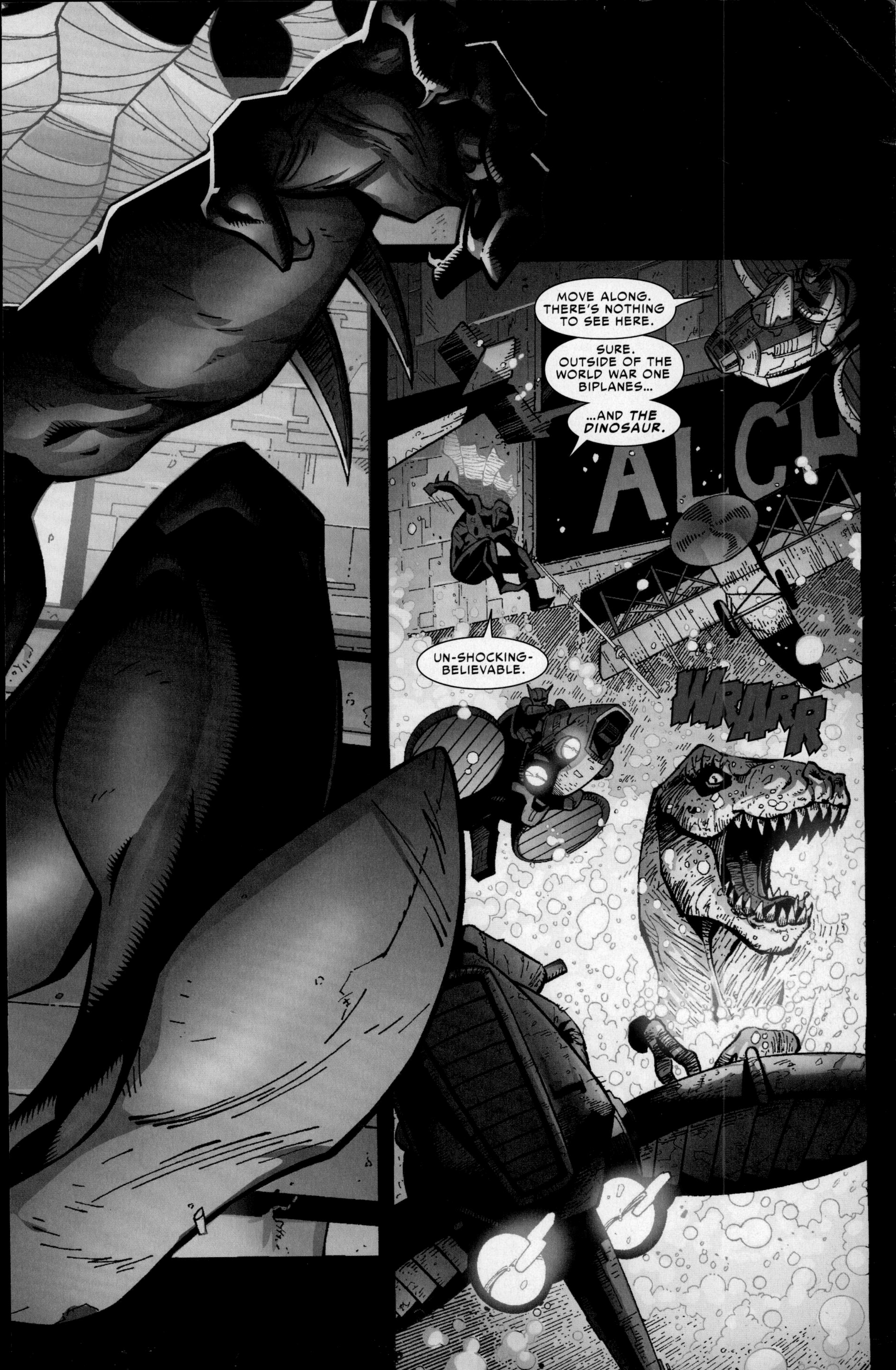
MOVE ALONG. THERE'S NOTHING TO SEE HERE.
SURE. OUTSIDE OF THE WORLD WAR ONE BIPLANES...
...AND *THE DINOSAUR*.
ALCH
UN-SHOCKING-BELIEVABLE.
WRARR

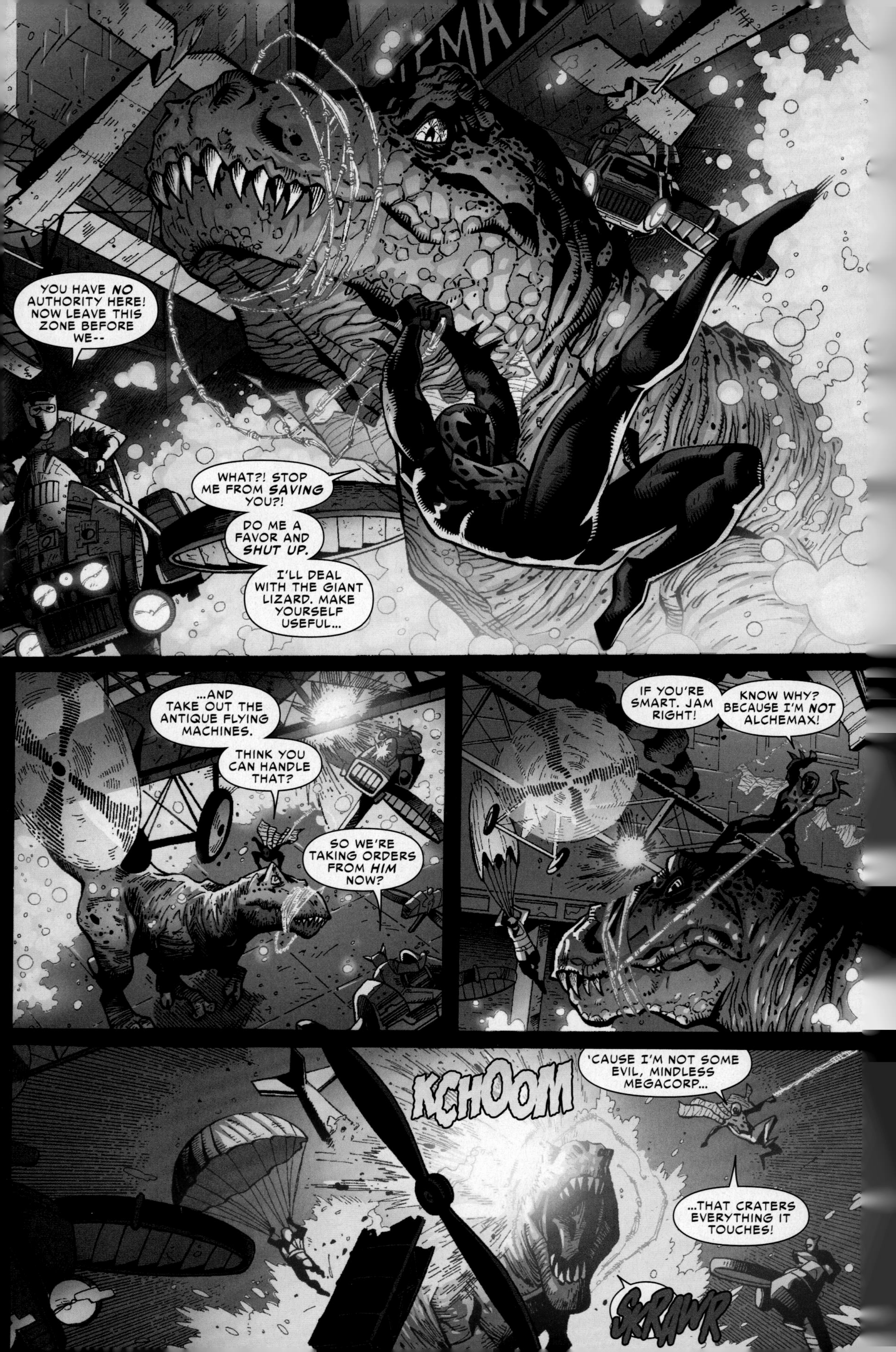

YOU HAVE NO AUTHORITY HERE! NOW LEAVE THIS ZONE BEFORE WE--
WHAT?! STOP ME FROM SAVING YOU?!
DO ME A FAVOR AND SHUT UP.
I'LL DEAL WITH THE GIANT LIZARD. MAKE YOURSELF USEFUL...
...AND TAKE OUT THE ANTIQUE FLYING MACHINES.
THINK YOU CAN HANDLE THAT?
SO WE'RE TAKING ORDERS FROM HIM NOW?
IF YOU'RE SMART. JAM RIGHT!
KNOW WHY? BECAUSE I'M NOT ALCHEMAX!
KCHOOM
'CAUSE I'M NOT SOME EVIL, MINDLESS MEGACORP...
...THAT CRATERS EVERYTHING IT TOUCHES!
SKRAWR

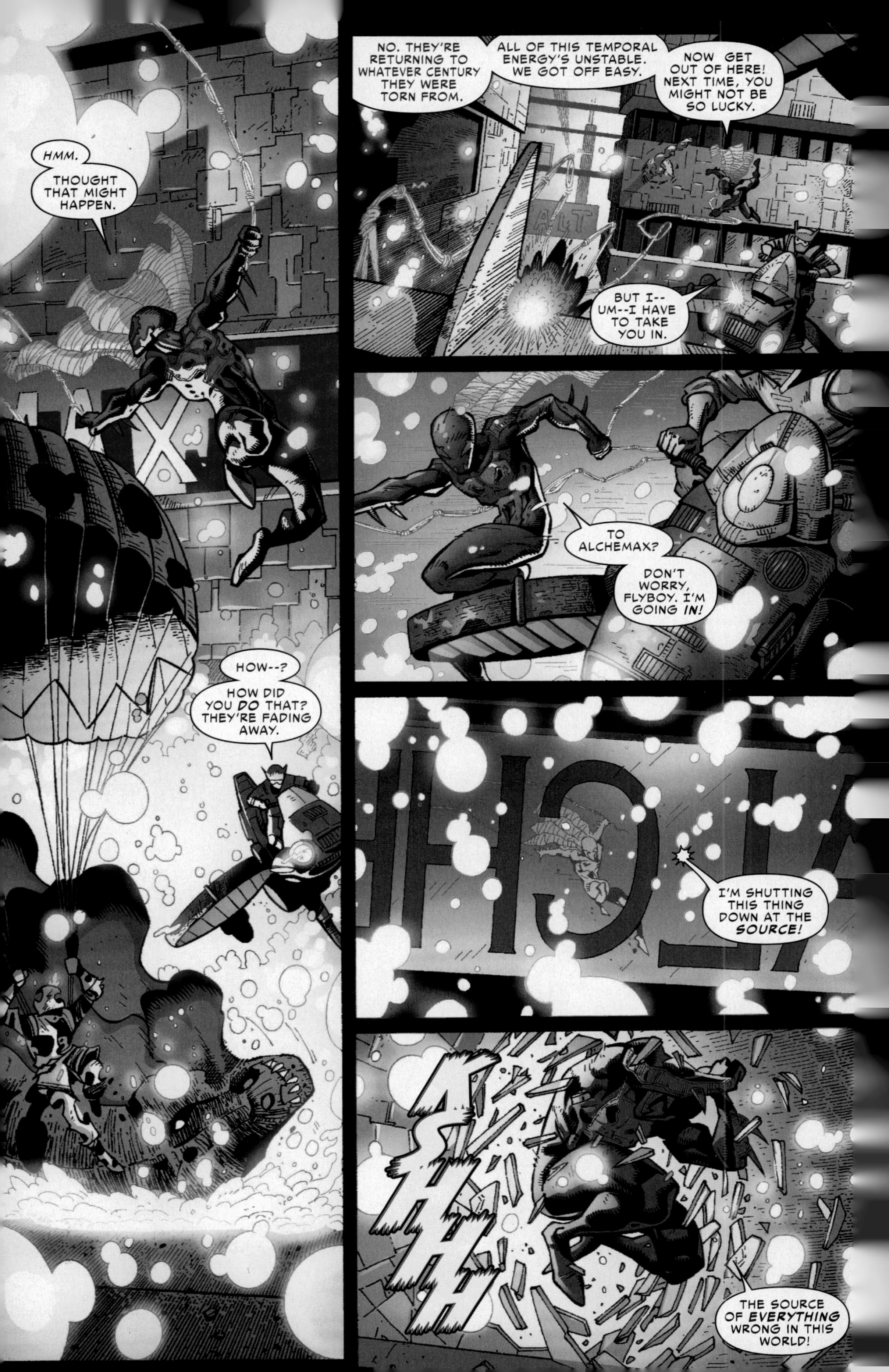
HMM.
THOUGHT THAT MIGHT HAPPEN.
HOW--?
HOW DID YOU DO THAT? THEY'RE FADING AWAY.
NO. THEY'RE RETURNING TO WHATEVER CENTURY THEY WERE TORN FROM.
ALL OF THIS TEMPORAL ENERGY'S UNSTABLE. WE GOT OFF EASY.
NOW GET OUT OF HERE! NEXT TIME, YOU MIGHT NOT BE SO LUCKY.
BUT I--UM--I HAVE TO TAKE YOU IN.
TO ALCHEMAX?
DON'T WORRY, FLYBOY. I'M GOING IN!
I'M SHUTTING THIS THING DOWN AT THE SOURCE!
THE SOURCE OF EVERYTHING WRONG IN THIS WORLD!

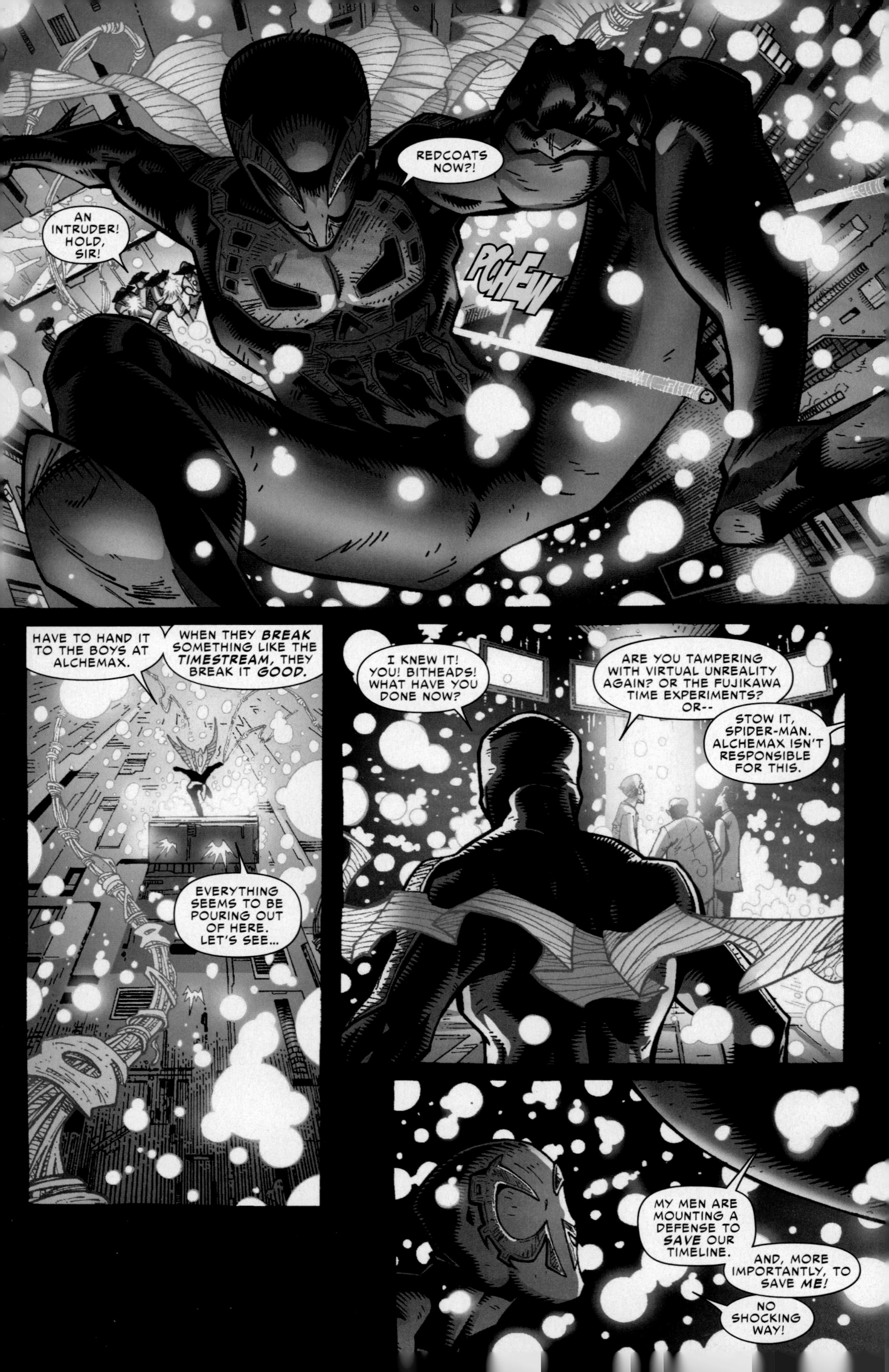
REDCOATS NOW?!
AN INTRUDER! HOLD, SIR!
PCHEW
HAVE TO HAND IT TO THE BOYS AT ALCHEMAX.
WHEN THEY BREAK SOMETHING LIKE THE TIMESTREAM, THEY BREAK IT GOOD.
EVERYTHING SEEMS TO BE POURING OUT OF HERE. LET'S SEE...
I KNEW IT! YOU! BITHEADS! WHAT HAVE YOU DONE NOW?
ARE YOU TAMPERING WITH VIRTUAL UNREALITY AGAIN? OR THE FUJIKAWA TIME EXPERIMENTS? OR--
STOW IT, SPIDER-MAN. ALCHEMAX ISN'T RESPONSIBLE FOR THIS.
MY MEN ARE MOUNTING A DEFENSE TO SAVE OUR TIMELINE.
AND, MORE IMPORTANTLY, TO SAVE ME!
NO SHOCKING WAY!

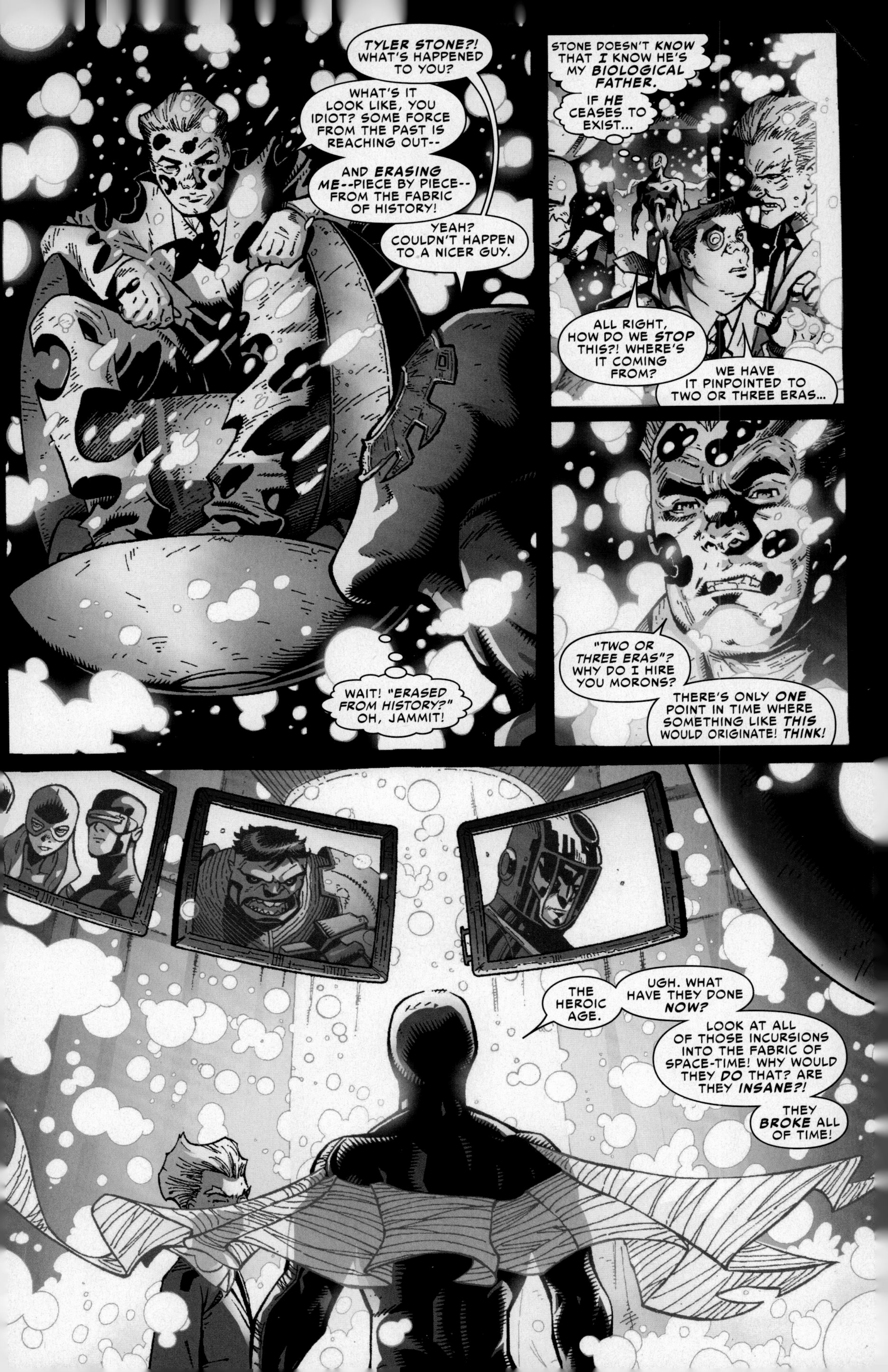
TYLER STONE?! WHAT'S HAPPENED TO YOU?
WHAT'S IT LOOK LIKE, YOU IDIOT? SOME FORCE FROM THE PAST IS REACHING OUT--
AND ERASING ME--PIECE BY PIECE--FROM THE FABRIC OF HISTORY!
YEAH? COULDN'T HAPPEN TO A NICER GUY.
WAIT! "ERASED FROM HISTORY?" OH, JAMMIT!
STONE DOESN'T KNOW THAT I KNOW HE'S MY BIOLOGICAL FATHER.
IF HE CEASES TO EXIST...
ALL RIGHT, HOW DO WE STOP THIS?! WHERE'S IT COMING FROM?
WE HAVE IT PINPOINTED TO TWO OR THREE ERAS...
"TWO OR THREE ERAS"? WHY DO I HIRE YOU MORONS?
THERE'S ONLY ONE POINT IN TIME WHERE SOMETHING LIKE THIS WOULD ORIGINATE! THINK!
THE HEROIC AGE.
UGH. WHAT HAVE THEY DONE NOW?
LOOK AT ALL OF THOSE INCURSIONS INTO THE FABRIC OF SPACE-TIME! WHY WOULD THEY DO THAT? ARE THEY INSANE?!
THEY BROKE ALL OF TIME!

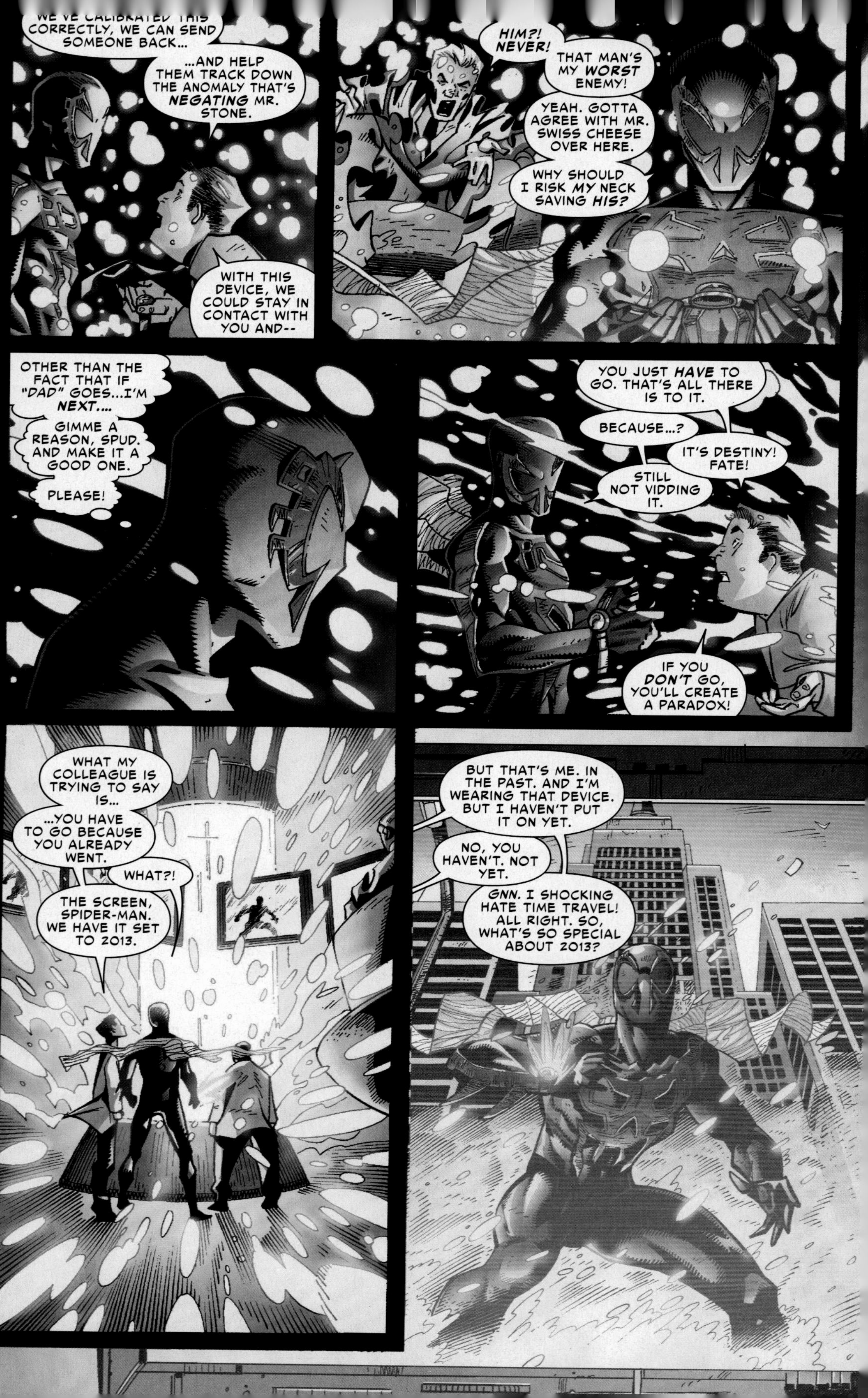
WE'VE CALIBRATED THIS CORRECTLY, WE CAN SEND SOMEONE BACK...
...AND HELP THEM TRACK DOWN THE ANOMALY THAT'S NEGATING MR. STONE.
WITH THIS DEVICE, WE COULD STAY IN CONTACT WITH YOU AND--
HIM?! NEVER!
THAT MAN'S MY WORST ENEMY!
YEAH. GOTTA AGREE WITH MR. SWISS CHEESE OVER HERE.
WHY SHOULD I RISK MY NECK SAVING HIS?
OTHER THAN THE FACT THAT IF "DAD" GOES...I'M NEXT....
GIMME A REASON, SPUD. AND MAKE IT A GOOD ONE.
PLEASE!
YOU JUST HAVE TO GO. THAT'S ALL THERE IS TO IT.
BECAUSE...?
IT'S DESTINY! FATE!
STILL NOT VIDDING IT.
IF YOU DON'T GO, YOU'LL CREATE A PARADOX!
WHAT MY COLLEAGUE IS TRYING TO SAY IS...
...YOU HAVE TO GO BECAUSE YOU ALREADY WENT.
WHAT?!
THE SCREEN, SPIDER-MAN. WE HAVE IT SET TO 2013.
BUT THAT'S ME. IN THE PAST. AND I'M WEARING THAT DEVICE. BUT I HAVEN'T PUT IT ON YET.
NO, YOU HAVEN'T. NOT YET.
GNN. I SHOCKING HATE TIME TRAVEL! ALL RIGHT. SO, WHAT'S SO SPECIAL ABOUT 2013?

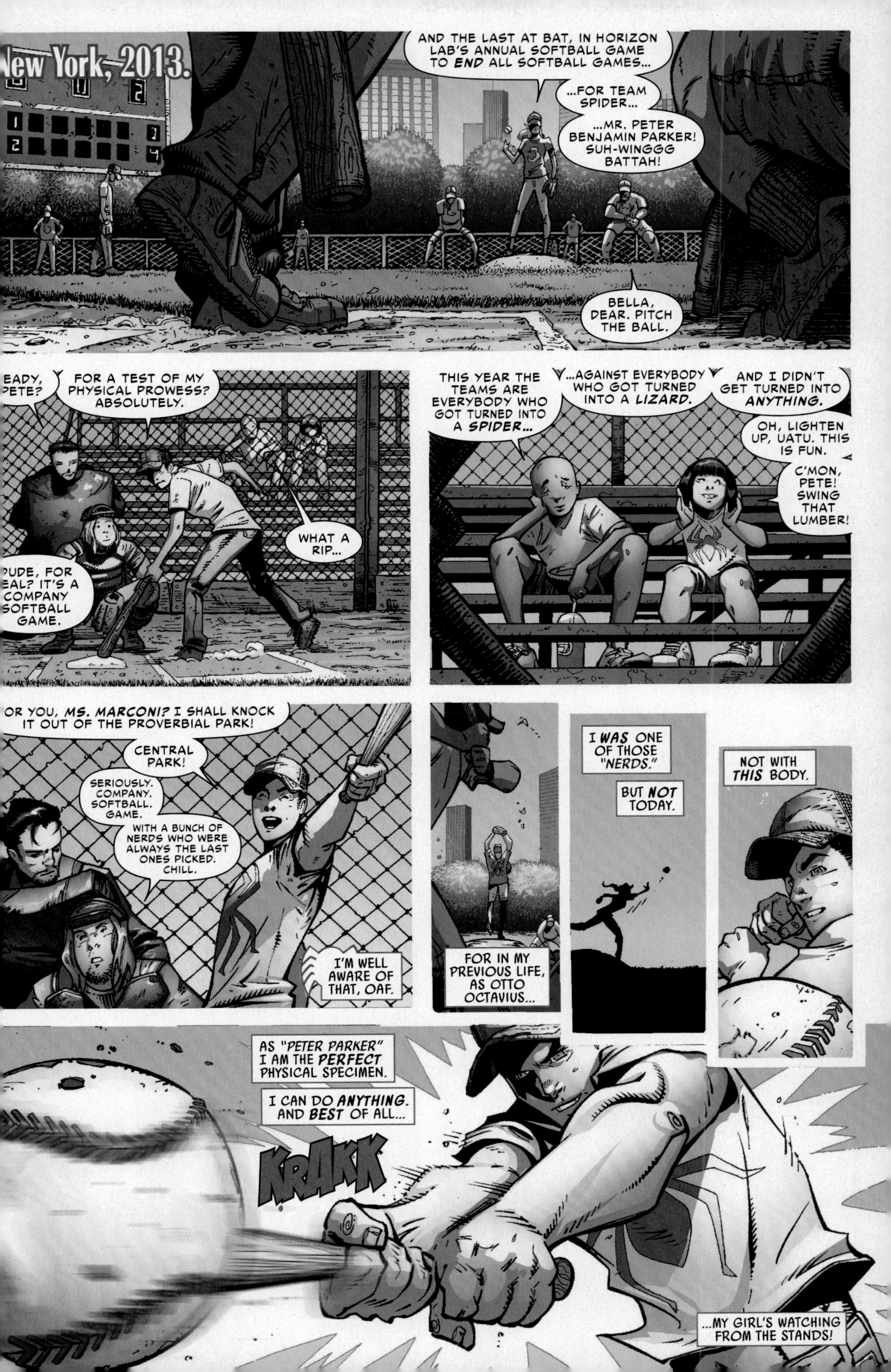

New York, 2013.
AND THE LAST AT BAT, IN HORIZON LAB'S ANNUAL SOFTBALL GAME TO END ALL SOFTBALL GAMES...
...FOR TEAM SPIDER...
...MR. PETER BENJAMIN PARKER! SUH-WINGGG BATTAH!
BELLA, DEAR. PITCH THE BALL.
EADY, PETE?
FOR A TEST OF MY PHYSICAL PROWESS? ABSOLUTELY.
WHAT A RIP...
UDE, FOR EAL? IT'S A COMPANY SOFTBALL GAME.
THIS YEAR THE TEAMS ARE EVERYBODY WHO GOT TURNED INTO A SPIDER...
...AGAINST EVERYBODY WHO GOT TURNED INTO A LIZARD.
AND I DIDN'T GET TURNED INTO ANYTHING.
OH, LIGHTEN UP, UATU. THIS IS FUN.
C'MON, PETE! SWING THAT LUMBER!
OR YOU, MS. MARCONI? I SHALL KNOCK IT OUT OF THE PROVERBIAL PARK!
CENTRAL PARK!
SERIOUSLY. COMPANY. SOFTBALL. GAME.
WITH A BUNCH OF NERDS WHO WERE ALWAYS THE LAST ONES PICKED. CHILL.
I'M WELL AWARE OF THAT, OAF.
FOR IN MY PREVIOUS LIFE, AS OTTO OCTAVIUS...
I WAS ONE OF THOSE "NERDS."
BUT NOT TODAY.
NOT WITH THIS BODY.
AS "PETER PARKER" I AM THE PERFECT PHYSICAL SPECIMEN.
I CAN DO ANYTHING. AND BEST OF ALL...
KRAKK
...MY GIRL'S WATCHING FROM THE STANDS!

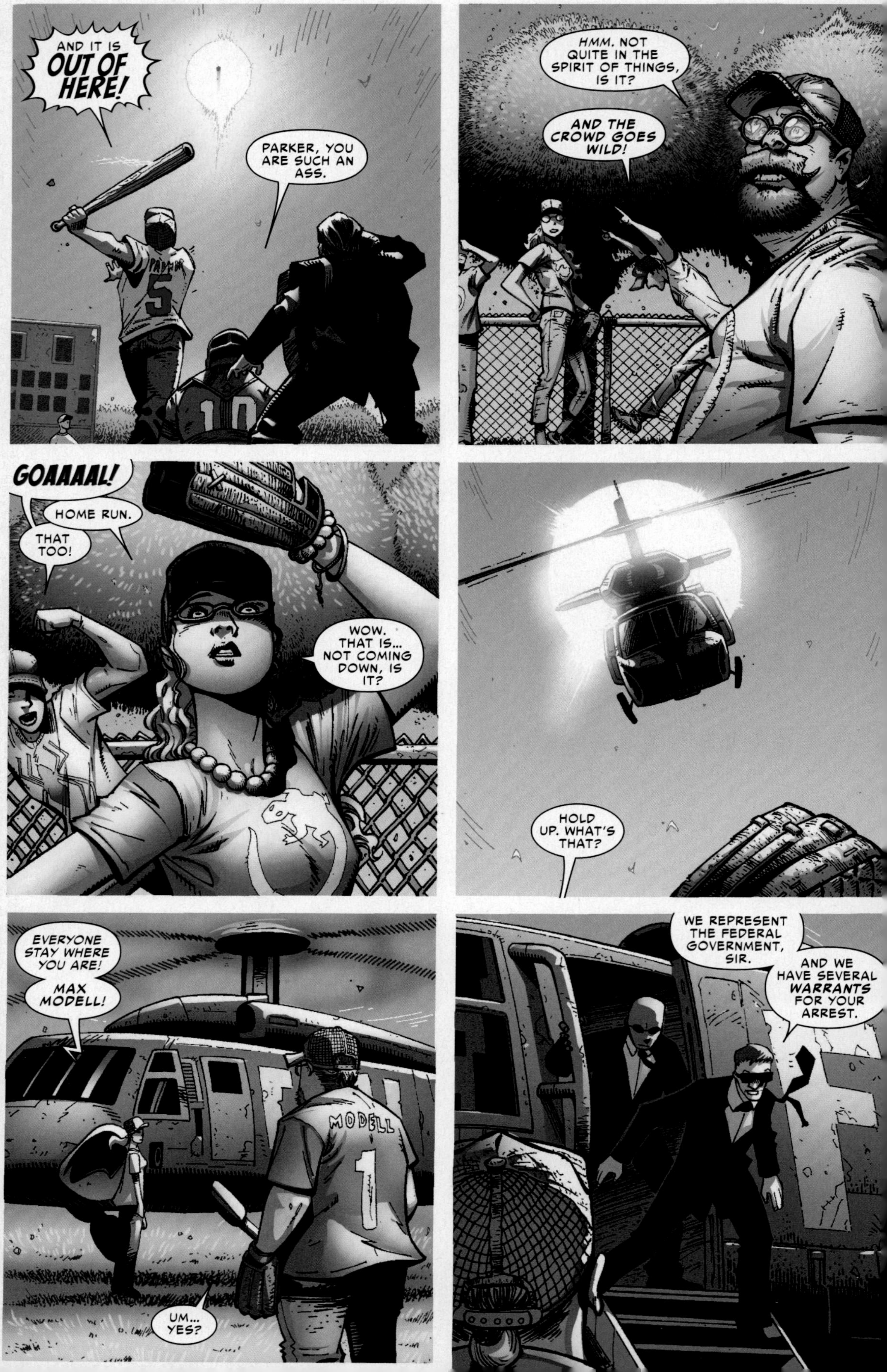
AND IT IS OUT OF HERE!
PARKER, YOU ARE SUCH AN ASS.
HMM. NOT QUITE IN THE SPIRIT OF THINGS, IS IT?
AND THE CROWD GOES WILD!
GOAAAAL!
HOME RUN.
THAT TOO!
WOW. THAT IS... NOT COMING DOWN, IS IT?
HOLD UP. WHAT'S THAT?
EVERYONE STAY WHERE YOU ARE!
MAX MODELL!
MODELL
1
UM... YES?
WE REPRESENT THE FEDERAL GOVERNMENT, SIR.
AND WE HAVE SEVERAL WARRANTS FOR YOUR ARREST.

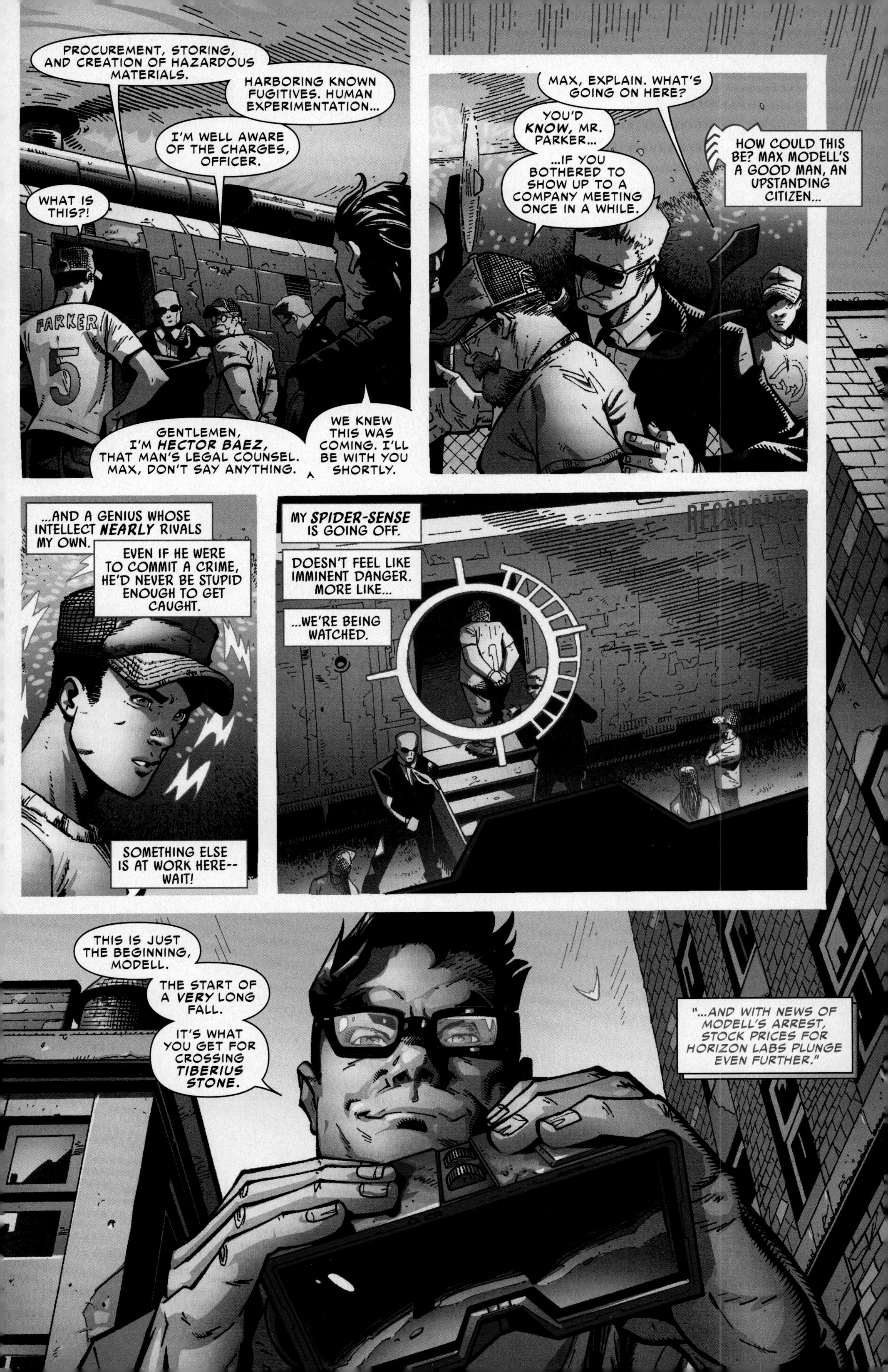
PROCUREMENT, STORING, AND CREATION OF HAZARDOUS MATERIALS.
HARBORING KNOWN FUGITIVES. HUMAN EXPERIMENTATION...
I'M WELL AWARE OF THE CHARGES, OFFICER.
WHAT IS THIS?!
PARKER
5
GENTLEMEN, I'M HECTOR BAEZ, THAT MAN'S LEGAL COUNSEL. MAX, DON'T SAY ANYTHING.
WE KNEW THIS WAS COMING. I'LL BE WITH YOU SHORTLY.
MAX, EXPLAIN. WHAT'S GOING ON HERE?
YOU'D KNOW, MR. PARKER...
...IF YOU BOTHERED TO SHOW UP TO A COMPANY MEETING ONCE IN A WHILE.
HOW COULD THIS BE? MAX MODELL'S A GOOD MAN, AN UPSTANDING CITIZEN...
...AND A GENIUS WHOSE INTELLECT NEARLY RIVALS MY OWN.
EVEN IF HE WERE TO COMMIT A CRIME, HE'D NEVER BE STUPID ENOUGH TO GET CAUGHT.
SOMETHING ELSE IS AT WORK HERE-- WAIT!
MY SPIDER-SENSE IS GOING OFF.
DOESN'T FEEL LIKE IMMINENT DANGER. MORE LIKE...
...WE'RE BEING WATCHED.
THIS IS JUST THE BEGINNING, MODELL.
THE START OF A VERY LONG FALL.
IT'S WHAT YOU GET FOR CROSSING TIBERIUS STONE.
"...AND WITH NEWS OF MODELL'S ARREST, STOCK PRICES FOR HORIZON LABS PLUNGE EVEN FURTHER."

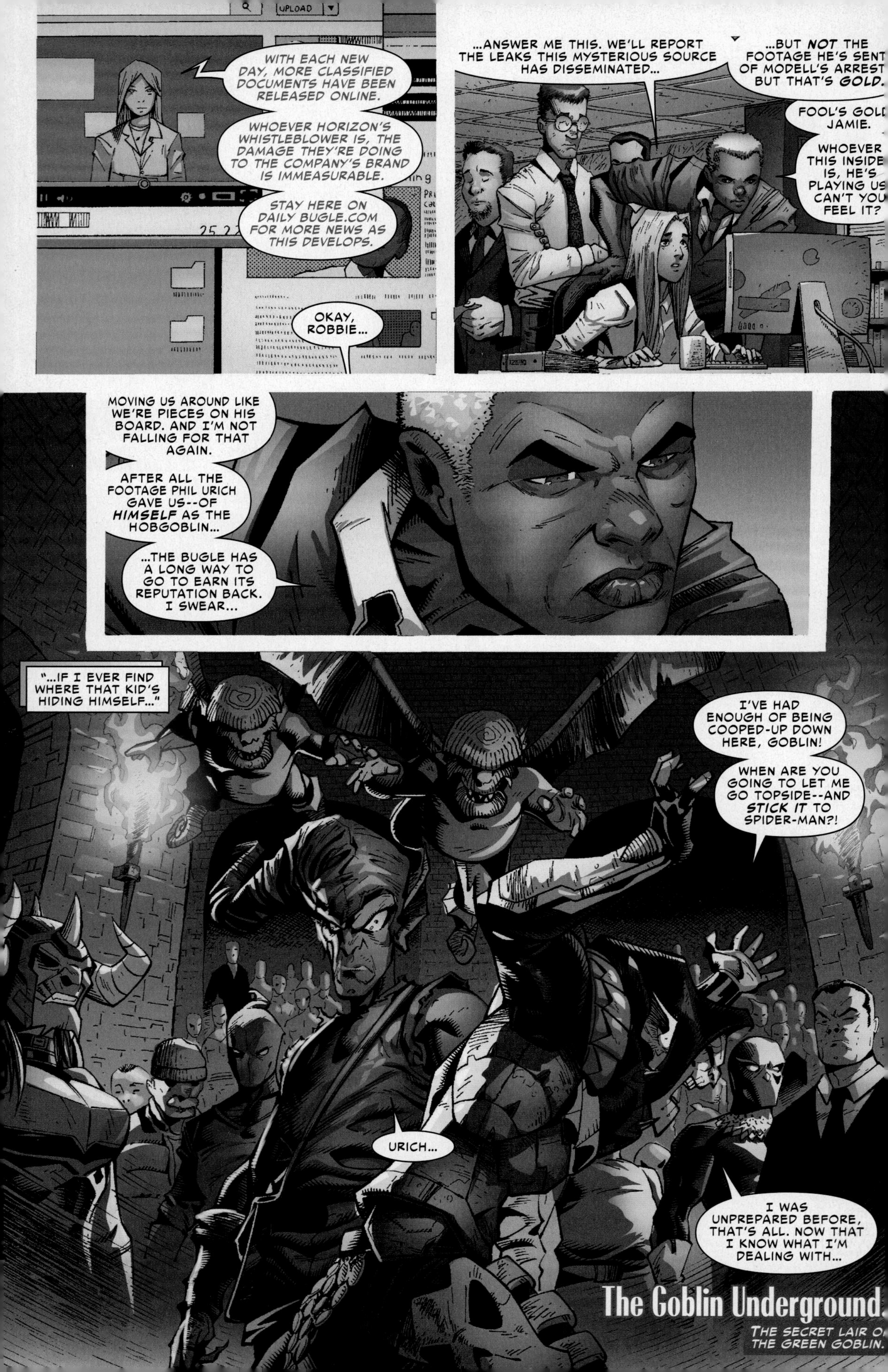
UPLOAD
WITH EACH NEW DAY, MORE CLASSIFIED DOCUMENTS HAVE BEEN RELEASED ONLINE.
WHOEVER HORIZON'S WHISTLEBLOWER IS, THE DAMAGE THEY'RE DOING TO THE COMPANY'S BRAND IS IMMEASURABLE.
STAY HERE ON DAILY BUGLE.COM FOR MORE NEWS AS THIS DEVELOPS.
OKAY, ROBBIE...
...ANSWER ME THIS. WE'LL REPORT THE LEAKS THIS MYSTERIOUS SOURCE HAS DISSEMINATED...
...BUT NOT THE FOOTAGE HE'S SENT OF MODELL'S ARREST BUT THAT'S GOLD.
FOOL'S GOLD JAMIE.
WHOEVER THIS INSIDE IS, HE'S PLAYING US CAN'T YOU FEEL IT?
MOVING US AROUND LIKE WE'RE PIECES ON HIS BOARD. AND I'M NOT FALLING FOR THAT AGAIN.
AFTER ALL THE FOOTAGE PHIL URICH GAVE US--OF HIMSELF AS THE HOBGOBLIN...
...THE BUGLE HAS A LONG WAY TO GO TO EARN ITS REPUTATION BACK. I SWEAR...
"...IF I EVER FIND WHERE THAT KID'S HIDING HIMSELF..."
I'VE HAD ENOUGH OF BEING COOPED-UP DOWN HERE, GOBLIN!
WHEN ARE YOU GOING TO LET ME GO TOPSIDE--AND STICK IT TO SPIDER-MAN?!
URICH...
I WAS UNPREPARED BEFORE, THAT'S ALL. NOW THAT I KNOW WHAT I'M DEALING WITH...
The Goblin Underground.
THE SECRET LAIR OF THE GREEN GOBLIN.

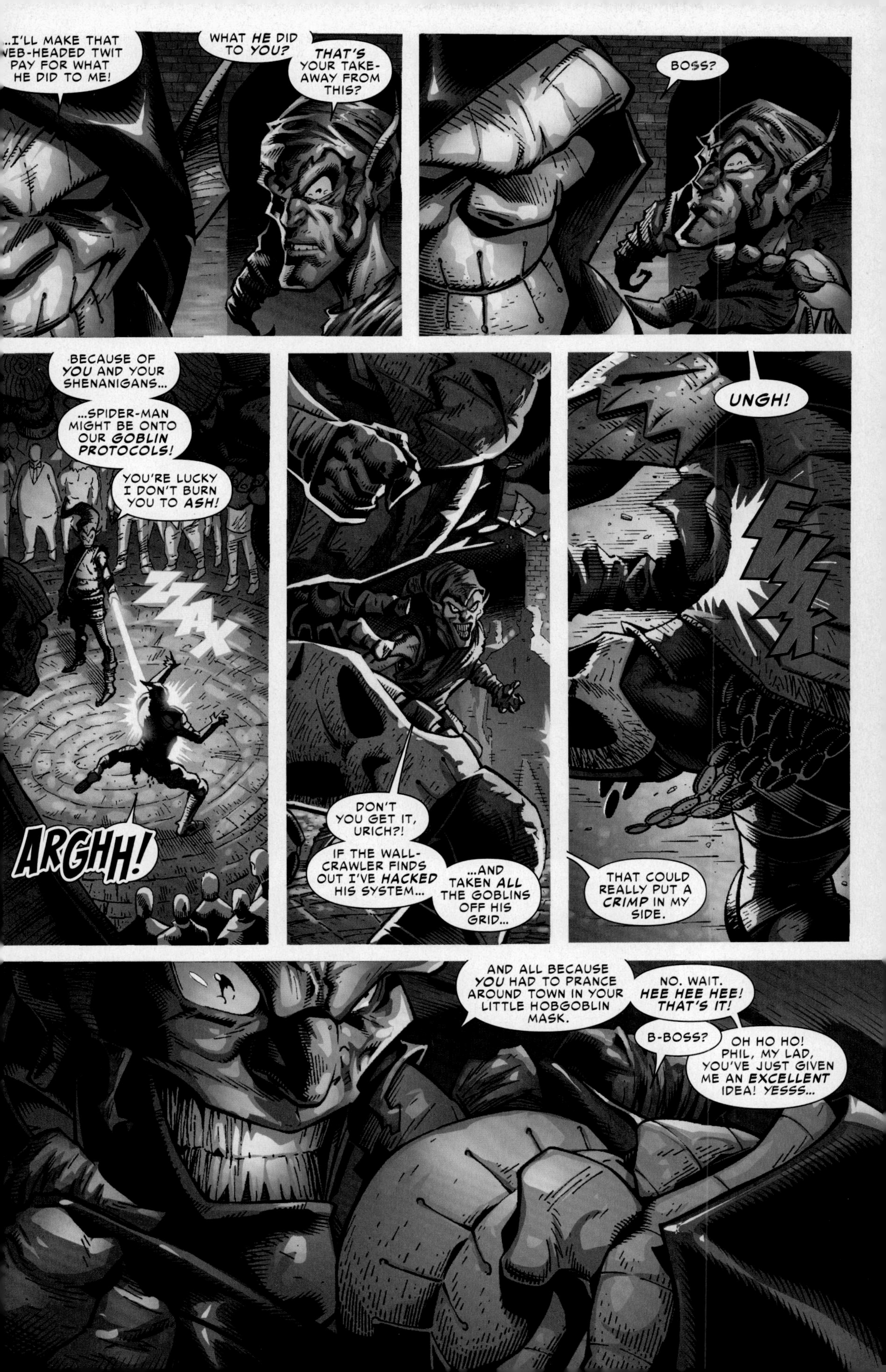
...I'LL MAKE THAT WEB-HEADED TWIT PAY FOR WHAT HE DID TO ME!
WHAT HE DID TO YOU?
THAT'S YOUR TAKE-AWAY FROM THIS?
BOSS?
BECAUSE OF YOU AND YOUR SHENANIGANS...
...SPIDER-MAN MIGHT BE ONTO OUR GOBLIN PROTOCOLS!
YOU'RE LUCKY I DON'T BURN YOU TO ASH!
ZZZAX
ARGHH!
DON'T YOU GET IT, URICH?!
IF THE WALL-CRAWLER FINDS OUT I'VE HACKED HIS SYSTEM...
...AND TAKEN ALL THE GOBLINS OFF HIS GRID...
UNGH!
THAT COULD REALLY PUT A CRIMP IN MY SIDE.
AND ALL BECAUSE YOU HAD TO PRANCE AROUND TOWN IN YOUR LITTLE HOBGOBLIN MASK.
NO. WAIT. HEE HEE HEE! THAT'S IT!
B-BOSS?
OH HO HO! PHIL, MY LAD, YOU'VE JUST GIVEN ME AN EXCELLENT IDEA! YESSS...

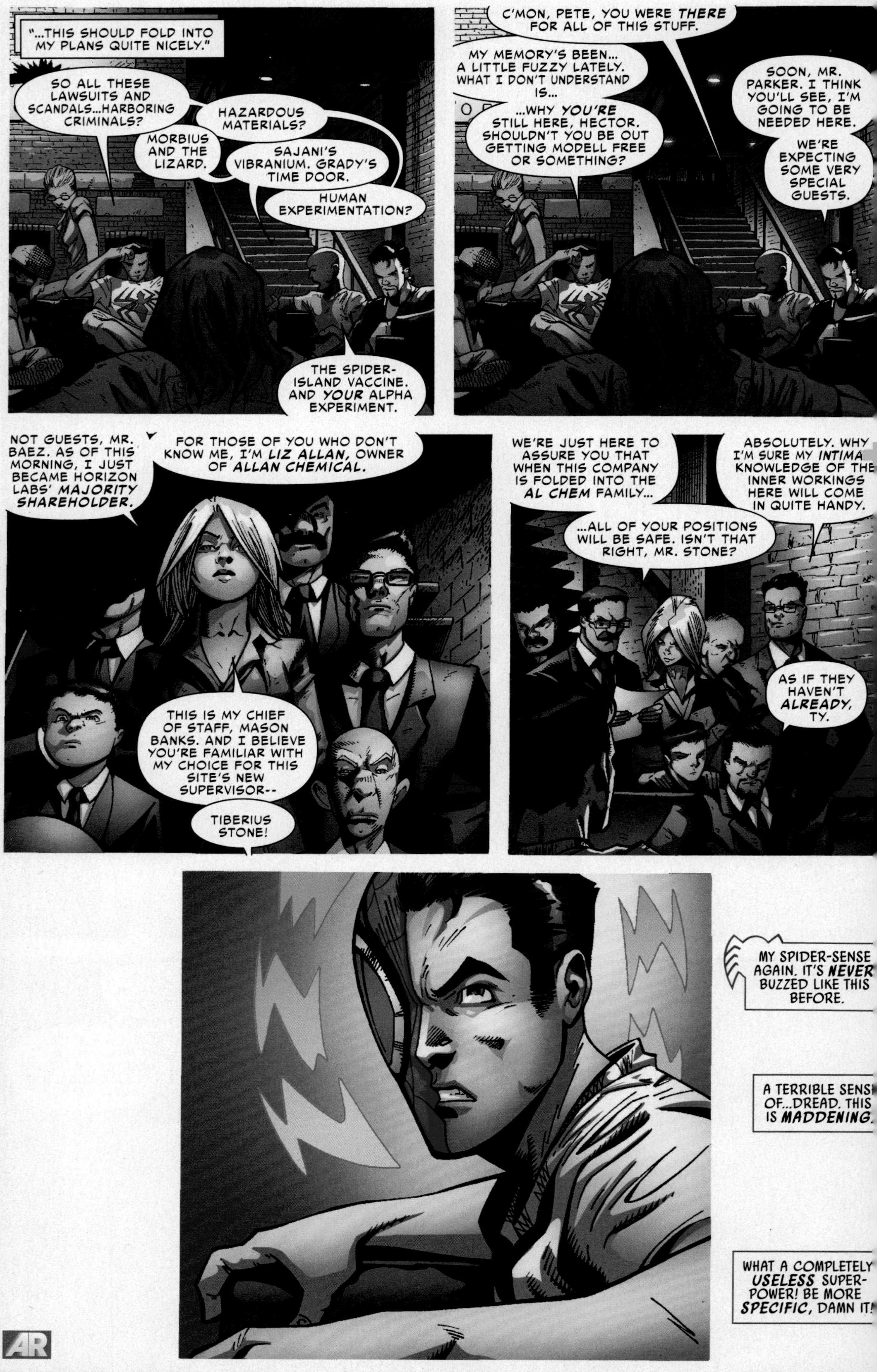
"...THIS SHOULD FOLD INTO MY PLANS QUITE NICELY."
SO ALL THESE LAWSUITS AND SCANDALS...HARBORING CRIMINALS?
HAZARDOUS MATERIALS?
MORBIUS AND THE LIZARD.
SAJANI'S VIBRANIUM. GRADY'S TIME DOOR.
HUMAN EXPERIMENTATION?
THE SPIDER-ISLAND VACCINE. AND YOUR ALPHA EXPERIMENT.
C'MON, PETE, YOU WERE THERE FOR ALL OF THIS STUFF.
MY MEMORY'S BEEN... A LITTLE FUZZY LATELY. WHAT I DON'T UNDERSTAND IS...
...WHY YOU'RE STILL HERE, HECTOR. SHOULDN'T YOU BE OUT GETTING MODELL FREE OR SOMETHING?
SOON, MR. PARKER. I THINK YOU'LL SEE, I'M GOING TO BE NEEDED HERE.
WE'RE EXPECTING SOME VERY SPECIAL GUESTS.
NOT GUESTS, MR. BAEZ. AS OF THIS MORNING, I JUST BECAME HORIZON LABS' MAJORITY SHAREHOLDER.
FOR THOSE OF YOU WHO DON'T KNOW ME, I'M LIZ ALLAN, OWNER OF ALLAN CHEMICAL.
THIS IS MY CHIEF OF STAFF, MASON BANKS. AND I BELIEVE YOU'RE FAMILIAR WITH MY CHOICE FOR THIS SITE'S NEW SUPERVISOR--
TIBERIUS STONE!
WE'RE JUST HERE TO ASSURE YOU THAT WHEN THIS COMPANY IS FOLDED INTO THE AL CHEM FAMILY...
...ALL OF YOUR POSITIONS WILL BE SAFE. ISN'T THAT RIGHT, MR. STONE?
ABSOLUTELY. WHY, I'M SURE MY INTIMA KNOWLEDGE OF THE INNER WORKINGS HERE WILL COME IN QUITE HANDY.
AS IF THEY HAVEN'T ALREADY, TY.
MY SPIDER-SENSE AGAIN. IT'S NEVER BUZZED LIKE THIS BEFORE.
A TERRIBLE SENS OF...DREAD. THIS IS MADDENING.
WHAT A COMPLETELY USELESS SUPER-POWER! BE MORE SPECIFIC, DAMN IT!

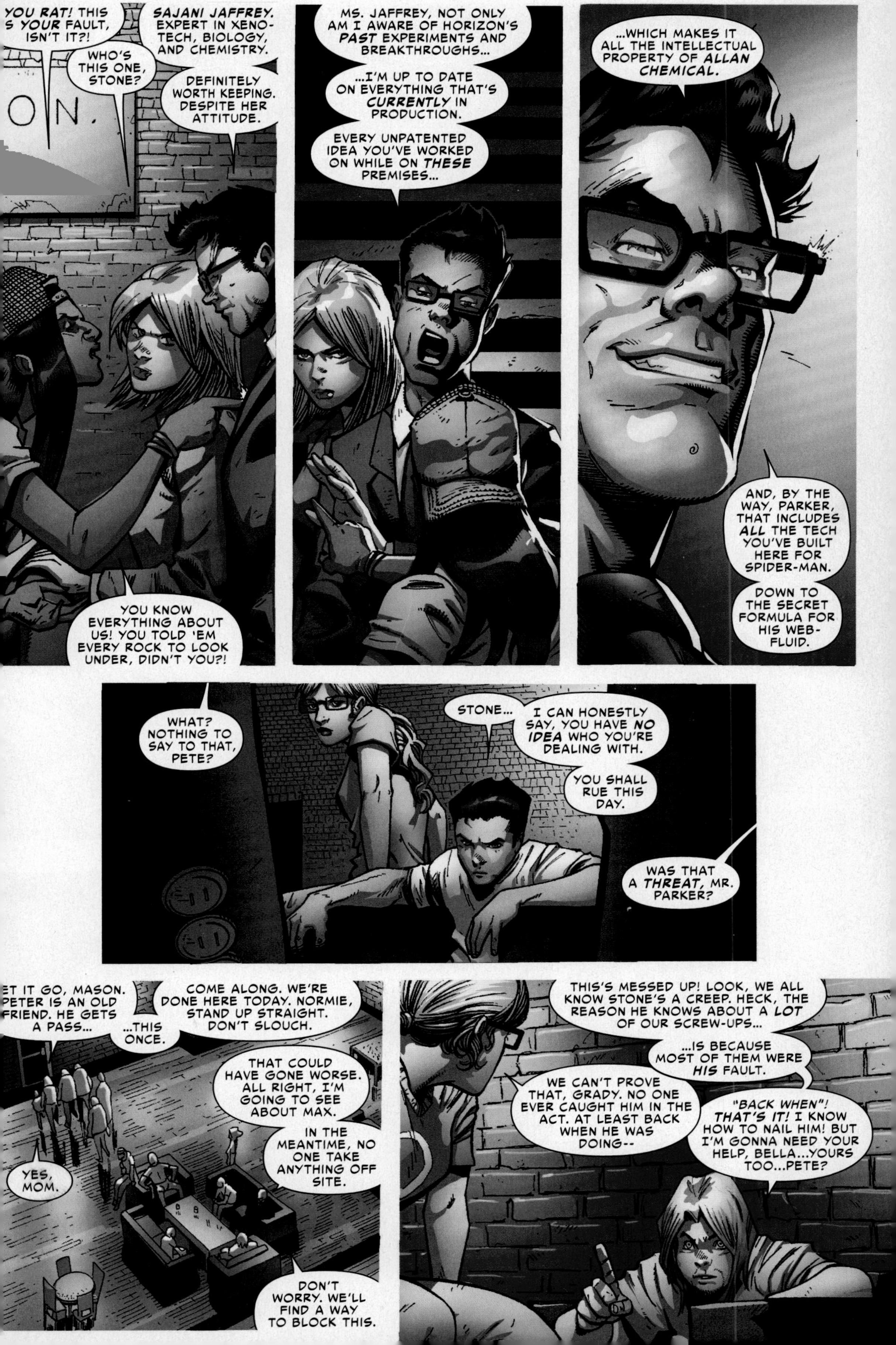

YOU RAT! THIS 'S YOUR FAULT, ISN'T IT?!
WHO'S THIS ONE, STONE?
SAJANI JAFFREY. EXPERT IN XENO-TECH, BIOLOGY, AND CHEMISTRY.
DEFINITELY WORTH KEEPING. DESPITE HER ATTITUDE.
YOU KNOW EVERYTHING ABOUT US! YOU TOLD 'EM EVERY ROCK TO LOOK UNDER, DIDN'T YOU?!
MS. JAFFREY, NOT ONLY AM I AWARE OF HORIZON'S PAST EXPERIMENTS AND BREAKTHROUGHS...
...I'M UP TO DATE ON EVERYTHING THAT'S CURRENTLY IN PRODUCTION.
EVERY UNPATENTED IDEA YOU'VE WORKED ON WHILE ON THESE PREMISES...
...WHICH MAKES IT ALL THE INTELLECTUAL PROPERTY OF ALLAN CHEMICAL.
AND, BY THE WAY, PARKER, THAT INCLUDES ALL THE TECH YOU'VE BUILT HERE FOR SPIDER-MAN.
DOWN TO THE SECRET FORMULA FOR HIS WEB-FLUID.
WHAT? NOTHING TO SAY TO THAT, PETE?
STONE...
I CAN HONESTLY SAY, YOU HAVE NO IDEA WHO YOU'RE DEALING WITH.
YOU SHALL RUE THIS DAY.
WAS THAT A THREAT, MR. PARKER?
ET IT GO, MASON. PETER IS AN OLD FRIEND. HE GETS A PASS...
...THIS ONCE.
COME ALONG. WE'RE DONE HERE TODAY. NORMIE, STAND UP STRAIGHT. DON'T SLOUCH.
YES, MOM.
THAT COULD HAVE GONE WORSE. ALL RIGHT, I'M GOING TO SEE ABOUT MAX.
IN THE MEANTIME, NO ONE TAKE ANYTHING OFF SITE.
DON'T WORRY. WE'LL FIND A WAY TO BLOCK THIS.
THIS'S MESSED UP! LOOK, WE ALL KNOW STONE'S A CREEP. HECK, THE REASON HE KNOWS ABOUT A LOT OF OUR SCREW-UPS...
...IS BECAUSE MOST OF THEM WERE HIS FAULT.
WE CAN'T PROVE THAT, GRADY. NO ONE EVER CAUGHT HIM IN THE ACT. AT LEAST BACK WHEN HE WAS DOING--
"BACK WHEN"! THAT'S IT! I KNOW HOW TO NAIL HIM! BUT I'M GONNA NEED YOUR HELP, BELLA...YOURS TOO...PETE?

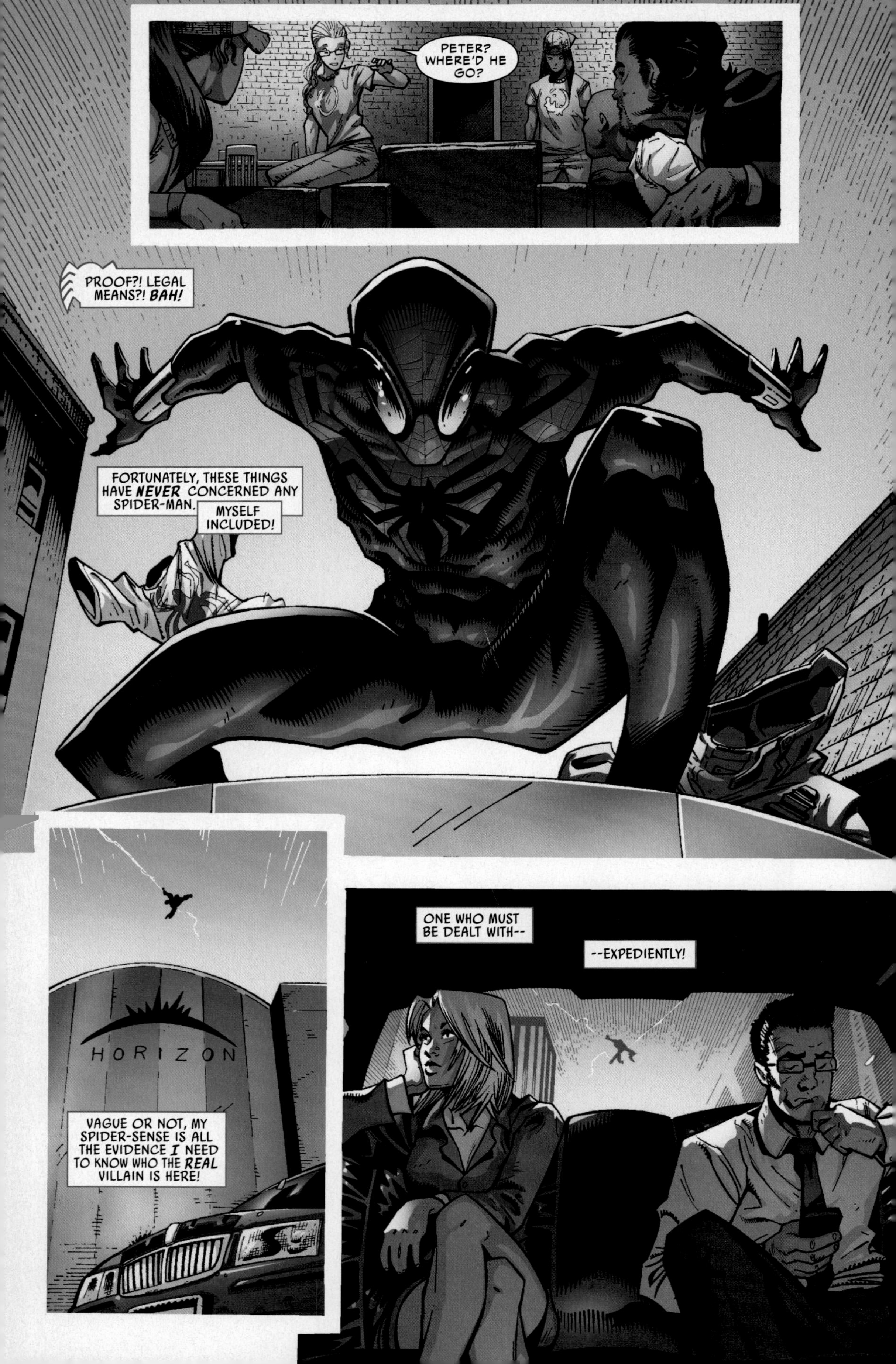
PETER? WHERE'D HE GO?
PROOF?! LEGAL MEANS?! BAH!
FORTUNATELY, THESE THINGS HAVE NEVER CONCERNED ANY SPIDER-MAN.
MYSELF INCLUDED!
HORIZON
VAGUE OR NOT, MY SPIDER-SENSE IS ALL THE EVIDENCE I NEED TO KNOW WHO THE REAL VILLAIN IS HERE!
ONE WHO MUST BE DEALT WITH--
--EXPEDIENTLY!

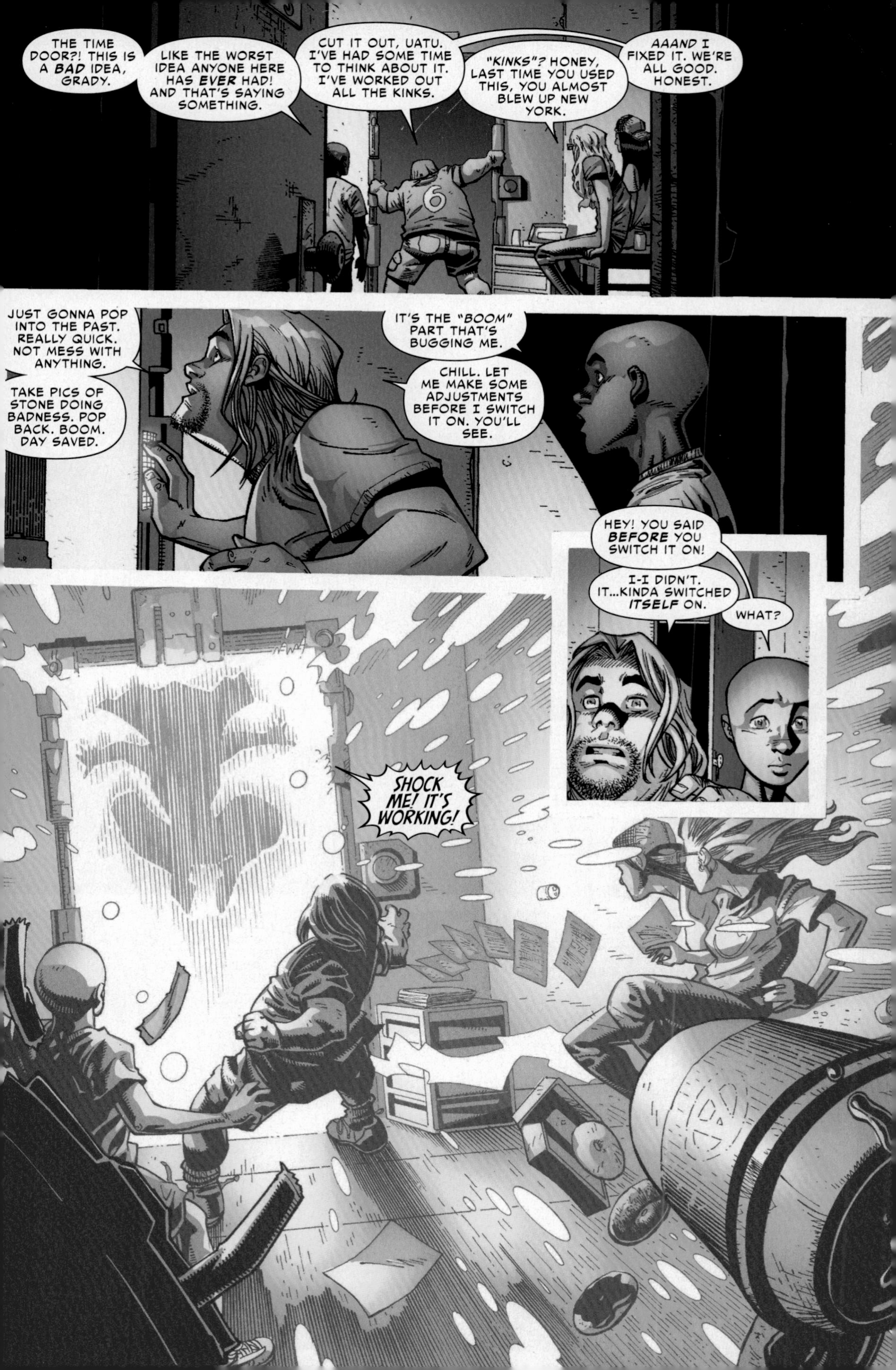
THE TIME DOOR?! THIS IS A BAD IDEA, GRADY.
LIKE THE WORST IDEA ANYONE HERE HAS EVER HAD! AND THAT'S SAYING SOMETHING.
CUT IT OUT, UATU. I'VE HAD SOME TIME TO THINK ABOUT IT. I'VE WORKED OUT ALL THE KINKS.
"KINKS"? HONEY, LAST TIME YOU USED THIS, YOU ALMOST BLEW UP NEW YORK.
AAAND I FIXED IT. WE'RE ALL GOOD. HONEST.
JUST GONNA POP INTO THE PAST. REALLY QUICK. NOT MESS WITH ANYTHING.
TAKE PICS OF STONE DOING BADNESS. POP BACK. BOOM. DAY SAVED.
IT'S THE "BOOM" PART THAT'S BUGGING ME.
CHILL. LET ME MAKE SOME ADJUSTMENTS BEFORE I SWITCH IT ON. YOU'LL SEE.
HEY! YOU SAID BEFORE YOU SWITCH IT ON!
I-I DIDN'T. IT...KINDA SWITCHED ITSELF ON.
WHAT?
SHOCK ME! IT'S WORKING!

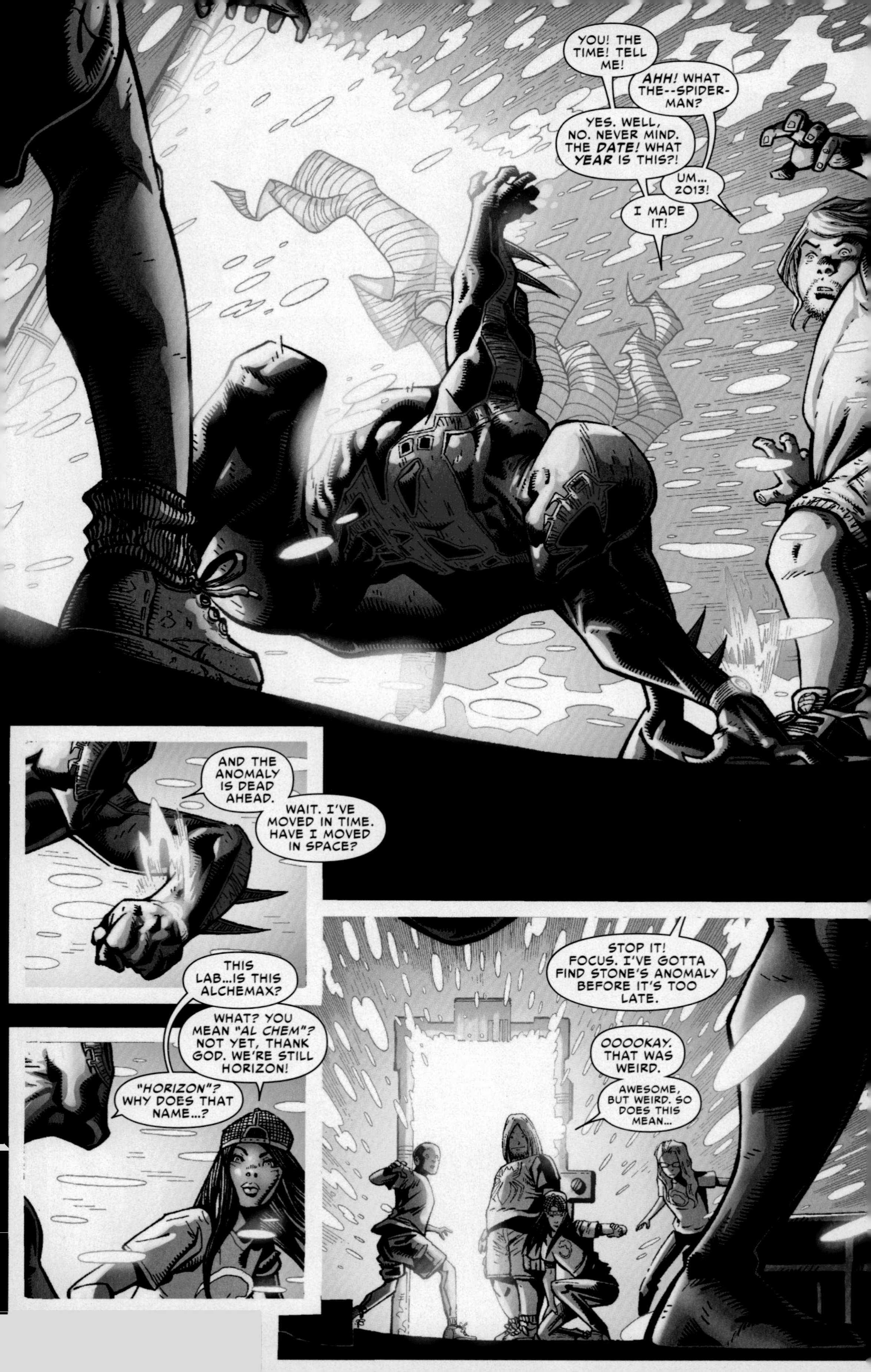
YOU! THE TIME! TELL ME!
AHH! WHAT THE--SPIDER-MAN?
YES. WELL, NO. NEVER MIND. THE DATE! WHAT YEAR IS THIS?!
UM... 2013!
I MADE IT!
AND THE ANOMALY IS DEAD AHEAD.
WAIT. I'VE MOVED IN TIME. HAVE I MOVED IN SPACE?
THIS LAB...IS THIS ALCHEMAX?
WHAT? YOU MEAN "AL CHEM"? NOT YET, THANK GOD. WE'RE STILL HORIZON!
"HORIZON"? WHY DOES THAT NAME...?
STOP IT! FOCUS. I'VE GOTTA FIND STONE'S ANOMALY BEFORE IT'S TOO LATE.
OOOOKAY. THAT WAS WEIRD.
AWESOME, BUT WEIRD. SO DOES THIS MEAN...

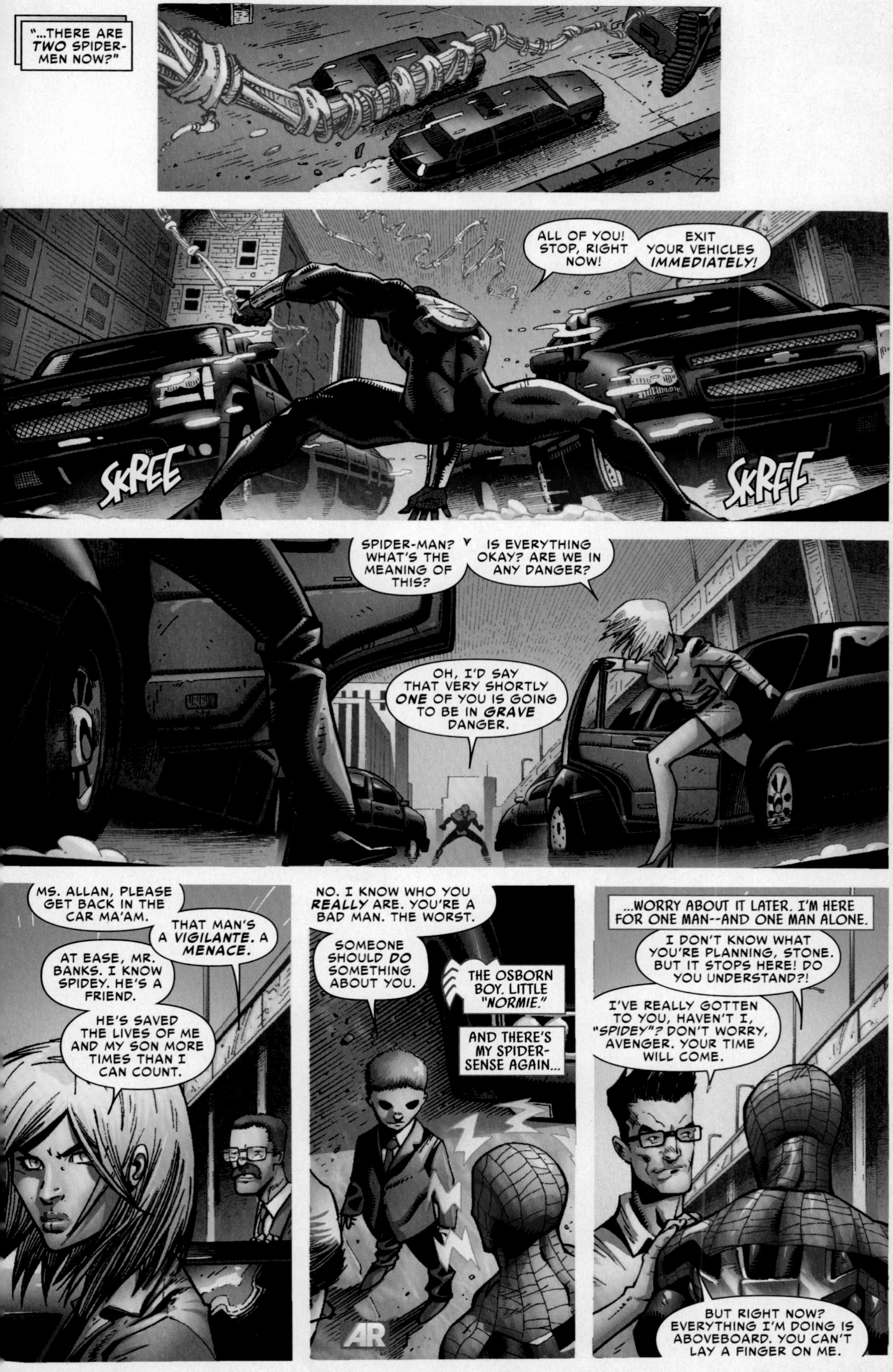
"...THERE ARE TWO SPIDER-MEN NOW?"
ALL OF YOU! STOP, RIGHT NOW!
EXIT YOUR VEHICLES IMMEDIATELY!
SKREE
SKRFF
SPIDER-MAN? WHAT'S THE MEANING OF THIS?
IS EVERYTHING OKAY? ARE WE IN ANY DANGER?
OH, I'D SAY THAT VERY SHORTLY ONE OF YOU IS GOING TO BE IN GRAVE DANGER.
MS. ALLAN, PLEASE GET BACK IN THE CAR MA'AM.
THAT MAN'S A VIGILANTE. A MENACE.
AT EASE, MR. BANKS. I KNOW SPIDEY. HE'S A FRIEND.
HE'S SAVED THE LIVES OF ME AND MY SON MORE TIMES THAN I CAN COUNT.
NO. I KNOW WHO YOU REALLY ARE. YOU'RE A BAD MAN. THE WORST.
SOMEONE SHOULD DO SOMETHING ABOUT YOU.
THE OSBORN BOY. LITTLE "NORMIE."
AND THERE'S MY SPIDER-SENSE AGAIN...
...WORRY ABOUT IT LATER. I'M HERE FOR ONE MAN--AND ONE MAN ALONE.
I DON'T KNOW WHAT YOU'RE PLANNING, STONE. BUT IT STOPS HERE! DO YOU UNDERSTAND?!
I'VE REALLY GOTTEN TO YOU, HAVEN'T I, "SPIDEY"? DON'T WORRY, AVENGER. YOUR TIME WILL COME.
BUT RIGHT NOW? EVERYTHING I'M DOING IS ABOVEBOARD. YOU CAN'T LAY A FINGER ON ME.

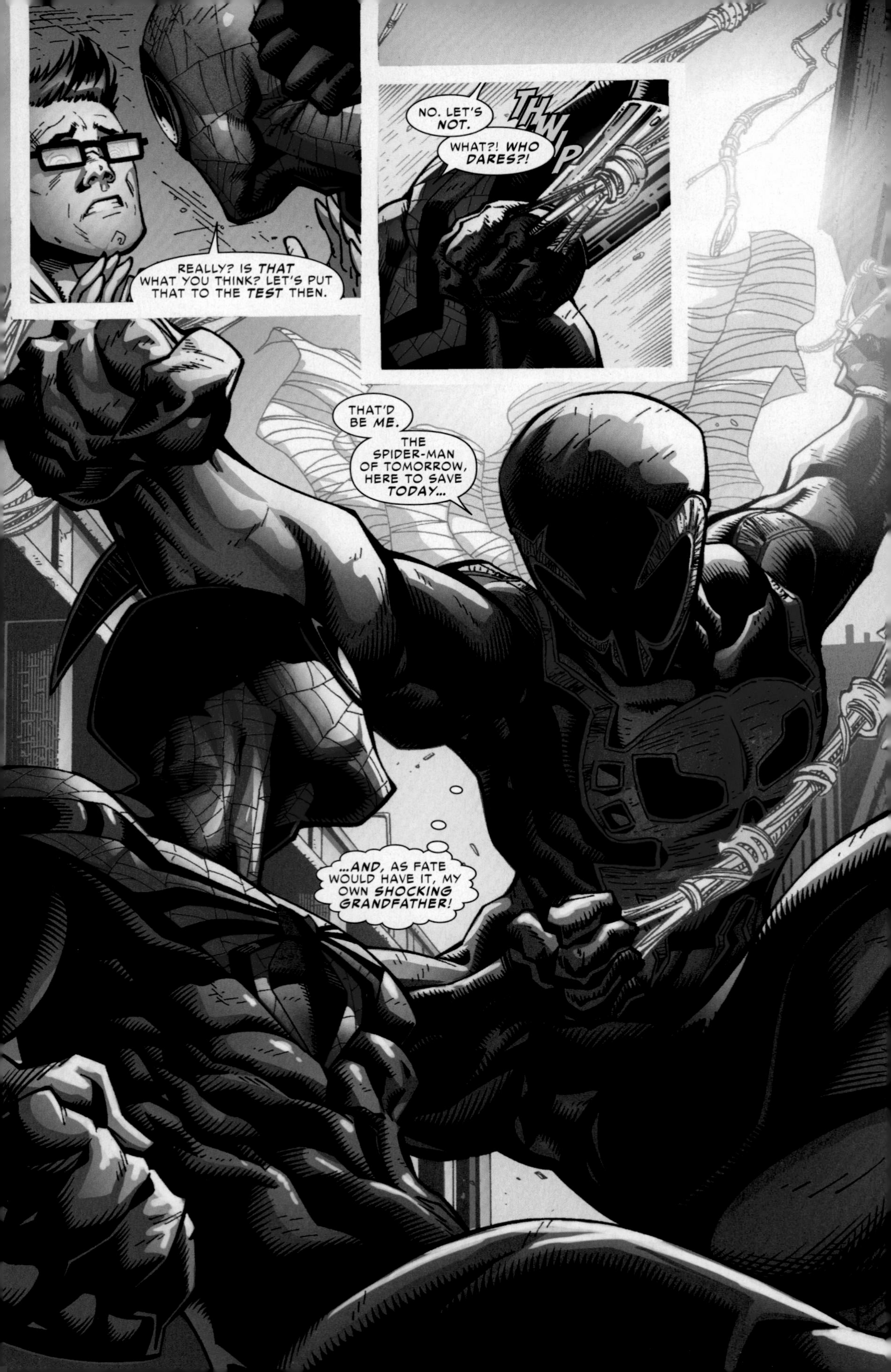
REALLY? IS THAT WHAT YOU THINK? LET'S PUT THAT TO THE TEST THEN.
NO. LET'S NOT.
THWIP
WHAT?! WHO DARES?!
THAT'D BE ME.
THE SPIDER-MAN OF TOMORROW, HERE TO SAVE TODAY...
...AND, AS FATE WOULD HAVE IT, MY OWN SHOCKING GRANDFATHER!

18

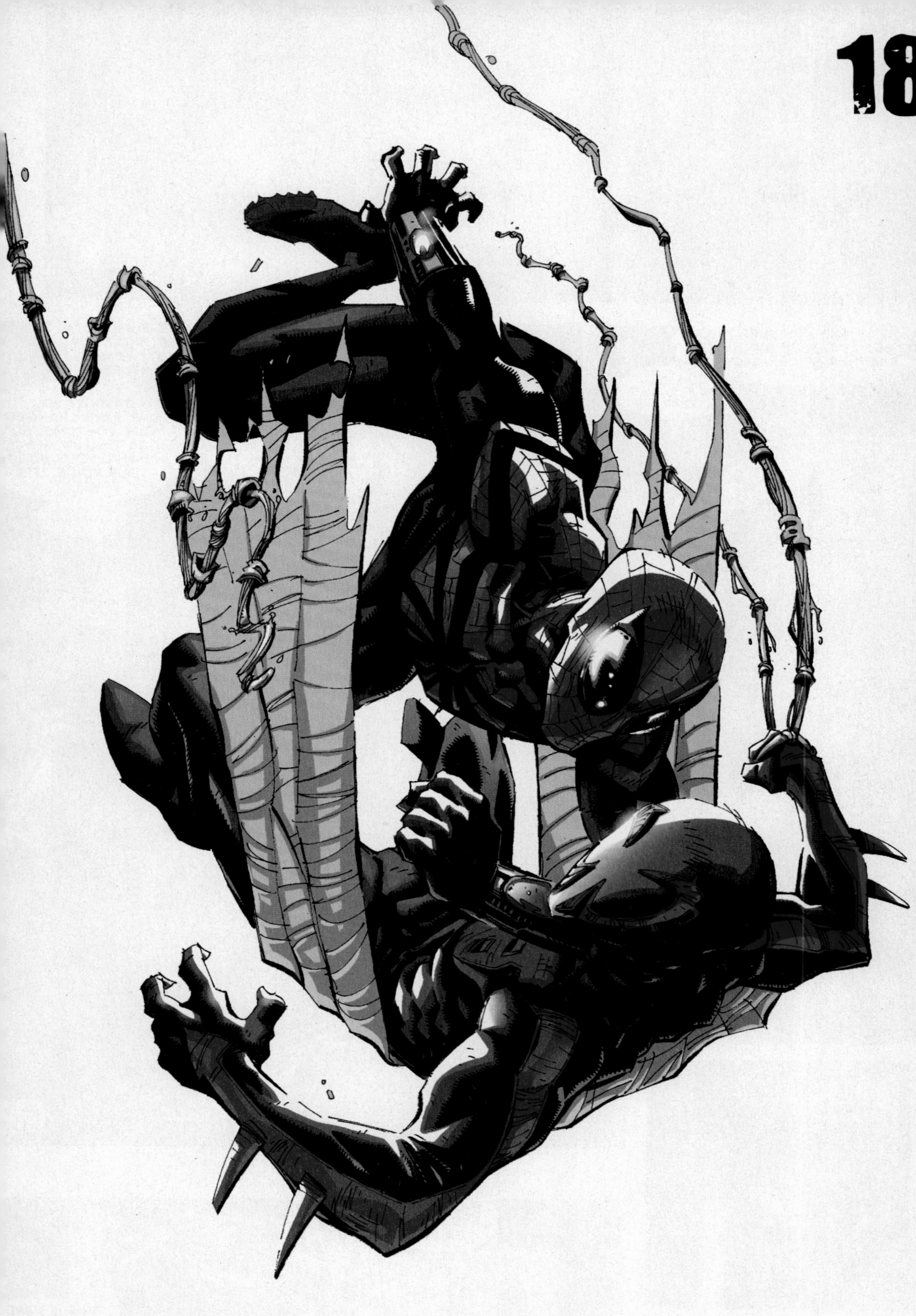

CAUSE & EFFECT

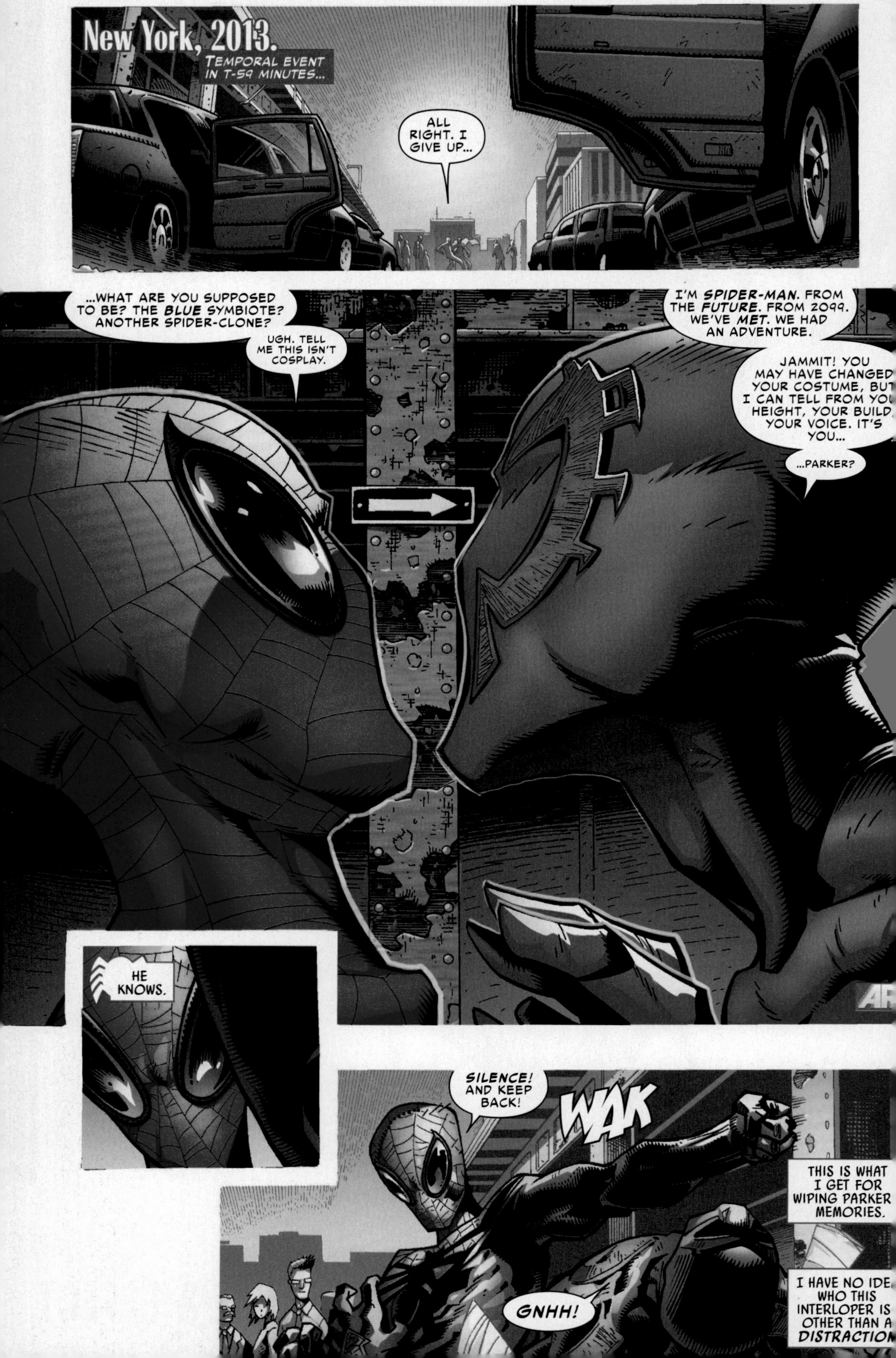
New York, 2013.
TEMPORAL EVENT IN T-59 MINUTES...
ALL RIGHT. I GIVE UP...
...WHAT ARE YOU SUPPOSED TO BE? THE BLUE SYMBIOTE? ANOTHER SPIDER-CLONE?
UGH. TELL ME THIS ISN'T COSPLAY.
I'M SPIDER-MAN. FROM THE FUTURE. FROM 2099. WE'VE MET. WE HAD AN ADVENTURE.
JAMMIT! YOU MAY HAVE CHANGED YOUR COSTUME, BUT I CAN TELL FROM YOU HEIGHT, YOUR BUILD, YOUR VOICE. IT'S YOU...
...PARKER?
HE KNOWS.
SILENCE! AND KEEP BACK!
WAK
THIS IS WHAT I GET FOR WIPING PARKER MEMORIES.
GNHH!
I HAVE NO IDE WHO THIS INTERLOPER IS OTHER THAN A DISTRACTIO

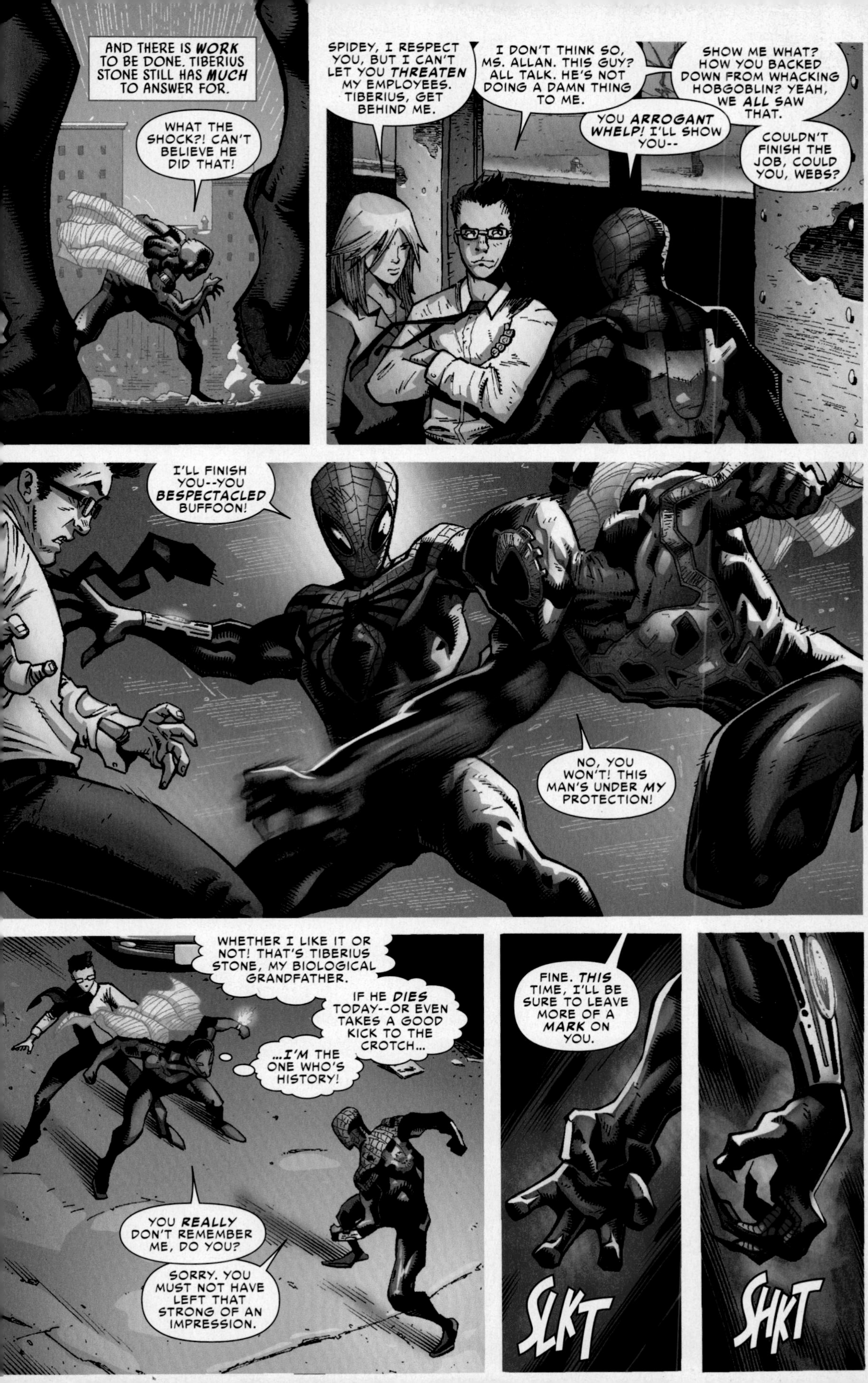
AND THERE IS WORK TO BE DONE. TIBERIUS STONE STILL HAS MUCH TO ANSWER FOR.
WHAT THE SHOCK?! CAN'T BELIEVE HE DID THAT!
SPIDEY, I RESPECT YOU, BUT I CAN'T LET YOU THREATEN MY EMPLOYEES. TIBERIUS, GET BEHIND ME.
I DON'T THINK SO, MS. ALLAN. THIS GUY? ALL TALK. HE'S NOT DOING A DAMN THING TO ME.
SHOW ME WHAT? HOW YOU BACKED DOWN FROM WHACKING HOBGOBLIN? YEAH, WE ALL SAW THAT.
YOU ARROGANT WHELP! I'LL SHOW YOU--
COULDN'T FINISH THE JOB, COULD YOU, WEBS?
I'LL FINISH YOU--YOU BESPECTACLED BUFFOON!
NO, YOU WON'T! THIS MAN'S UNDER MY PROTECTION!
WHETHER I LIKE IT OR NOT! THAT'S TIBERIUS STONE, MY BIOLOGICAL GRANDFATHER.
IF HE DIES TODAY--OR EVEN TAKES A GOOD KICK TO THE CROTCH...
...I'M THE ONE WHO'S HISTORY!
YOU REALLY DON'T REMEMBER ME, DO YOU?
SORRY. YOU MUST NOT HAVE LEFT THAT STRONG OF AN IMPRESSION.
FINE. THIS TIME, I'LL BE SURE TO LEAVE MORE OF A MARK ON YOU.
SLKT
SHKT

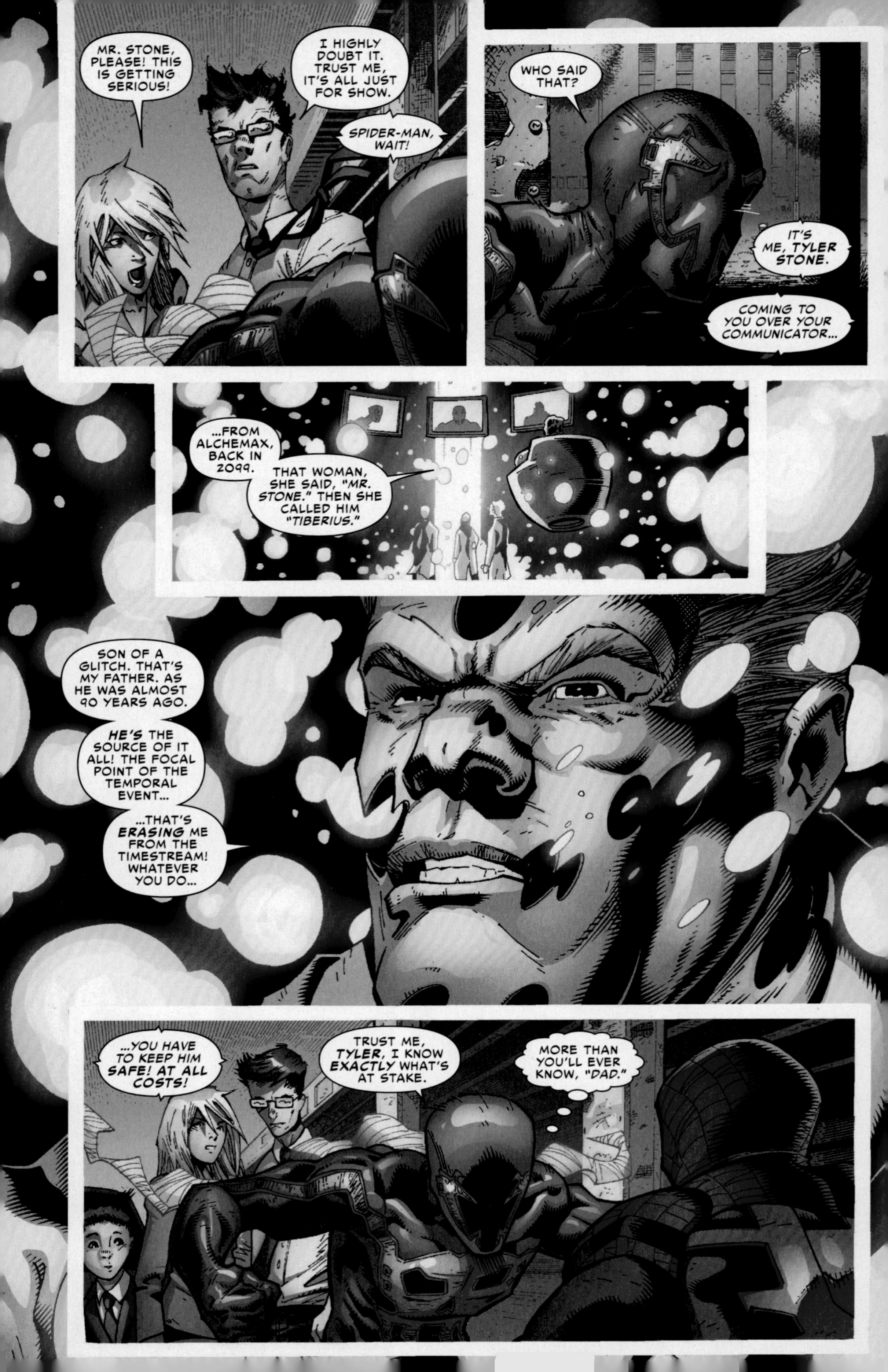
MR. STONE, PLEASE! THIS IS GETTING SERIOUS!
I HIGHLY DOUBT IT. TRUST ME, IT'S ALL JUST FOR SHOW.
SPIDER-MAN, WAIT!
WHO SAID THAT?
IT'S ME, TYLER STONE.
COMING TO YOU OVER YOUR COMMUNICATOR...
...FROM ALCHEMAX, BACK IN 2099.
THAT WOMAN, SHE SAID, "MR. STONE." THEN SHE CALLED HIM "TIBERIUS."
SON OF A GLITCH. THAT'S MY FATHER. AS HE WAS ALMOST 90 YEARS AGO.
HE'S THE SOURCE OF IT ALL! THE FOCAL POINT OF THE TEMPORAL EVENT...
...THAT'S ERASING ME FROM THE TIMESTREAM! WHATEVER YOU DO...
...YOU HAVE TO KEEP HIM SAFE! AT ALL COSTS!
TRUST ME, TYLER, I KNOW EXACTLY WHAT'S AT STAKE.
MORE THAN YOU'LL EVER KNOW, "DAD."

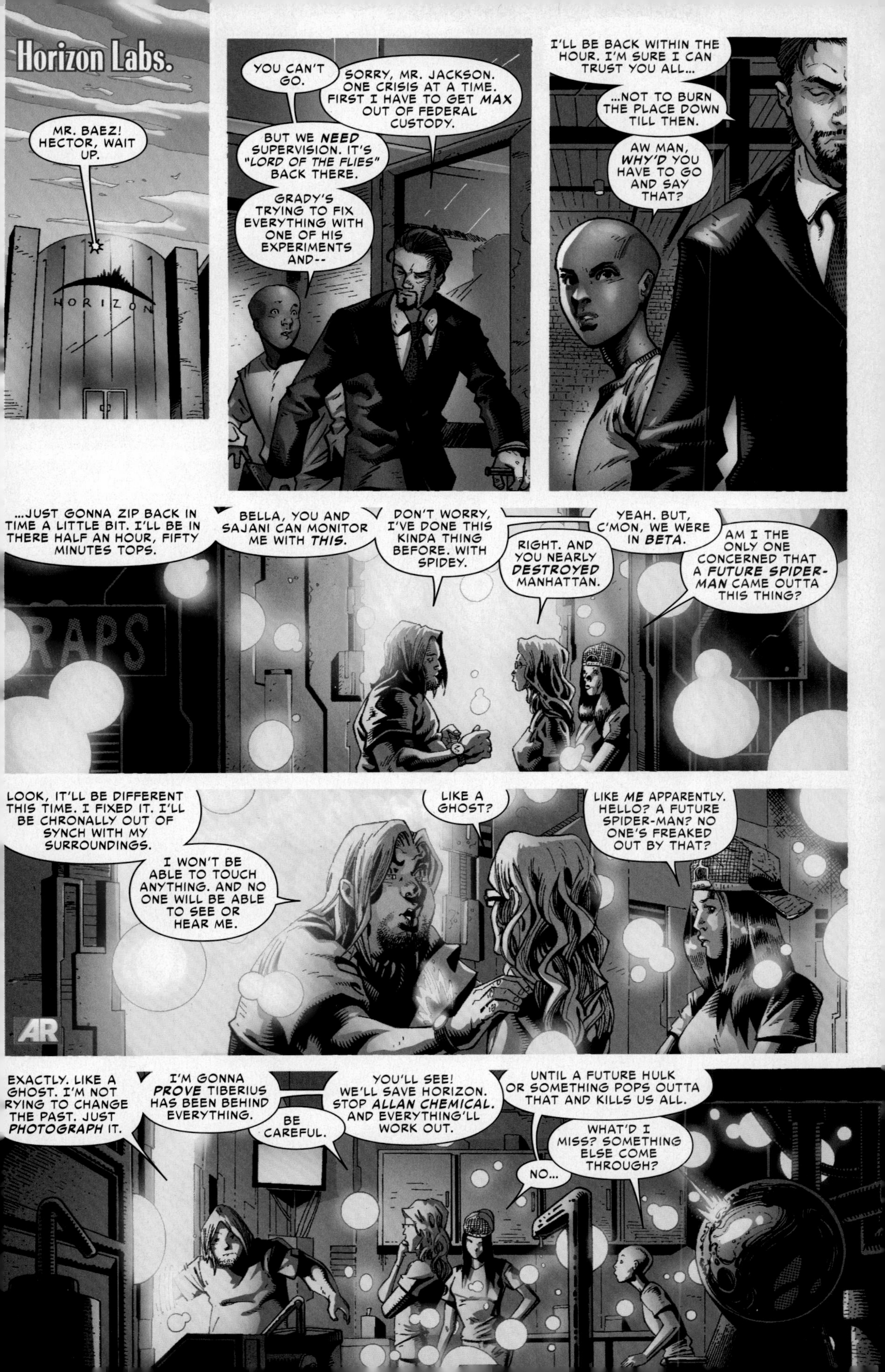

Horizon Labs.
MR. BAEZ! HECTOR, WAIT UP.
HORIZON
YOU CAN'T GO.
SORRY, MR. JACKSON. ONE CRISIS AT A TIME. FIRST I HAVE TO GET MAX OUT OF FEDERAL CUSTODY.
BUT WE NEED SUPERVISION. IT'S "LORD OF THE FLIES" BACK THERE.
GRADY'S TRYING TO FIX EVERYTHING WITH ONE OF HIS EXPERIMENTS AND--
I'LL BE BACK WITHIN THE HOUR. I'M SURE I CAN TRUST YOU ALL...
...NOT TO BURN THE PLACE DOWN TILL THEN.
AW MAN, WHY'D YOU HAVE TO GO AND SAY THAT?
...JUST GONNA ZIP BACK IN TIME A LITTLE BIT. I'LL BE IN THERE HALF AN HOUR, FIFTY MINUTES TOPS.
BELLA, YOU AND SAJANI CAN MONITOR ME WITH THIS.
DON'T WORRY, I'VE DONE THIS KINDA THING BEFORE. WITH SPIDEY.
RIGHT. AND YOU NEARLY DESTROYED MANHATTAN.
YEAH. BUT, C'MON, WE WERE IN BETA.
AM I THE ONLY ONE CONCERNED THAT A FUTURE SPIDER-MAN CAME OUTTA THIS THING?
RAPS
LOOK, IT'LL BE DIFFERENT THIS TIME. I FIXED IT. I'LL BE CHRONALLY OUT OF SYNCH WITH MY SURROUNDINGS.
I WON'T BE ABLE TO TOUCH ANYTHING. AND NO ONE WILL BE ABLE TO SEE OR HEAR ME.
LIKE A GHOST?
LIKE ME APPARENTLY. HELLO? A FUTURE SPIDER-MAN? NO ONE'S FREAKED OUT BY THAT?
AR
EXACTLY. LIKE A GHOST. I'M NOT RYING TO CHANGE THE PAST. JUST PHOTOGRAPH IT.
I'M GONNA PROVE TIBERIUS HAS BEEN BEHIND EVERYTHING.
BE CAREFUL.
YOU'LL SEE! WE'LL SAVE HORIZON. STOP ALLAN CHEMICAL. AND EVERYTHING'LL WORK OUT.
UNTIL A FUTURE HULK OR SOMETHING POPS OUTTA THAT AND KILLS US ALL.
NO...
WHAT'D I MISS? SOMETHING ELSE COME THROUGH?

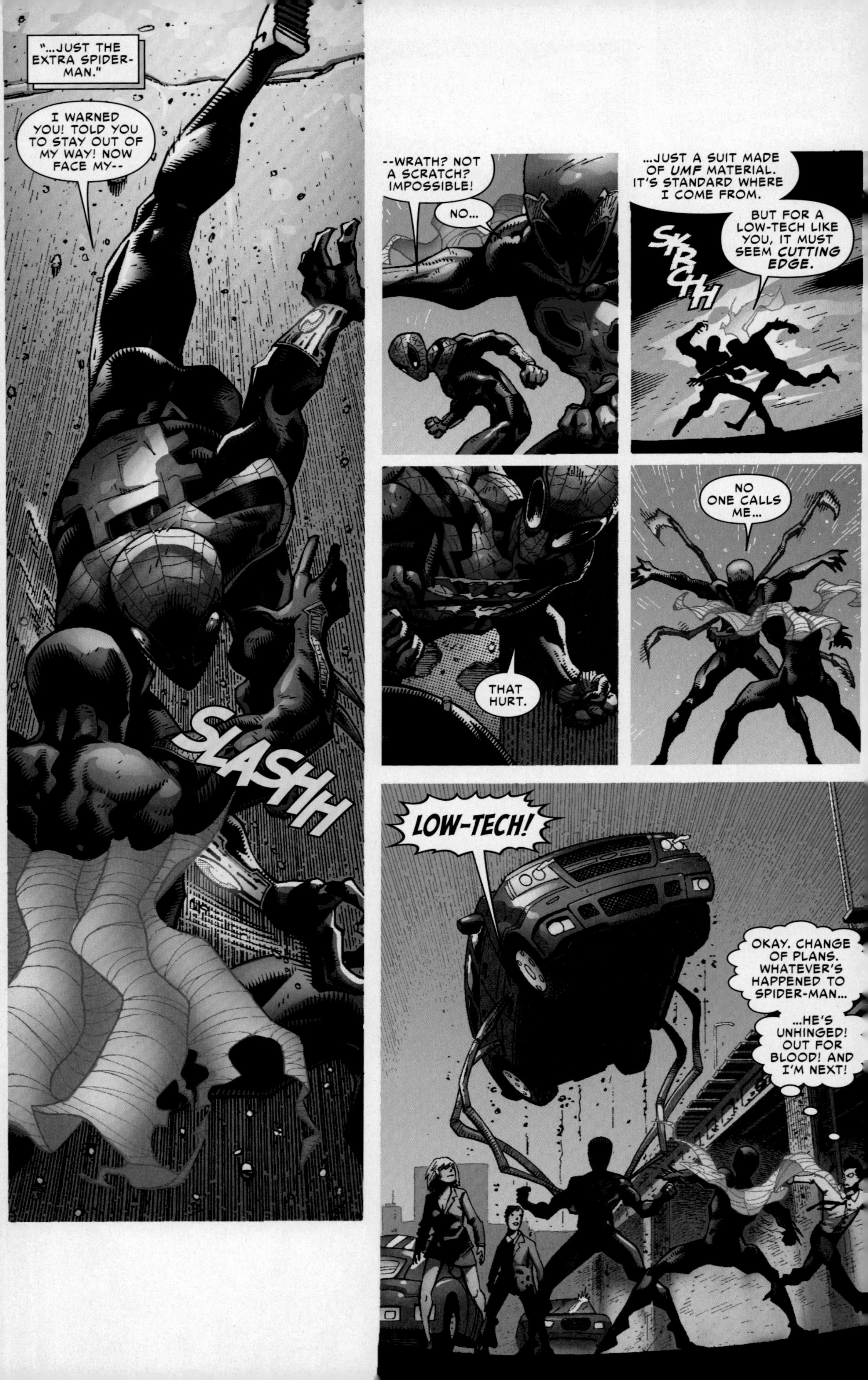
"...JUST THE EXTRA SPIDER-MAN."
I WARNED YOU! TOLD YOU TO STAY OUT OF MY WAY! NOW FACE MY--
SLASHH
--WRATH? NOT A SCRATCH? IMPOSSIBLE!
NO...
...JUST A SUIT MADE OF UMF MATERIAL. IT'S STANDARD WHERE I COME FROM.
BUT FOR A LOW-TECH LIKE YOU, IT MUST SEEM CUTTING EDGE.
SKRCHH
THAT HURT.
NO ONE CALLS ME...
LOW-TECH!
OKAY. CHANGE OF PLANS. WHATEVER'S HAPPENED TO SPIDER-MAN...
...HE'S UNHINGED! OUT FOR BLOOD! AND I'M NEXT!

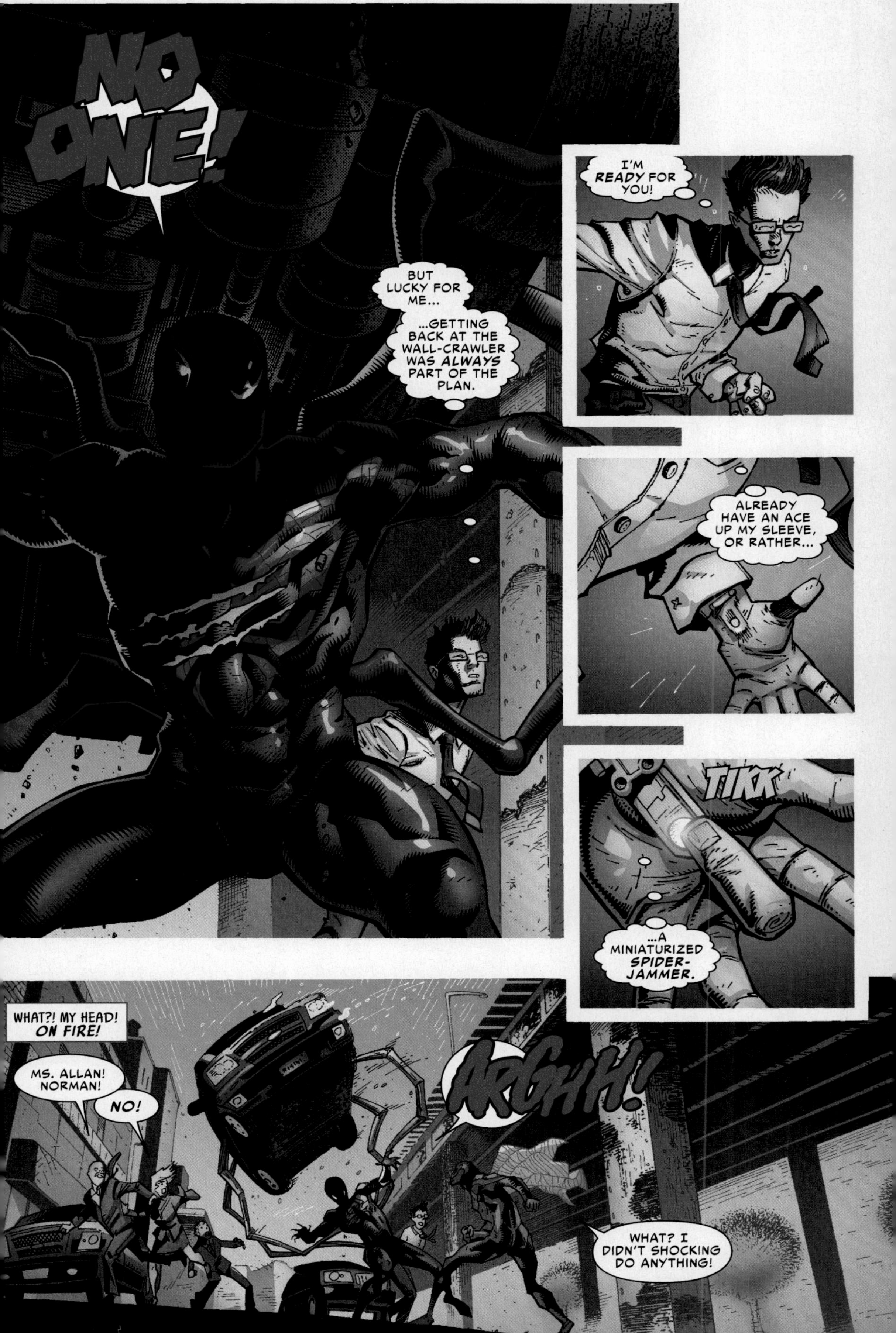
NO ONE!
BUT LUCKY FOR ME...
...GETTING BACK AT THE WALL-CRAWLER WAS ALWAYS PART OF THE PLAN.
I'M READY FOR YOU!
ALREADY HAVE AN ACE UP MY SLEEVE, OR RATHER...
TIKK
...A MINIATURIZED SPIDER-JAMMER.
WHAT?! MY HEAD! ON FIRE!
MS. ALLAN! NORMAN!
NO!
ARGHH!
WHAT? I DIDN'T SHOCKING DO ANYTHING!

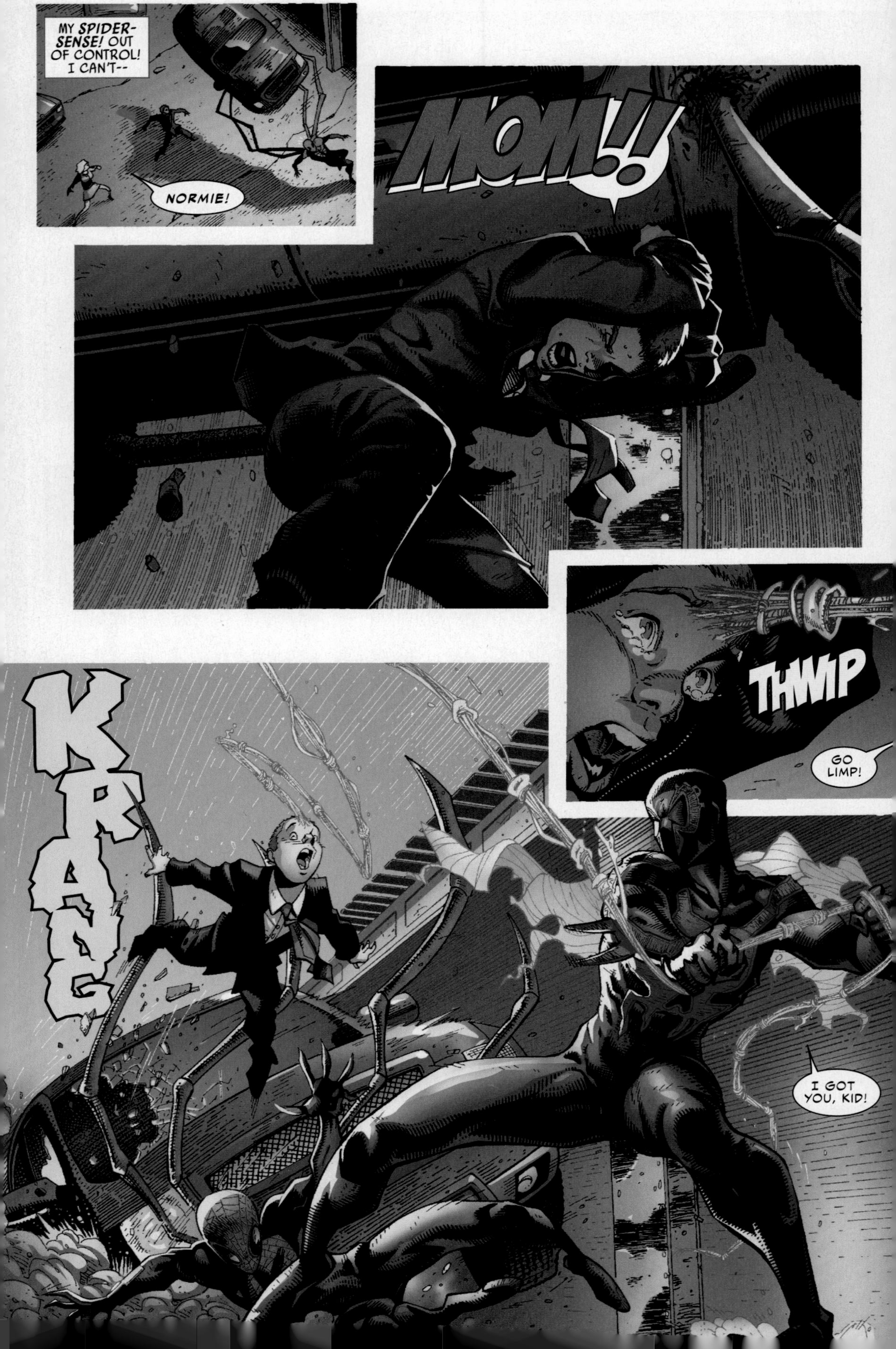
MY SPIDER-SENSE! OUT OF CONTROL! I CAN'T--
NORMIE!
MOM!!
THWIP
GO LIMP!
KRANG
I GOT YOU, KID!

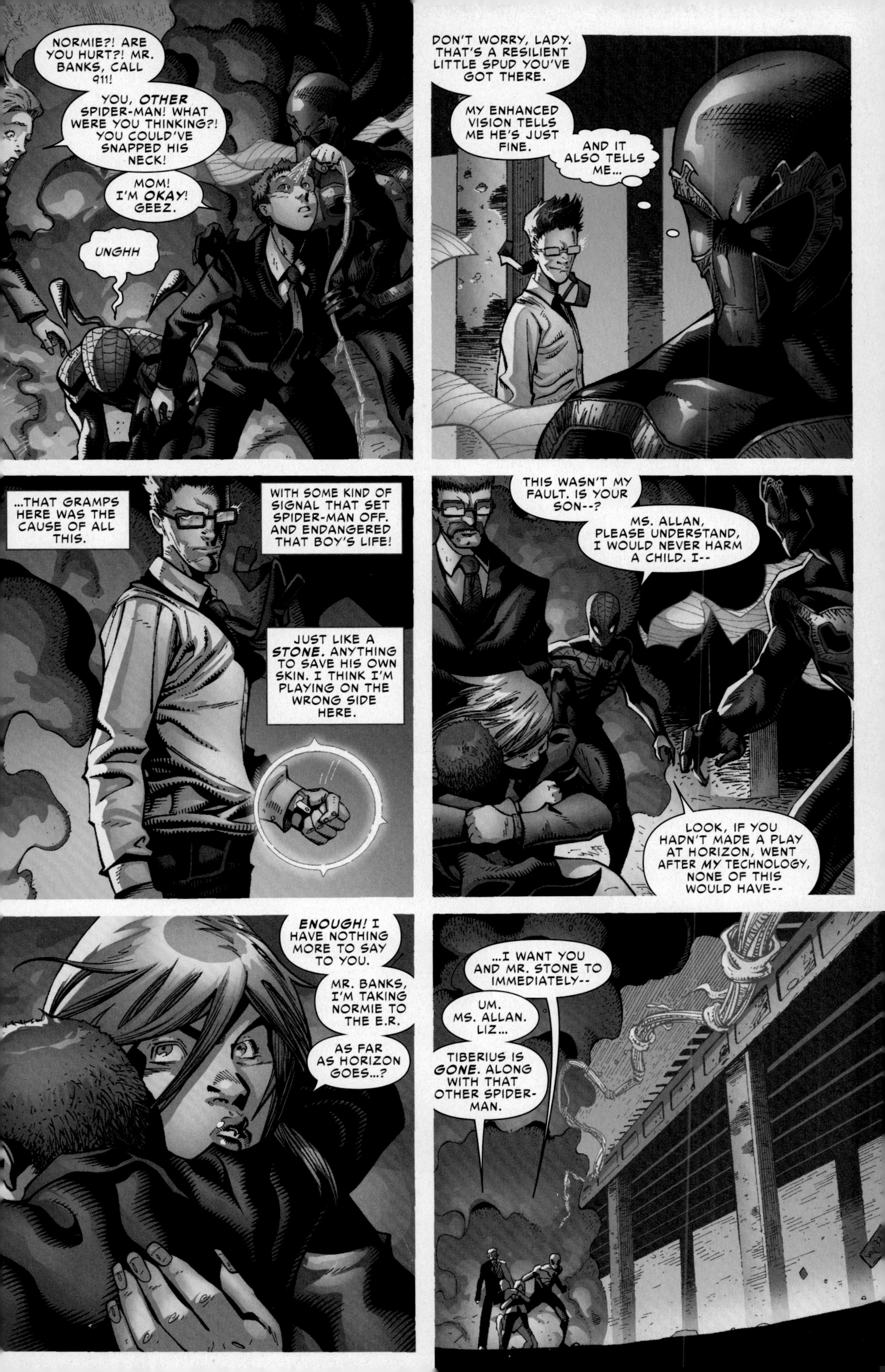
NORMIE?! ARE YOU HURT?! MR. BANKS, CALL 911!
YOU, OTHER SPIDER-MAN! WHAT WERE YOU THINKING?! YOU COULD'VE SNAPPED HIS NECK!
MOM! I'M OKAY! GEEZ.
UNGHH
DON'T WORRY, LADY. THAT'S A RESILIENT LITTLE SPUD YOU'VE GOT THERE.
MY ENHANCED VISION TELLS ME HE'S JUST FINE.
AND IT ALSO TELLS ME...
...THAT GRAMPS HERE WAS THE CAUSE OF ALL THIS.
WITH SOME KIND OF SIGNAL THAT SET SPIDER-MAN OFF. AND ENDANGERED THAT BOY'S LIFE!
JUST LIKE A STONE. ANYTHING TO SAVE HIS OWN SKIN. I THINK I'M PLAYING ON THE WRONG SIDE HERE.
THIS WASN'T MY FAULT. IS YOUR SON--?
MS. ALLAN, PLEASE UNDERSTAND, I WOULD NEVER HARM A CHILD. I--
LOOK, IF YOU HADN'T MADE A PLAY AT HORIZON, WENT AFTER MY TECHNOLOGY, NONE OF THIS WOULD HAVE--
ENOUGH! I HAVE NOTHING MORE TO SAY TO YOU.
MR. BANKS, I'M TAKING NORMIE TO THE E.R.
AS FAR AS HORIZON GOES...?
...I WANT YOU AND MR. STONE TO IMMEDIATELY--
UM. MS. ALLAN. LIZ...
TIBERIUS IS GONE. ALONG WITH THAT OTHER SPIDER-MAN.

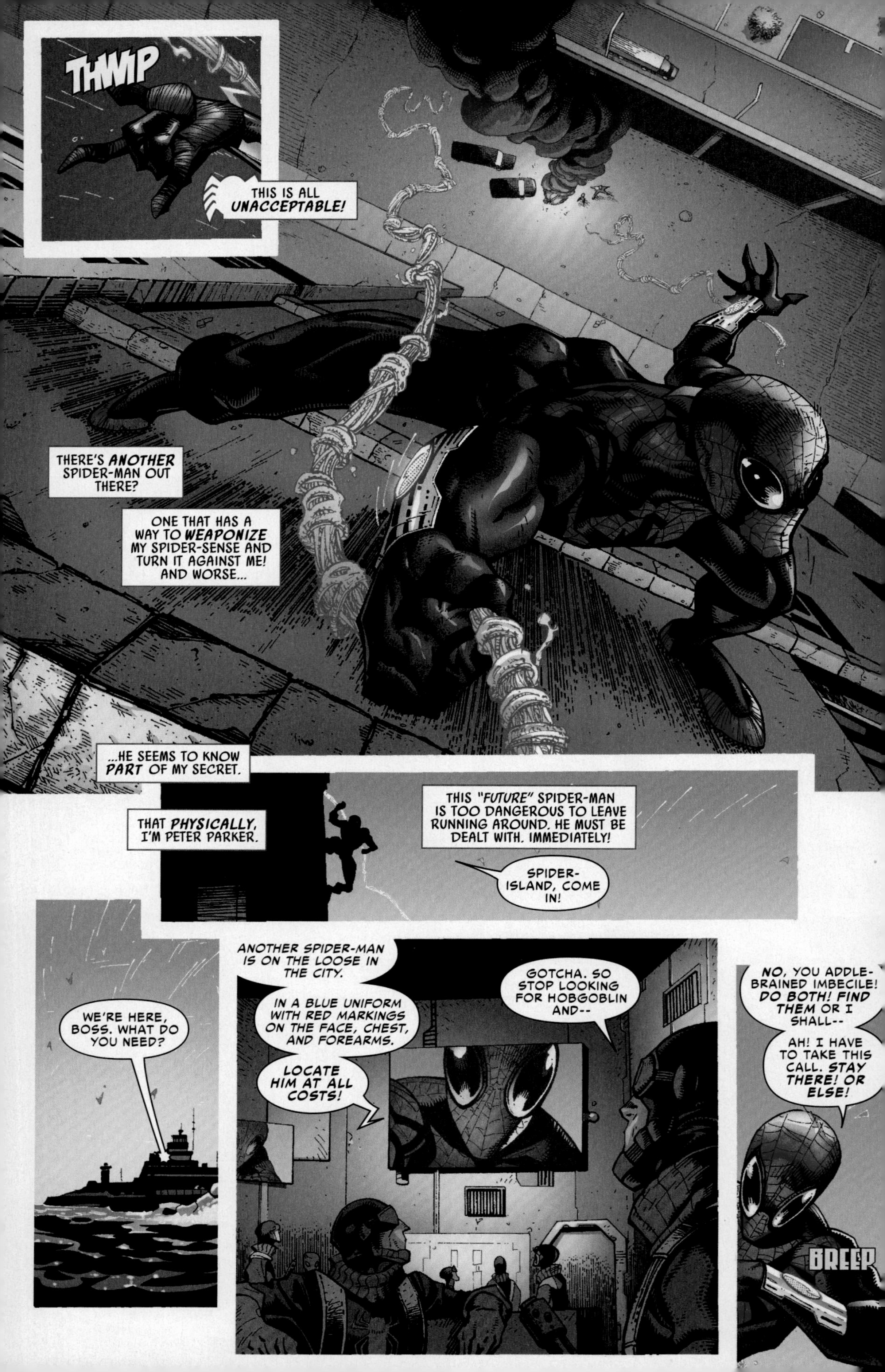
THWIP
THIS IS ALL UNACCEPTABLE!
THERE'S ANOTHER SPIDER-MAN OUT THERE?
ONE THAT HAS A WAY TO WEAPONIZE MY SPIDER-SENSE AND TURN IT AGAINST ME! AND WORSE...
...HE SEEMS TO KNOW PART OF MY SECRET.
THAT PHYSICALLY, I'M PETER PARKER.
THIS "FUTURE" SPIDER-MAN IS TOO DANGEROUS TO LEAVE RUNNING AROUND. HE MUST BE DEALT WITH. IMMEDIATELY!
SPIDER-ISLAND, COME IN!
WE'RE HERE, BOSS. WHAT DO YOU NEED?
ANOTHER SPIDER-MAN IS ON THE LOOSE IN THE CITY.
IN A BLUE UNIFORM WITH RED MARKINGS ON THE FACE, CHEST, AND FOREARMS.
LOCATE HIM AT ALL COSTS!
GOTCHA. SO STOP LOOKING FOR HOBGOBLIN AND--
NO, YOU ADDLE-BRAINED IMBECILE! DO BOTH! FIND THEM OR I SHALL--
AH! I HAVE TO TAKE THIS CALL. STAY THERE! OR ELSE!
BREEP

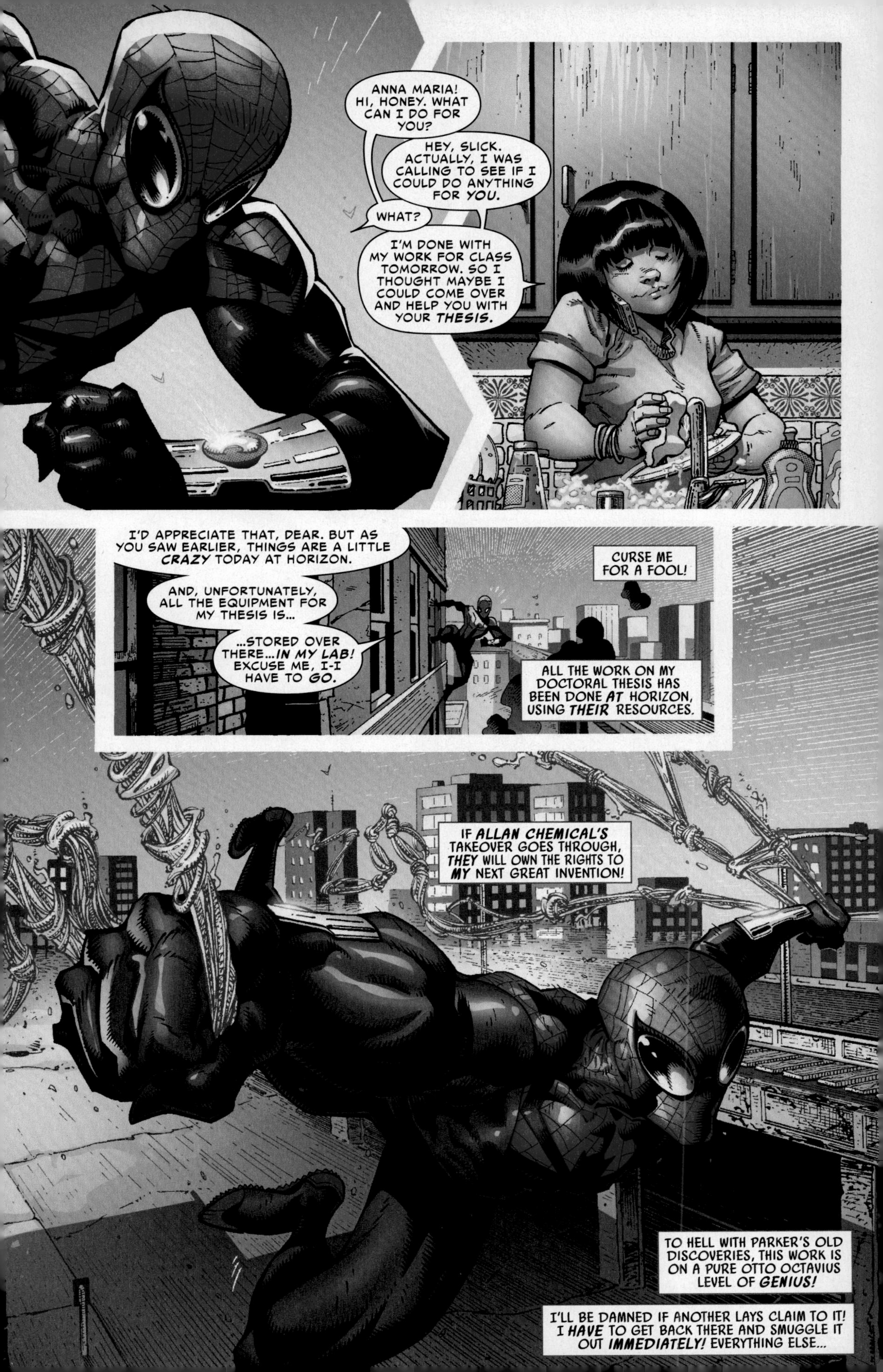

ANNA MARIA! HI, HONEY. WHAT CAN I DO FOR YOU?
HEY, SLICK. ACTUALLY, I WAS CALLING TO SEE IF I COULD DO ANYTHING FOR YOU.
WHAT?
I'M DONE WITH MY WORK FOR CLASS TOMORROW. SO I THOUGHT MAYBE I COULD COME OVER AND HELP YOU WITH YOUR THESIS.
I'D APPRECIATE THAT, DEAR. BUT AS YOU SAW EARLIER, THINGS ARE A LITTLE CRAZY TODAY AT HORIZON.
AND, UNFORTUNATELY, ALL THE EQUIPMENT FOR MY THESIS IS...
...STORED OVER THERE...IN MY LAB! EXCUSE ME, I-I HAVE TO GO.
CURSE ME FOR A FOOL!
ALL THE WORK ON MY DOCTORAL THESIS HAS BEEN DONE AT HORIZON, USING THEIR RESOURCES.
IF ALLAN CHEMICAL'S TAKEOVER GOES THROUGH, THEY WILL OWN THE RIGHTS TO MY NEXT GREAT INVENTION!
TO HELL WITH PARKER'S OLD DISCOVERIES, THIS WORK IS ON A PURE OTTO OCTAVIUS LEVEL OF GENIUS!
I'LL BE DAMNED IF ANOTHER LAYS CLAIM TO IT! I HAVE TO GET BACK THERE AND SMUGGLE IT OUT IMMEDIATELY! EVERYTHING ELSE...

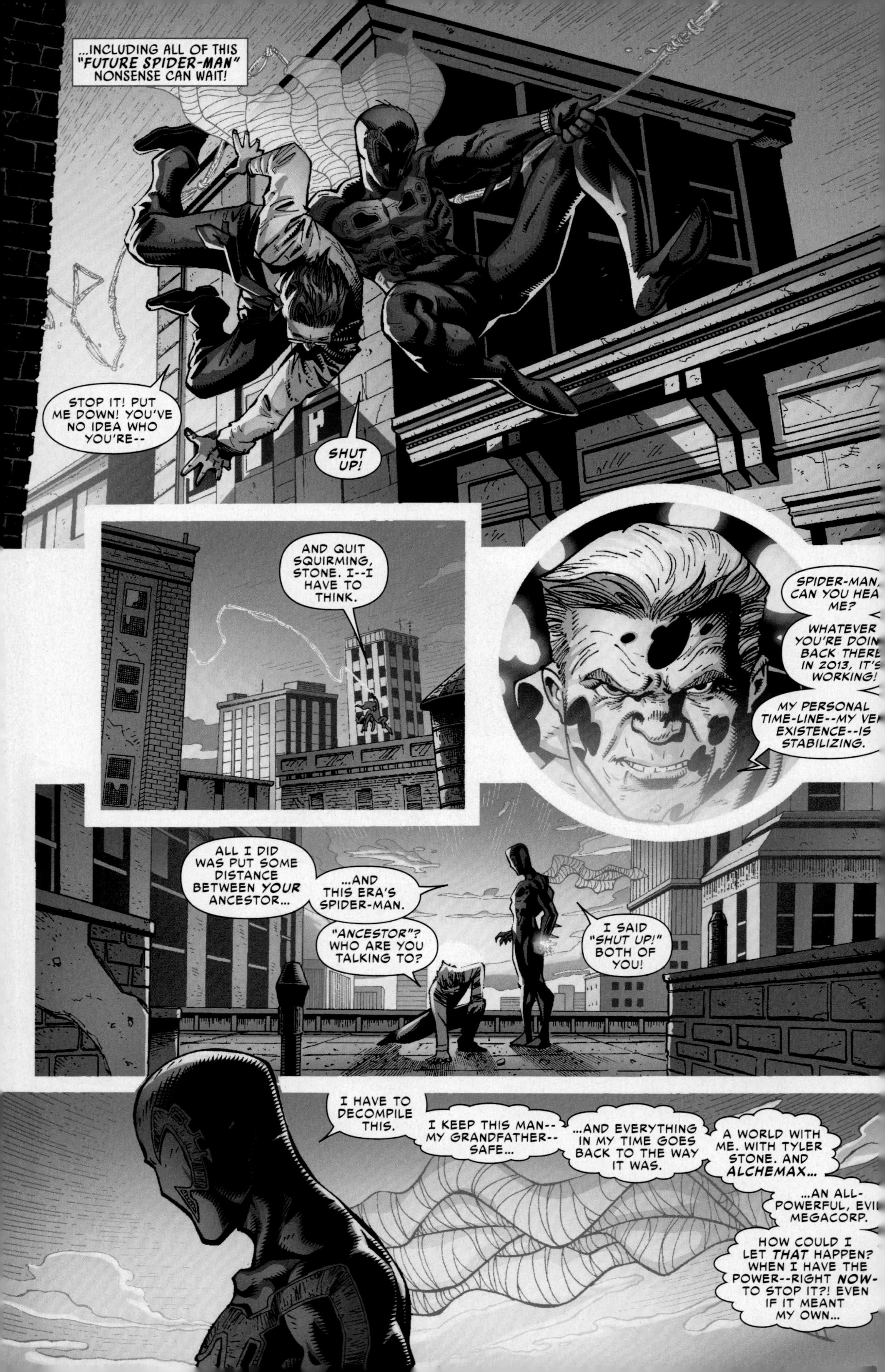
...INCLUDING ALL OF THIS *"FUTURE SPIDER-MAN"* NONSENSE CAN WAIT!
STOP IT! PUT ME DOWN! YOU'VE NO IDEA WHO YOU'RE--
SHUT UP!
AND QUIT SQUIRMING, STONE. I--I HAVE TO THINK.
SPIDER-MAN, CAN YOU HEA ME?
WHATEVER YOU'RE DOIN BACK THERE IN 2013, IT'S WORKING!
MY PERSONAL TIME-LINE--MY VE EXISTENCE--IS STABILIZING.
ALL I DID WAS PUT SOME DISTANCE BETWEEN *YOUR* ANCESTOR...
...AND THIS ERA'S SPIDER-MAN.
"ANCESTOR"? WHO ARE YOU TALKING TO?
I SAID *"SHUT UP!"* BOTH OF YOU!
I HAVE TO DECOMPILE THIS.
I KEEP THIS MAN-- MY GRANDFATHER-- SAFE...
...AND EVERYTHING IN MY TIME GOES BACK TO THE WAY IT WAS.
A WORLD WITH ME. WITH TYLER STONE. AND *ALCHEMAX*...
...AN ALL-POWERFUL, EVI MEGACORP.
HOW COULD I LET *THAT* HAPPEN? WHEN I HAVE THE POWER--RIGHT *NOW*-- TO STOP IT?! EVEN IF IT MEANT MY OWN...

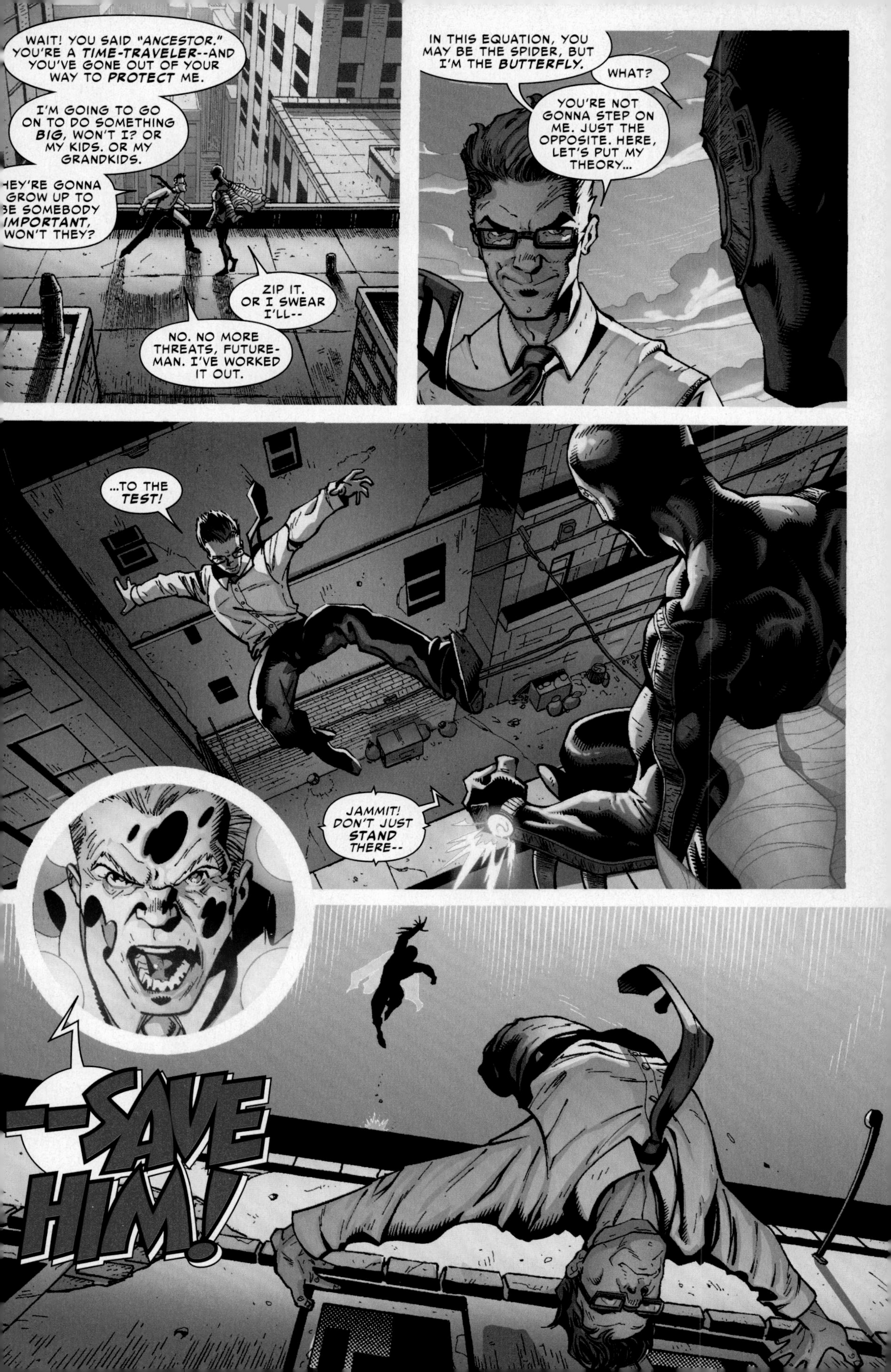
WAIT! YOU SAID "ANCESTOR." YOU'RE A TIME-TRAVELER--AND YOU'VE GONE OUT OF YOUR WAY TO PROTECT ME.
I'M GOING TO GO ON TO DO SOMETHING BIG, WON'T I? OR MY KIDS. OR MY GRANDKIDS.
HEY'RE GONNA GROW UP TO BE SOMEBODY IMPORTANT, WON'T THEY?
ZIP IT. OR I SWEAR I'LL--
NO. NO MORE THREATS, FUTURE-MAN. I'VE WORKED IT OUT.
IN THIS EQUATION, YOU MAY BE THE SPIDER, BUT I'M THE BUTTERFLY.
WHAT?
YOU'RE NOT GONNA STEP ON ME. JUST THE OPPOSITE. HERE, LET'S PUT MY THEORY...
...TO THE TEST!
JAMMIT! DON'T JUST STAND THERE--
--SAVE HIM!

THWIP

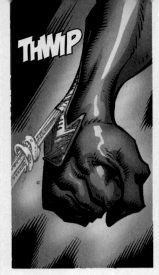

HA!

THWIP

I KNEW IT! THANKS FOR PERFECTLY PROVING MY--

POIMPHH--

YOU CRAZY, SHOCKING LUNATIC! I'VE HAD ENOUGH OF YOUR--

WHAT ARE YOU DOING?! UNHAND HIM!

THAT MAN'S A STONE, YOU DOWNTOWN PIECE OF TRASH!

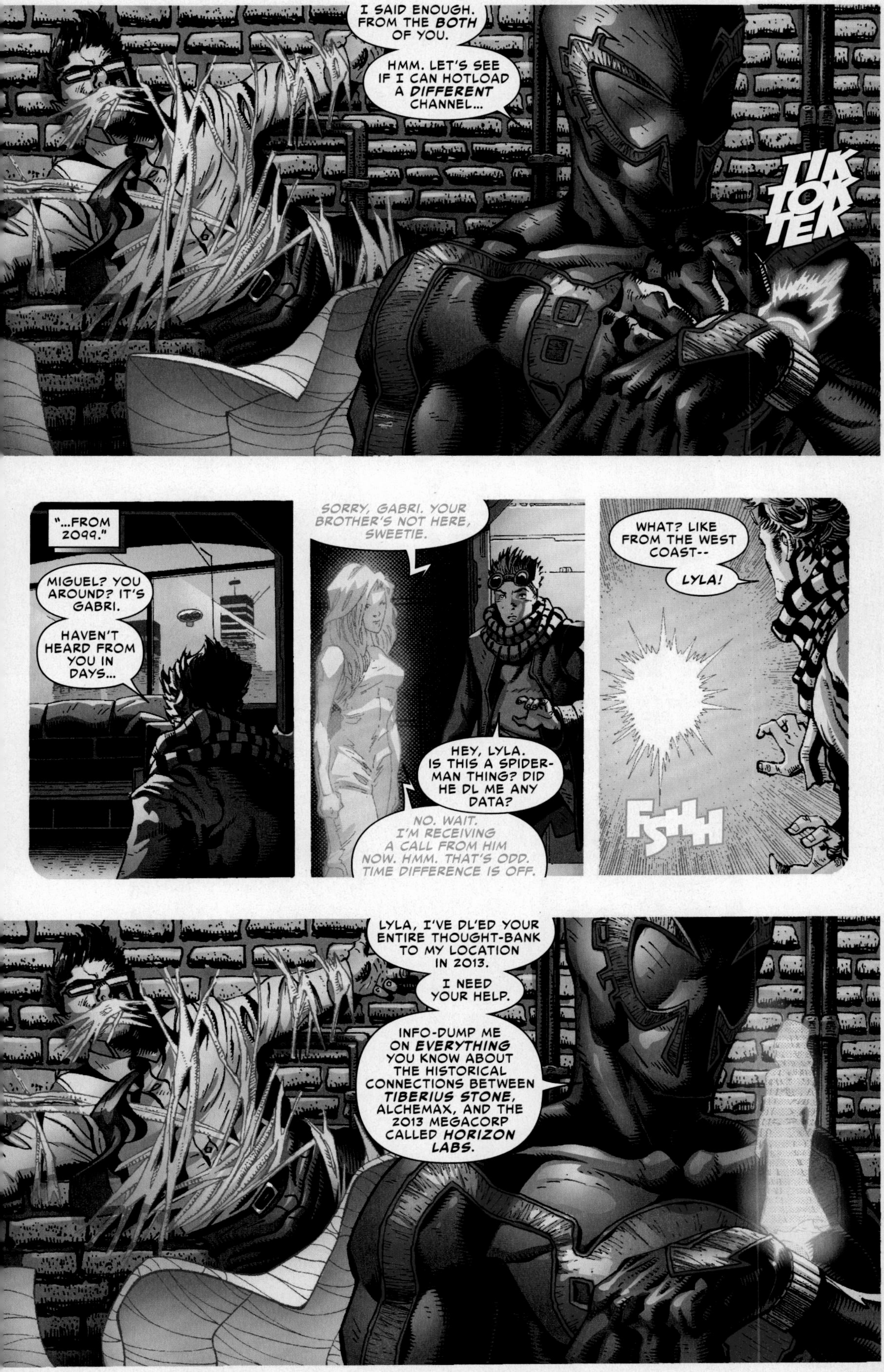
I SAID ENOUGH. FROM THE BOTH OF YOU.
HMM. LET'S SEE IF I CAN HOTLOAD A DIFFERENT CHANNEL...
TIK TOK TEK
"...FROM 2099."
MIGUEL? YOU AROUND? IT'S GABRI.
HAVEN'T HEARD FROM YOU IN DAYS...
SORRY, GABRI. YOUR BROTHER'S NOT HERE, SWEETIE.
HEY, LYLA. IS THIS A SPIDER-MAN THING? DID HE DL ME ANY DATA?
NO. WAIT. I'M RECEIVING A CALL FROM HIM NOW. HMM. THAT'S ODD. TIME DIFFERENCE IS OFF.
WHAT? LIKE FROM THE WEST COAST--
LYLA!
FSHH
LYLA, I'VE DL'ED YOUR ENTIRE THOUGHT-BANK TO MY LOCATION IN 2013.
I NEED YOUR HELP.
INFO-DUMP ME ON EVERYTHING YOU KNOW ABOUT THE HISTORICAL CONNECTIONS BETWEEN TIBERIUS STONE, ALCHEMAX, AND THE 2013 MEGACORP CALLED HORIZON LABS.

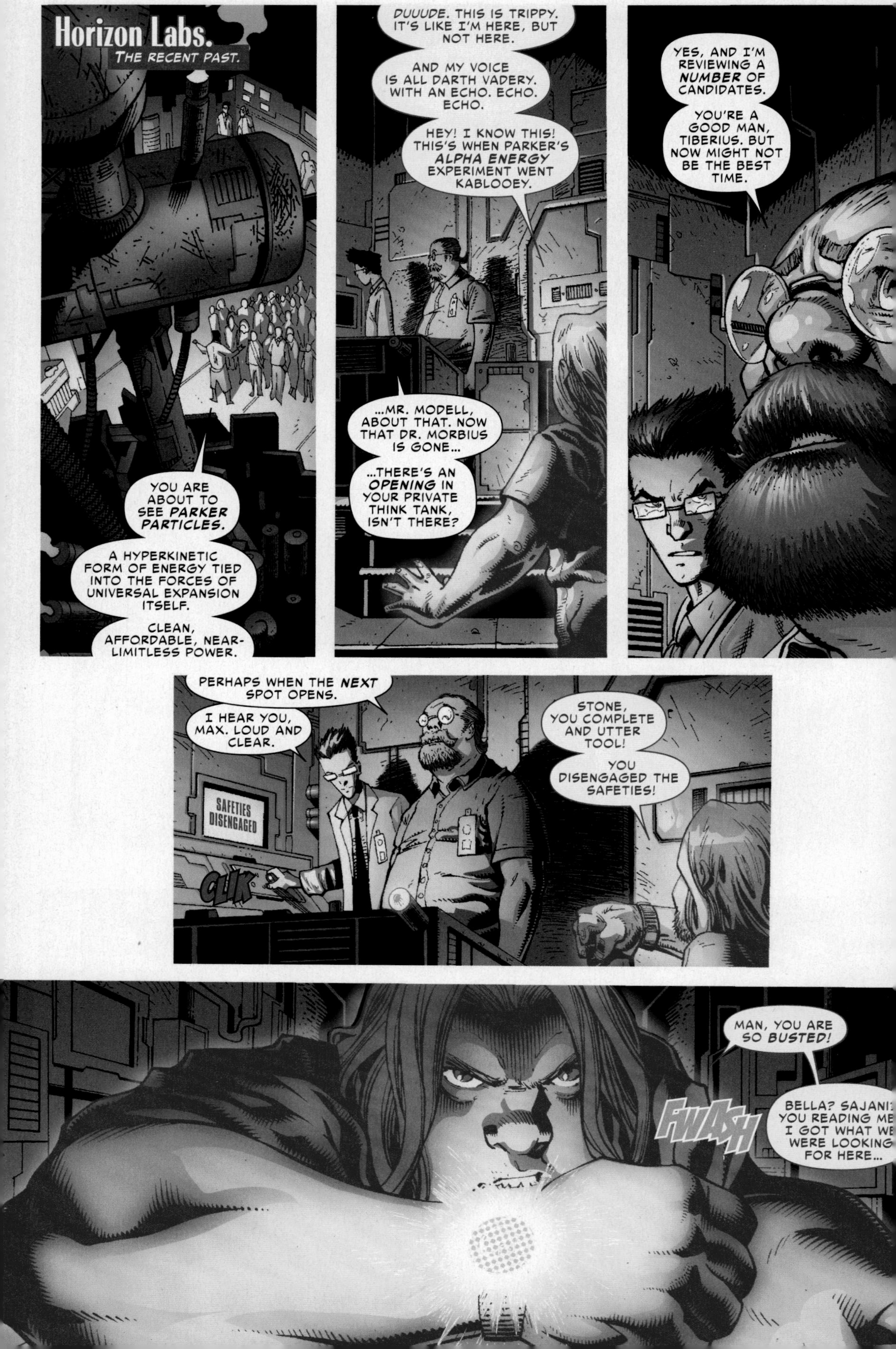
Horizon Labs.
THE RECENT PAST.
YOU ARE ABOUT TO SEE PARKER PARTICLES.
A HYPERKINETIC FORM OF ENERGY TIED INTO THE FORCES OF UNIVERSAL EXPANSION ITSELF.
CLEAN, AFFORDABLE, NEAR-LIMITLESS POWER.
DUUUDE. THIS IS TRIPPY. IT'S LIKE I'M HERE, BUT NOT HERE.
AND MY VOICE IS ALL DARTH VADERY. WITH AN ECHO. ECHO. ECHO.
HEY! I KNOW THIS! THIS'S WHEN PARKER'S ALPHA ENERGY EXPERIMENT WENT KABLOOEY.
...MR. MODELL, ABOUT THAT. NOW THAT DR. MORBIUS IS GONE...
...THERE'S AN OPENING IN YOUR PRIVATE THINK TANK, ISN'T THERE?
YES, AND I'M REVIEWING A NUMBER OF CANDIDATES.
YOU'RE A GOOD MAN, TIBERIUS. BUT NOW MIGHT NOT BE THE BEST TIME.
PERHAPS WHEN THE NEXT SPOT OPENS.
I HEAR YOU, MAX. LOUD AND CLEAR.
SAFETIES DISENGAGED
CLIK
STONE, YOU COMPLETE AND UTTER TOOL!
YOU DISENGAGED THE SAFETIES!
MAN, YOU ARE SO BUSTED!
FWASH
BELLA? SAJANI? YOU READING ME? I GOT WHAT WE WERE LOOKING FOR HERE...

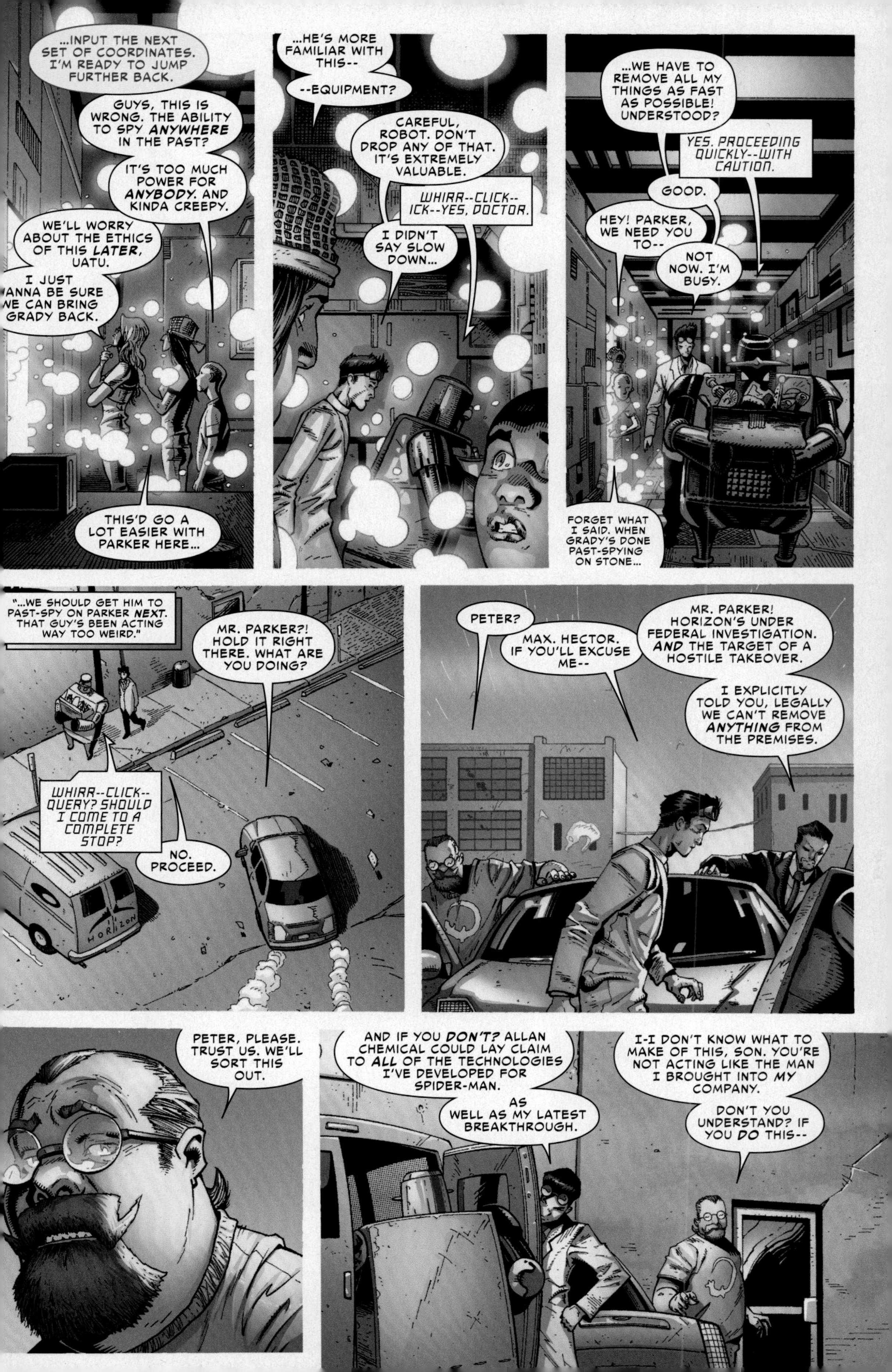
...INPUT THE NEXT SET OF COORDINATES. I'M READY TO JUMP FURTHER BACK.
GUYS, THIS IS WRONG. THE ABILITY TO SPY ANYWHERE IN THE PAST?
IT'S TOO MUCH POWER FOR ANYBODY. AND KINDA CREEPY.
WE'LL WORRY ABOUT THE ETHICS OF THIS LATER, UATU.
I JUST WANNA BE SURE WE CAN BRING GRADY BACK.
THIS'D GO A LOT EASIER WITH PARKER HERE...
...HE'S MORE FAMILIAR WITH THIS--
--EQUIPMENT?
CAREFUL, ROBOT. DON'T DROP ANY OF THAT. IT'S EXTREMELY VALUABLE.
WHIRR--CLICK--ICK--YES, DOCTOR.
I DIDN'T SAY SLOW DOWN...
...WE HAVE TO REMOVE ALL MY THINGS AS FAST AS POSSIBLE! UNDERSTOOD?
YES. PROCEEDING QUICKLY--WITH CAUTION.
GOOD.
HEY! PARKER, WE NEED YOU TO--
NOT NOW. I'M BUSY.
FORGET WHAT I SAID. WHEN GRADY'S DONE PAST-SPYING ON STONE...
"...WE SHOULD GET HIM TO PAST-SPY ON PARKER NEXT. THAT GUY'S BEEN ACTING WAY TOO WEIRD."
MR. PARKER?! HOLD IT RIGHT THERE. WHAT ARE YOU DOING?
WHIRR--CLICK--QUERY? SHOULD I COME TO A COMPLETE STOP?
NO. PROCEED.
HORIZON
PETER?
MAX. HECTOR. IF YOU'LL EXCUSE ME--
MR. PARKER! HORIZON'S UNDER FEDERAL INVESTIGATION. AND THE TARGET OF A HOSTILE TAKEOVER.
I EXPLICITLY TOLD YOU, LEGALLY WE CAN'T REMOVE ANYTHING FROM THE PREMISES.
PETER, PLEASE. TRUST US. WE'LL SORT THIS OUT.
AND IF YOU DON'T? ALLAN CHEMICAL COULD LAY CLAIM TO ALL OF THE TECHNOLOGIES I'VE DEVELOPED FOR SPIDER-MAN.
AS WELL AS MY LATEST BREAKTHROUGH.
I-I DON'T KNOW WHAT TO MAKE OF THIS, SON. YOU'RE NOT ACTING LIKE THE MAN I BROUGHT INTO MY COMPANY.
DON'T YOU UNDERSTAND? IF YOU DO THIS--

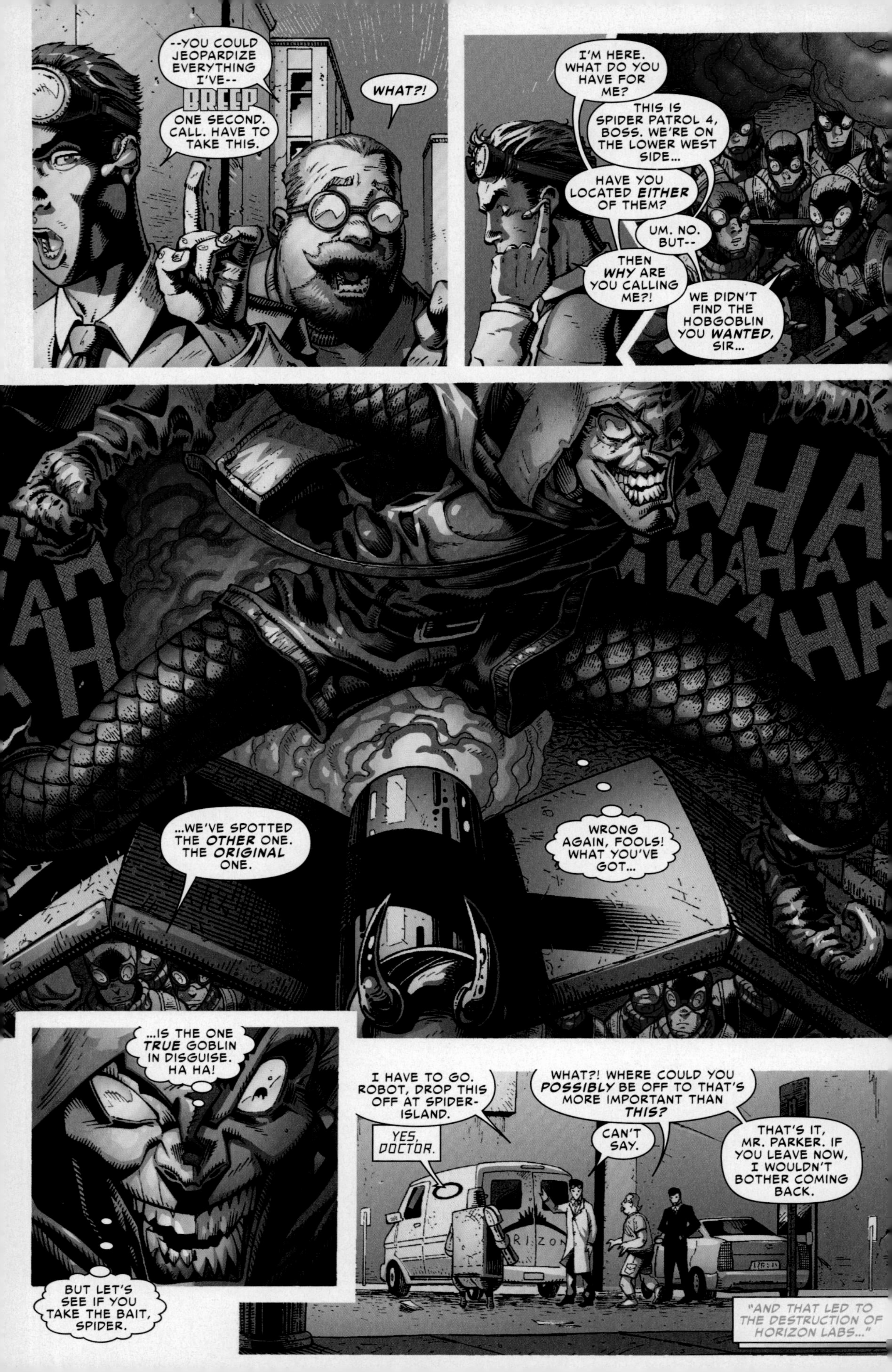
--YOU COULD JEOPARDIZE EVERYTHING I'VE--
BREEP
ONE SECOND. CALL. HAVE TO TAKE THIS.
WHAT?!
I'M HERE. WHAT DO YOU HAVE FOR ME?
THIS IS SPIDER PATROL 4, BOSS. WE'RE ON THE LOWER WEST SIDE...
HAVE YOU LOCATED EITHER OF THEM?
UM. NO. BUT--
THEN WHY ARE YOU CALLING ME?!
WE DIDN'T FIND THE HOBGOBLIN YOU WANTED, SIR...
...WE'VE SPOTTED THE OTHER ONE. THE ORIGINAL ONE.
WRONG AGAIN, FOOLS! WHAT YOU'VE GOT...
...IS THE ONE TRUE GOBLIN IN DISGUISE. HA HA!
BUT LET'S SEE IF YOU TAKE THE BAIT, SPIDER.
I HAVE TO GO. ROBOT, DROP THIS OFF AT SPIDER-ISLAND.
YES, DOCTOR.
WHAT?! WHERE COULD YOU POSSIBLY BE OFF TO THAT'S MORE IMPORTANT THAN THIS?
CAN'T SAY.
THAT'S IT, MR. PARKER. IF YOU LEAVE NOW, I WOULDN'T BOTHER COMING BACK.
"AND THAT LED TO THE DESTRUCTION OF HORIZON LABS..."

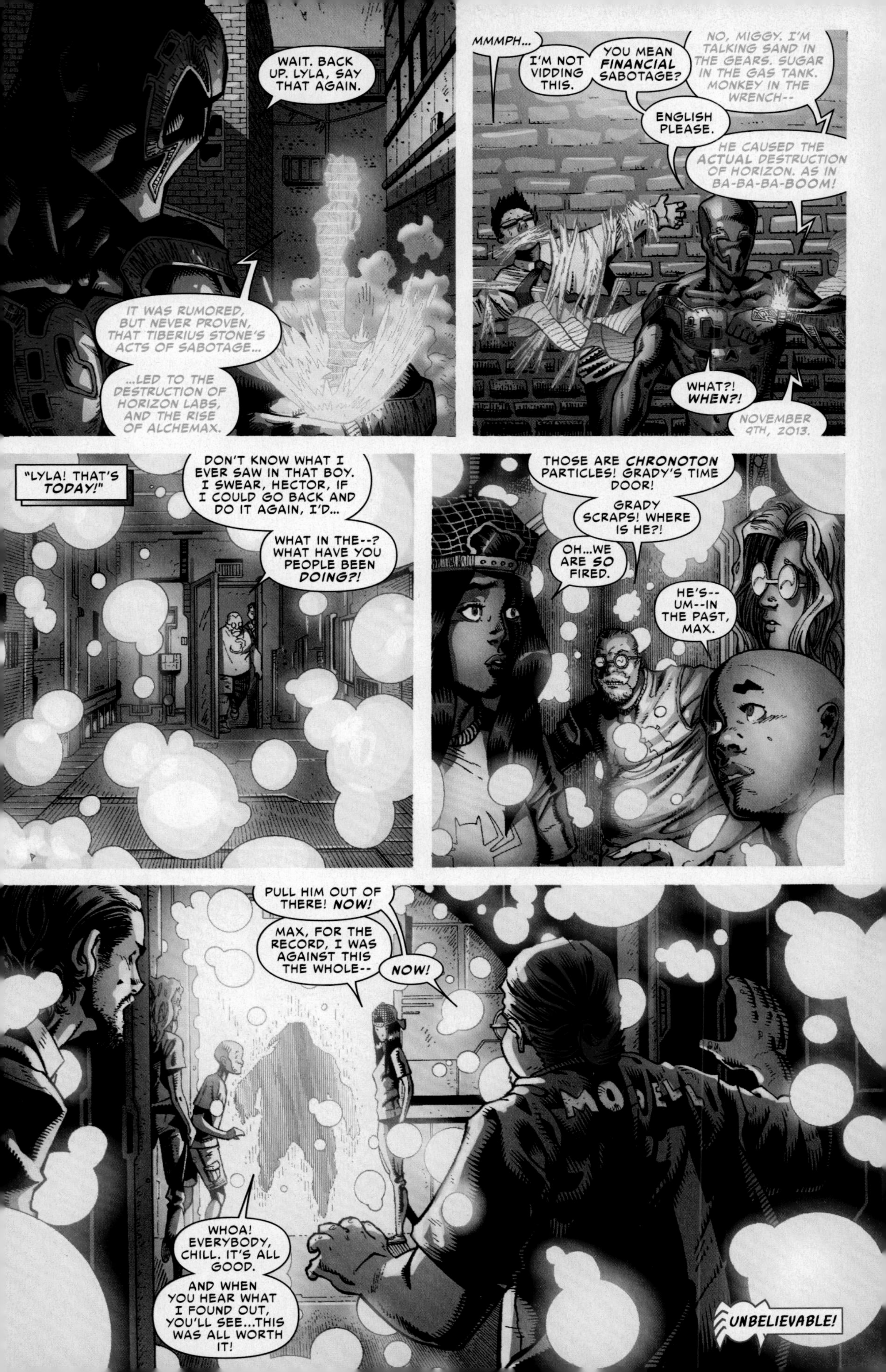
WAIT. BACK UP. LYLA, SAY THAT AGAIN.
IT WAS RUMORED, BUT NEVER PROVEN, THAT TIBERIUS STONE'S ACTS OF SABOTAGE...
...LED TO THE DESTRUCTION OF HORIZON LABS, AND THE RISE OF ALCHEMAX.
MMMPH...
I'M NOT VIDDING THIS.
YOU MEAN FINANCIAL SABOTAGE?
NO, MIGGY. I'M TALKING SAND IN THE GEARS. SUGAR IN THE GAS TANK. MONKEY IN THE WRENCH--
ENGLISH PLEASE.
HE CAUSED THE ACTUAL DESTRUCTION OF HORIZON. AS IN BA-BA-BA-BOOM!
WHAT?! WHEN?!
NOVEMBER 9TH, 2013.
"LYLA! THAT'S TODAY!"
DON'T KNOW WHAT I EVER SAW IN THAT BOY. I SWEAR, HECTOR, IF I COULD GO BACK AND DO IT AGAIN, I'D...
WHAT IN THE--? WHAT HAVE YOU PEOPLE BEEN DOING?!
THOSE ARE CHRONOTON PARTICLES! GRADY'S TIME DOOR!
GRADY SCRAPS! WHERE IS HE?!
OH...WE ARE SO FIRED.
HE'S--UM--IN THE PAST, MAX.
PULL HIM OUT OF THERE! NOW!
MAX, FOR THE RECORD, I WAS AGAINST THIS THE WHOLE--
NOW!
WHOA! EVERYBODY, CHILL. IT'S ALL GOOD.
AND WHEN YOU HEAR WHAT I FOUND OUT, YOU'LL SEE...THIS WAS ALL WORTH IT!
UNBELIEVABLE!

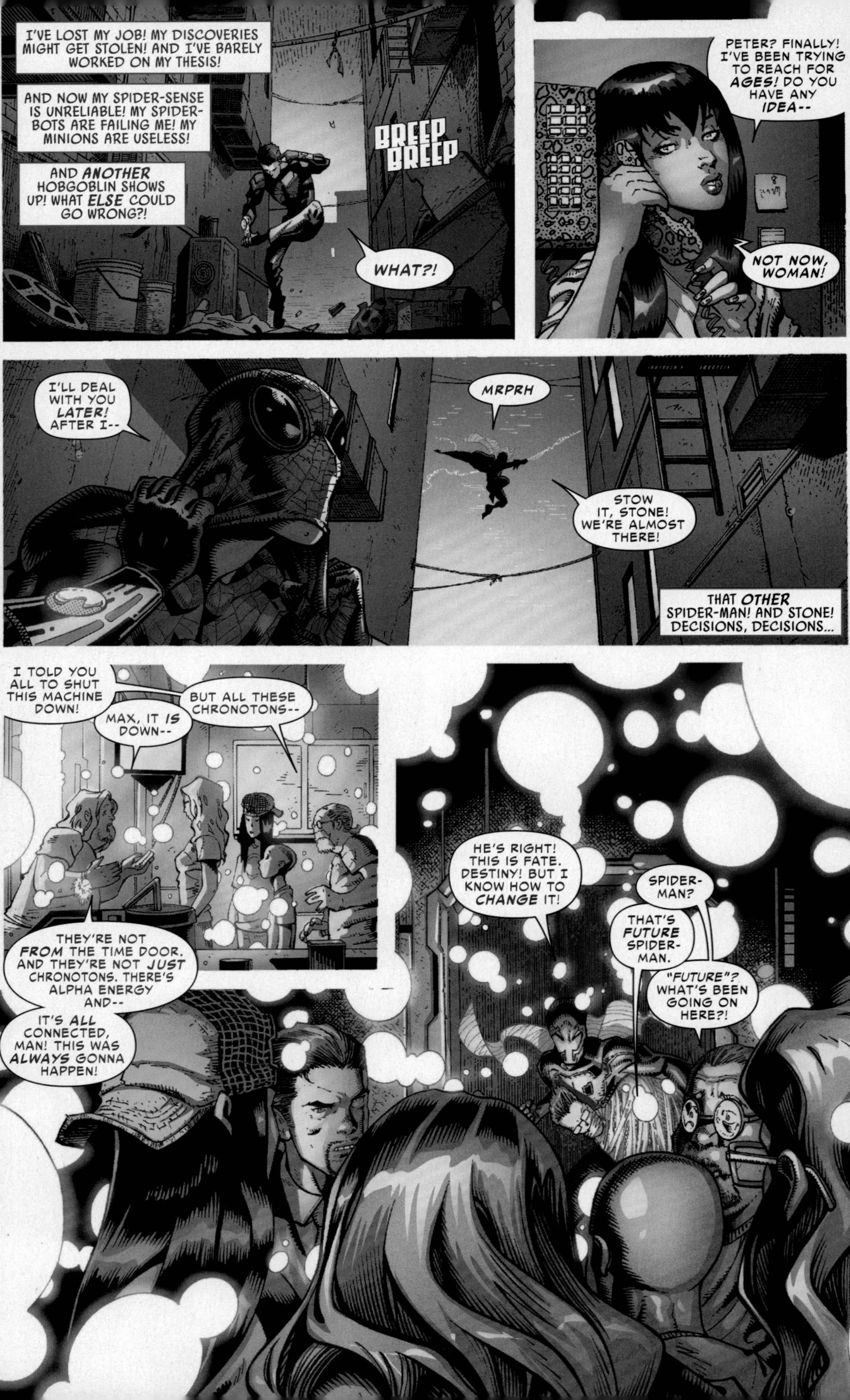
I'VE LOST MY JOB! MY DISCOVERIES MIGHT GET STOLEN! AND I'VE BARELY WORKED ON MY THESIS!
AND NOW MY SPIDER-SENSE IS UNRELIABLE! MY SPIDER-BOTS ARE FAILING ME! MY MINIONS ARE USELESS!
AND ANOTHER HOBGOBLIN SHOWS UP! WHAT ELSE COULD GO WRONG?!
BREEP BREEP
WHAT?!
PETER? FINALLY! I'VE BEEN TRYING TO REACH FOR AGES! DO YOU HAVE ANY IDEA--
NOT NOW, WOMAN!
I'LL DEAL WITH YOU LATER! AFTER I--
MRPRH
STOW IT, STONE! WE'RE ALMOST THERE!
THAT OTHER SPIDER-MAN! AND STONE! DECISIONS, DECISIONS...
I TOLD YOU ALL TO SHUT THIS MACHINE DOWN!
MAX, IT IS DOWN--
BUT ALL THESE CHRONOTONS--
THEY'RE NOT FROM THE TIME DOOR. AND THEY'RE NOT JUST CHRONOTONS. THERE'S ALPHA ENERGY AND--
IT'S ALL CONNECTED, MAN! THIS WAS ALWAYS GONNA HAPPEN!
HE'S RIGHT! THIS IS FATE. DESTINY! BUT I KNOW HOW TO CHANGE IT!
SPIDER-MAN?
THAT'S FUTURE SPIDER-MAN.
"FUTURE"? WHAT'S BEEN GOING ON HERE?!

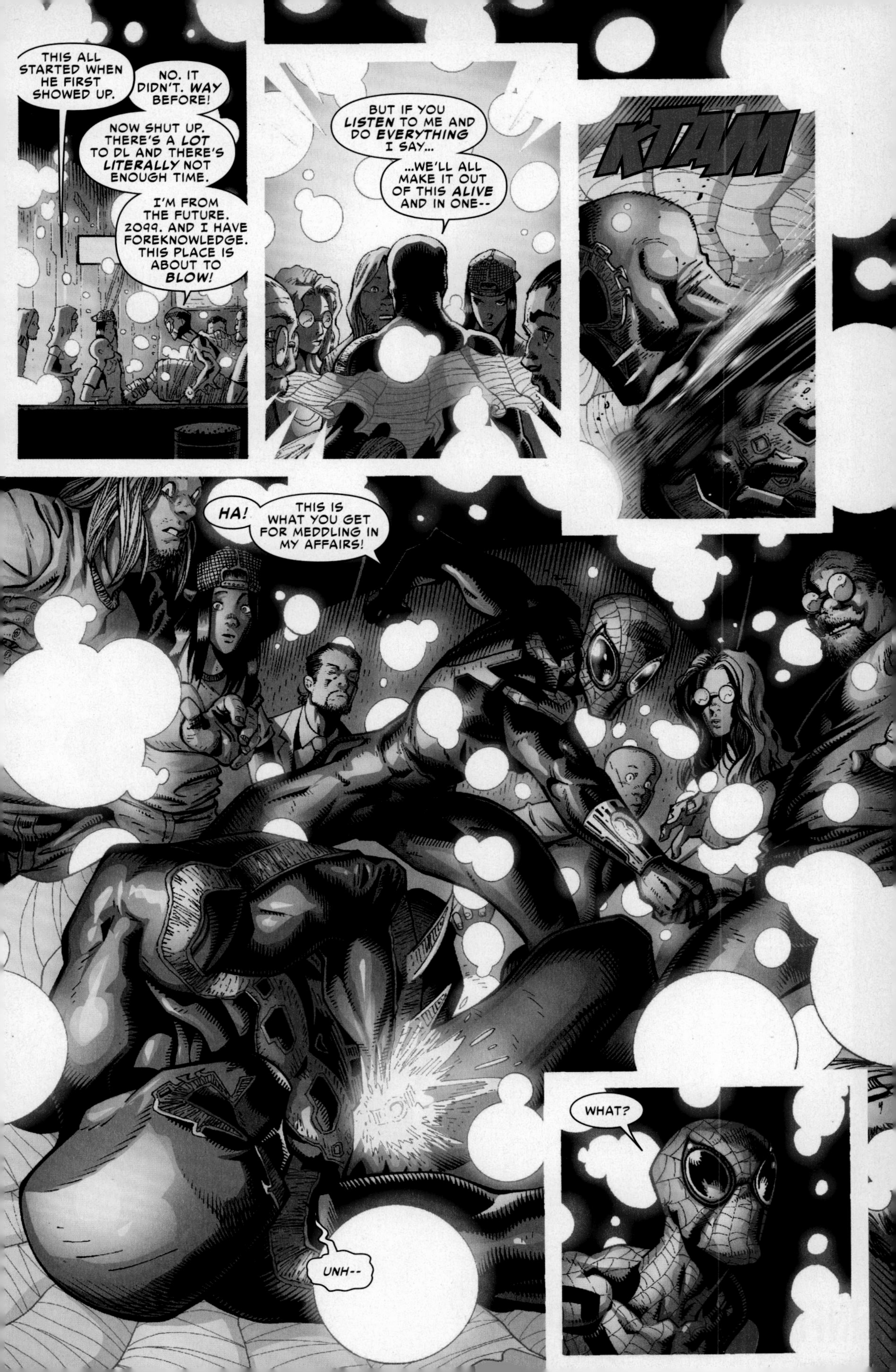

THIS ALL STARTED WHEN HE FIRST SHOWED UP.
NO. IT DIDN'T. WAY BEFORE!
NOW SHUT UP. THERE'S A LOT TO DL AND THERE'S LITERALLY NOT ENOUGH TIME.
I'M FROM THE FUTURE. 2099. AND I HAVE FOREKNOWLEDGE. THIS PLACE IS ABOUT TO BLOW!
BUT IF YOU LISTEN TO ME AND DO EVERYTHING I SAY...
...WE'LL ALL MAKE IT OUT OF THIS ALIVE AND IN ONE--
KTAM
HA!
THIS IS WHAT YOU GET FOR MEDDLING IN MY AFFAIRS!
WHAT?
UNH--

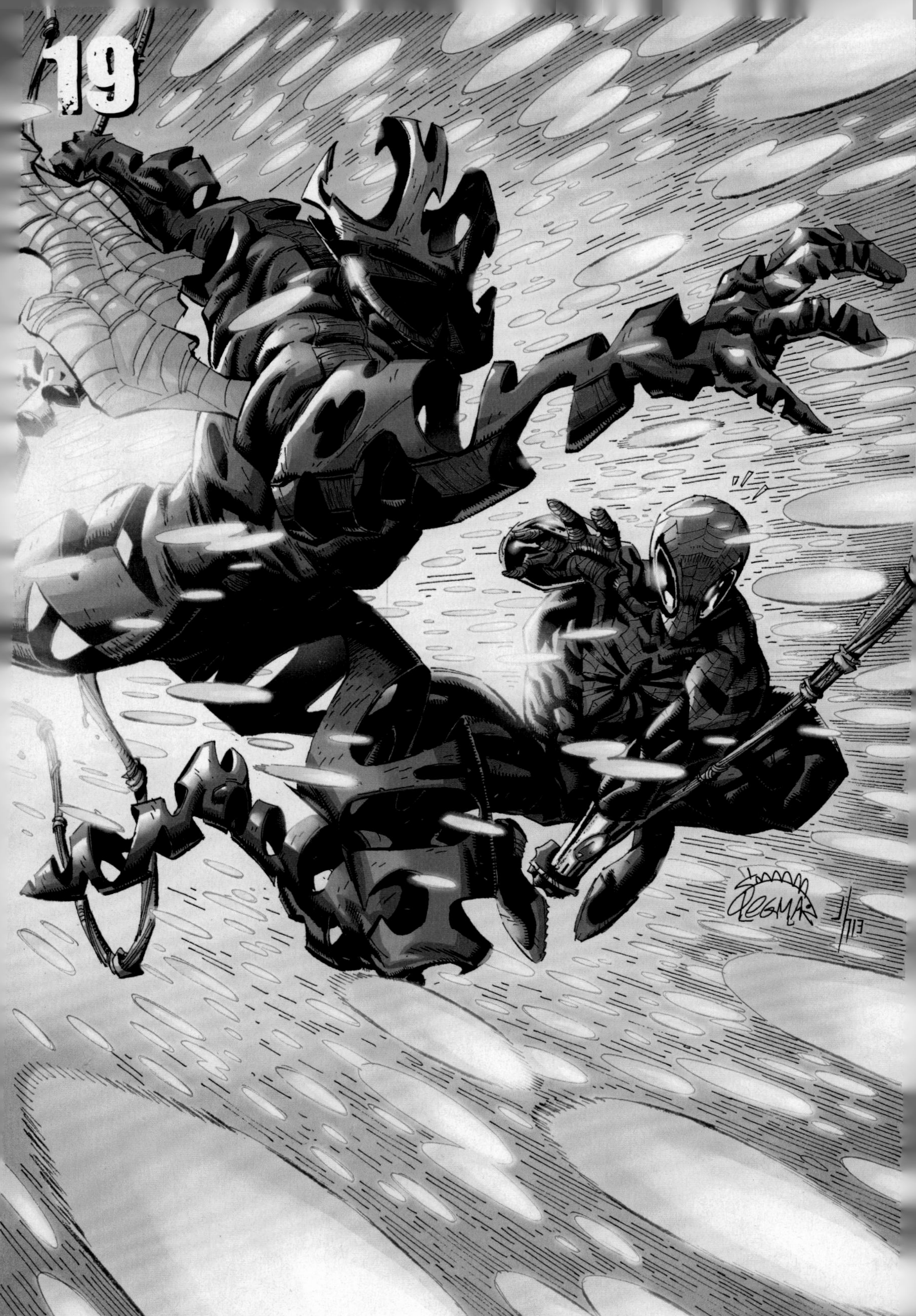
19

NFERIORITY COMPLEX

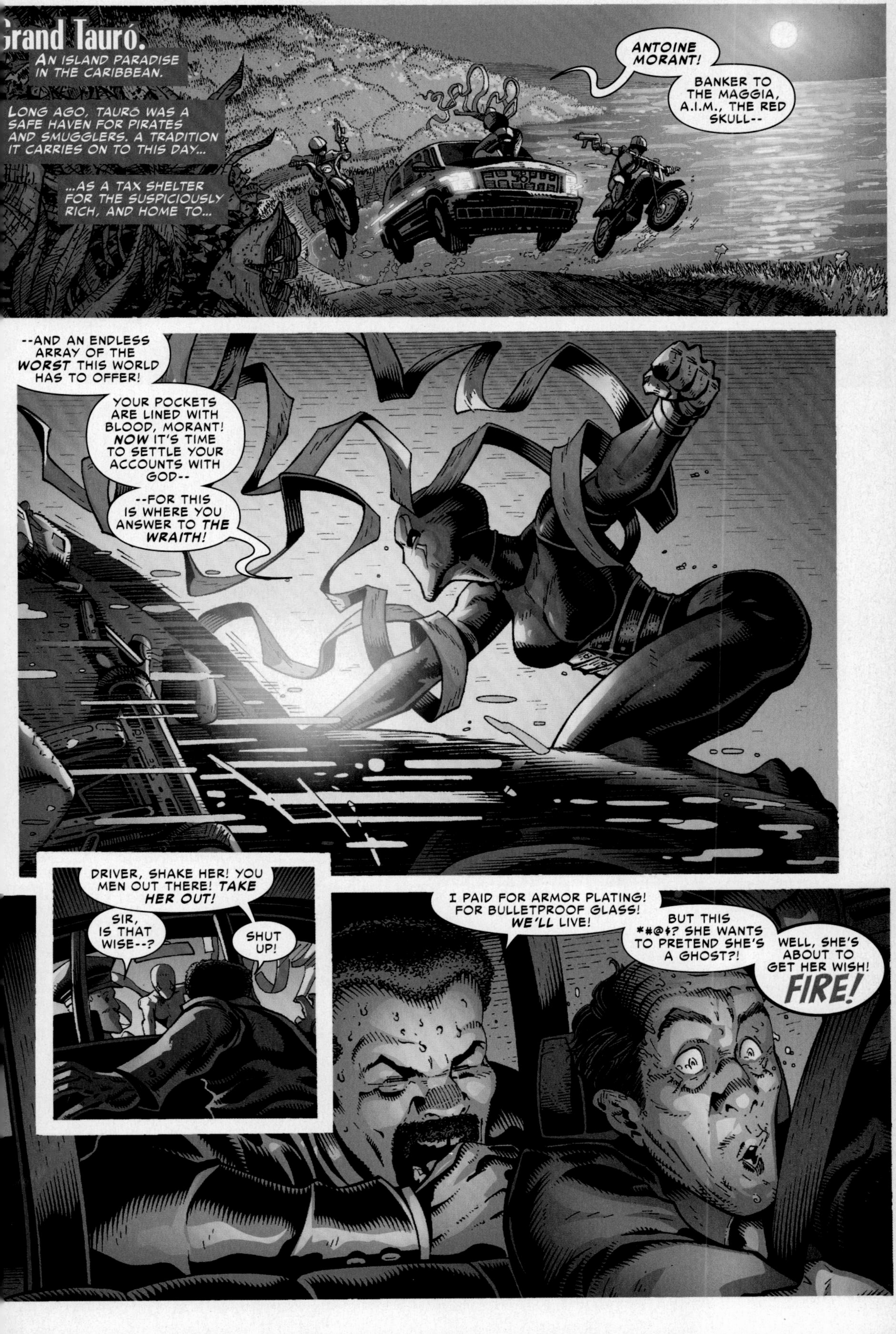
Grand Tauró.
AN ISLAND PARADISE IN THE CARIBBEAN.
LONG AGO, TAURÓ WAS A SAFE HAVEN FOR PIRATES AND SMUGGLERS. A TRADITION IT CARRIES ON TO THIS DAY...
...AS A TAX SHELTER FOR THE SUSPICIOUSLY RICH, AND HOME TO...
ANTOINE MORANT!
BANKER TO THE MAGGIA, A.I.M., THE RED SKULL--
--AND AN ENDLESS ARRAY OF THE WORST THIS WORLD HAS TO OFFER!
YOUR POCKETS ARE LINED WITH BLOOD, MORANT! NOW IT'S TIME TO SETTLE YOUR ACCOUNTS WITH GOD--
--FOR THIS IS WHERE YOU ANSWER TO THE WRAITH!
DRIVER, SHAKE HER! YOU MEN OUT THERE! TAKE HER OUT!
SIR, IS THAT WISE--?
SHUT UP!
I PAID FOR ARMOR PLATING! FOR BULLETPROOF GLASS! WE'LL LIVE!
BUT THIS *#@$? SHE WANTS TO PRETEND SHE'S A GHOST?!
WELL, SHE'S ABOUT TO GET HER WISH! FIRE!

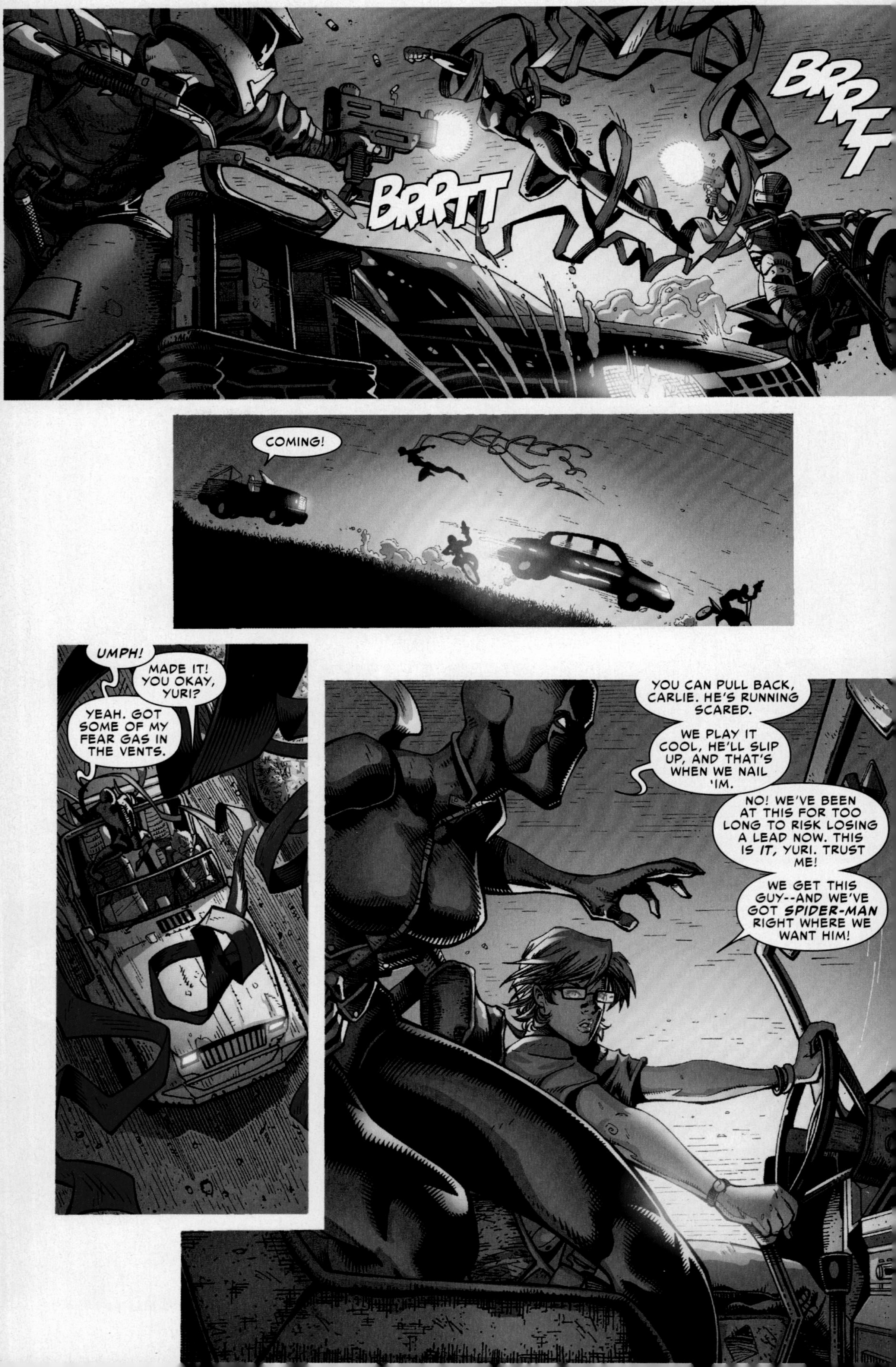
BRRTT
BRRTT
COMING!
UMPH!
MADE IT! YOU OKAY, YURI?
YEAH. GOT SOME OF MY FEAR GAS IN THE VENTS.
YOU CAN PULL BACK, CARLIE. HE'S RUNNING SCARED.
WE PLAY IT COOL, HE'LL SLIP UP, AND THAT'S WHEN WE NAIL 'IM.
NO! WE'VE BEEN AT THIS FOR TOO LONG TO RISK LOSING A LEAD NOW. THIS IS IT, YURI. TRUST ME!
WE GET THIS GUY--AND WE'VE GOT SPIDER-MAN RIGHT WHERE WE WANT HIM!

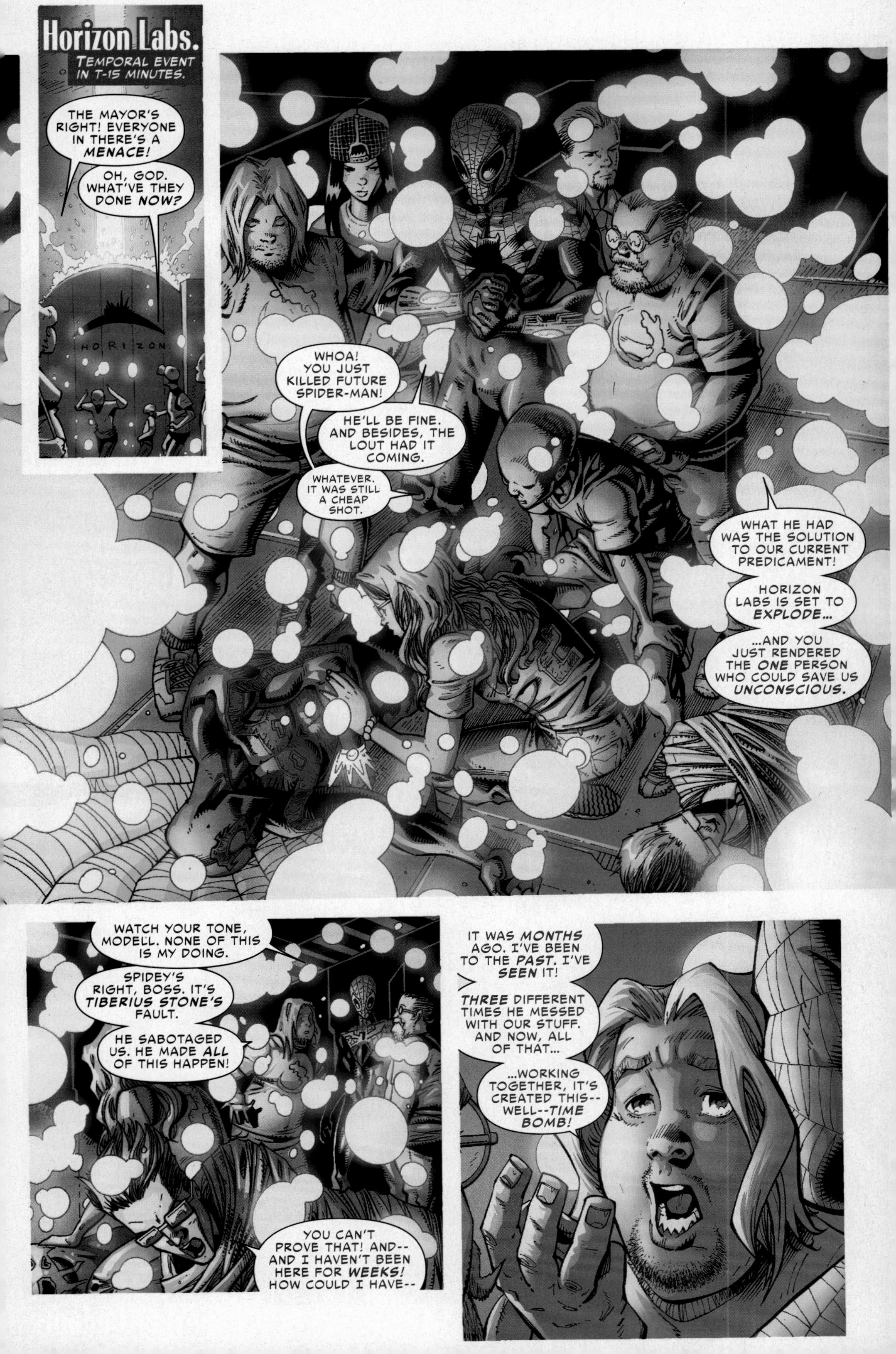
Horizon Labs.
TEMPORAL EVENT IN T-15 MINUTES.
THE MAYOR'S RIGHT! EVERYONE IN THERE'S A MENACE!
OH, GOD. WHAT'VE THEY DONE NOW?
HORIZON
WHOA! YOU JUST KILLED FUTURE SPIDER-MAN!
HE'LL BE FINE. AND BESIDES, THE LOUT HAD IT COMING.
WHATEVER. IT WAS STILL A CHEAP SHOT.
WHAT HE HAD WAS THE SOLUTION TO OUR CURRENT PREDICAMENT!
HORIZON LABS IS SET TO EXPLODE...
...AND YOU JUST RENDERED THE ONE PERSON WHO COULD SAVE US UNCONSCIOUS.
WATCH YOUR TONE, MODELL. NONE OF THIS IS MY DOING.
SPIDEY'S RIGHT, BOSS. IT'S TIBERIUS STONE'S FAULT.
HE SABOTAGED US. HE MADE ALL OF THIS HAPPEN!
YOU CAN'T PROVE THAT! AND-- AND I HAVEN'T BEEN HERE FOR WEEKS! HOW COULD I HAVE--
IT WAS MONTHS AGO. I'VE BEEN TO THE PAST. I'VE SEEN IT!
THREE DIFFERENT TIMES HE MESSED WITH OUR STUFF. AND NOW, ALL OF THAT...
...WORKING TOGETHER, IT'S CREATED THIS-- WELL--TIME BOMB!

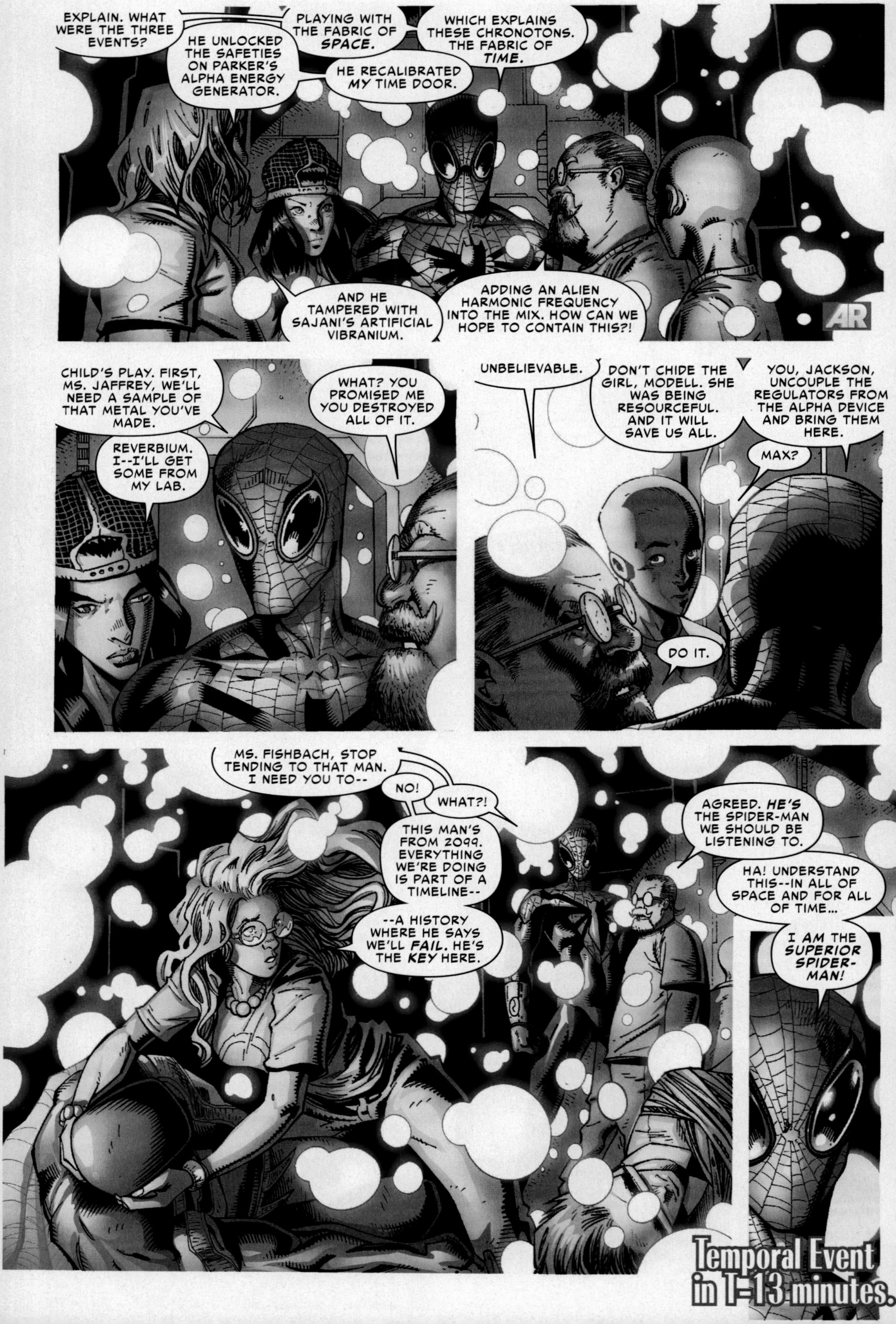
EXPLAIN. WHAT WERE THE THREE EVENTS?
HE UNLOCKED THE SAFETIES ON PARKER'S ALPHA ENERGY GENERATOR.
PLAYING WITH THE FABRIC OF SPACE.
HE RECALIBRATED MY TIME DOOR.
WHICH EXPLAINS THESE CHRONOTONS. THE FABRIC OF TIME.
AND HE TAMPERED WITH SAJANI'S ARTIFICIAL VIBRANIUM.
ADDING AN ALIEN HARMONIC FREQUENCY INTO THE MIX. HOW CAN WE HOPE TO CONTAIN THIS?!
AR
CHILD'S PLAY. FIRST, MS. JAFFREY, WE'LL NEED A SAMPLE OF THAT METAL YOU'VE MADE.
REVERBIUM. I--I'LL GET SOME FROM MY LAB.
WHAT? YOU PROMISED ME YOU DESTROYED ALL OF IT.
UNBELIEVABLE.
DON'T CHIDE THE GIRL, MODELL. SHE WAS BEING RESOURCEFUL. AND IT WILL SAVE US ALL.
YOU, JACKSON, UNCOUPLE THE REGULATORS FROM THE ALPHA DEVICE AND BRING THEM HERE.
MAX?
DO IT.
MS. FISHBACH, STOP TENDING TO THAT MAN. I NEED YOU TO--
NO!
WHAT?!
THIS MAN'S FROM 2099. EVERYTHING WE'RE DOING IS PART OF A TIMELINE--
--A HISTORY WHERE HE SAYS WE'LL FAIL. HE'S THE KEY HERE.
AGREED. HE'S THE SPIDER-MAN WE SHOULD BE LISTENING TO.
HA! UNDERSTAND THIS--IN ALL OF SPACE AND FOR ALL OF TIME...
I AM THE SUPERIOR SPIDER-MAN!
Temporal Event in T-13 minutes.

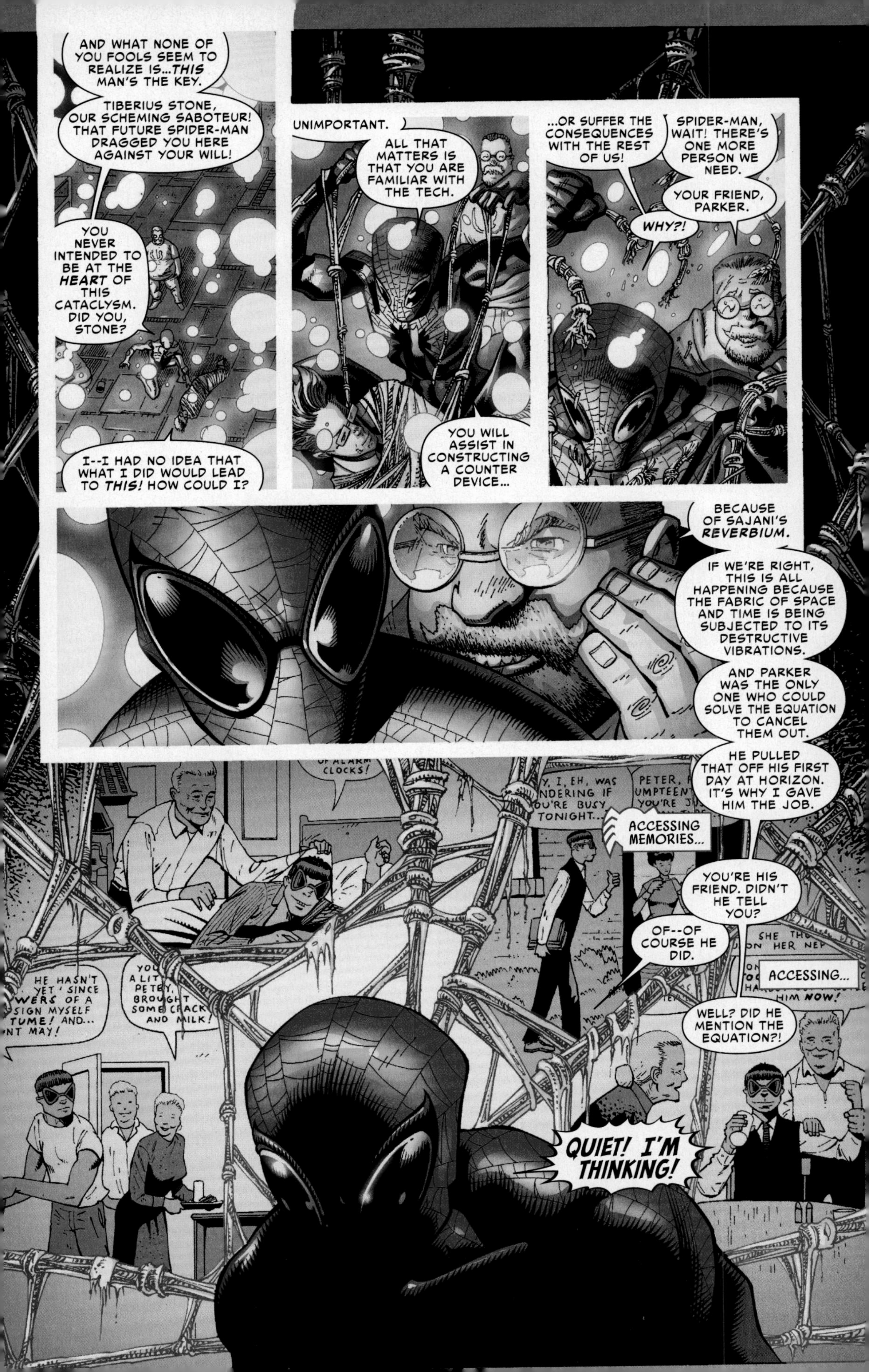

AND WHAT NONE OF YOU FOOLS SEEM TO REALIZE IS...THIS MAN'S THE KEY.
TIBERIUS STONE, OUR SCHEMING SABOTEUR! THAT FUTURE SPIDER-MAN DRAGGED YOU HERE AGAINST YOUR WILL!
YOU NEVER INTENDED TO BE AT THE HEART OF THIS CATACLYSM. DID YOU, STONE?
I--I HAD NO IDEA THAT WHAT I DID WOULD LEAD TO THIS! HOW COULD I?
UNIMPORTANT.
ALL THAT MATTERS IS THAT YOU ARE FAMILIAR WITH THE TECH.
YOU WILL ASSIST IN CONSTRUCTING A COUNTER DEVICE...
...OR SUFFER THE CONSEQUENCES WITH THE REST OF US!
SPIDER-MAN, WAIT! THERE'S ONE MORE PERSON WE NEED.
YOUR FRIEND, PARKER.
WHY?!
BECAUSE OF SAJANI'S REVERBIUM.
IF WE'RE RIGHT, THIS IS ALL HAPPENING BECAUSE THE FABRIC OF SPACE AND TIME IS BEING SUBJECTED TO ITS DESTRUCTIVE VIBRATIONS.
AND PARKER WAS THE ONLY ONE WHO COULD SOLVE THE EQUATION TO CANCEL THEM OUT.
HE PULLED THAT OFF HIS FIRST DAY AT HORIZON. IT'S WHY I GAVE HIM THE JOB.
ACCESSING MEMORIES...
YOU'RE HIS FRIEND. DIDN'T HE TELL YOU?
OF--OF COURSE HE DID.
ACCESSING...
WELL? DID HE MENTION THE EQUATION?!
QUIET! I'M THINKING!

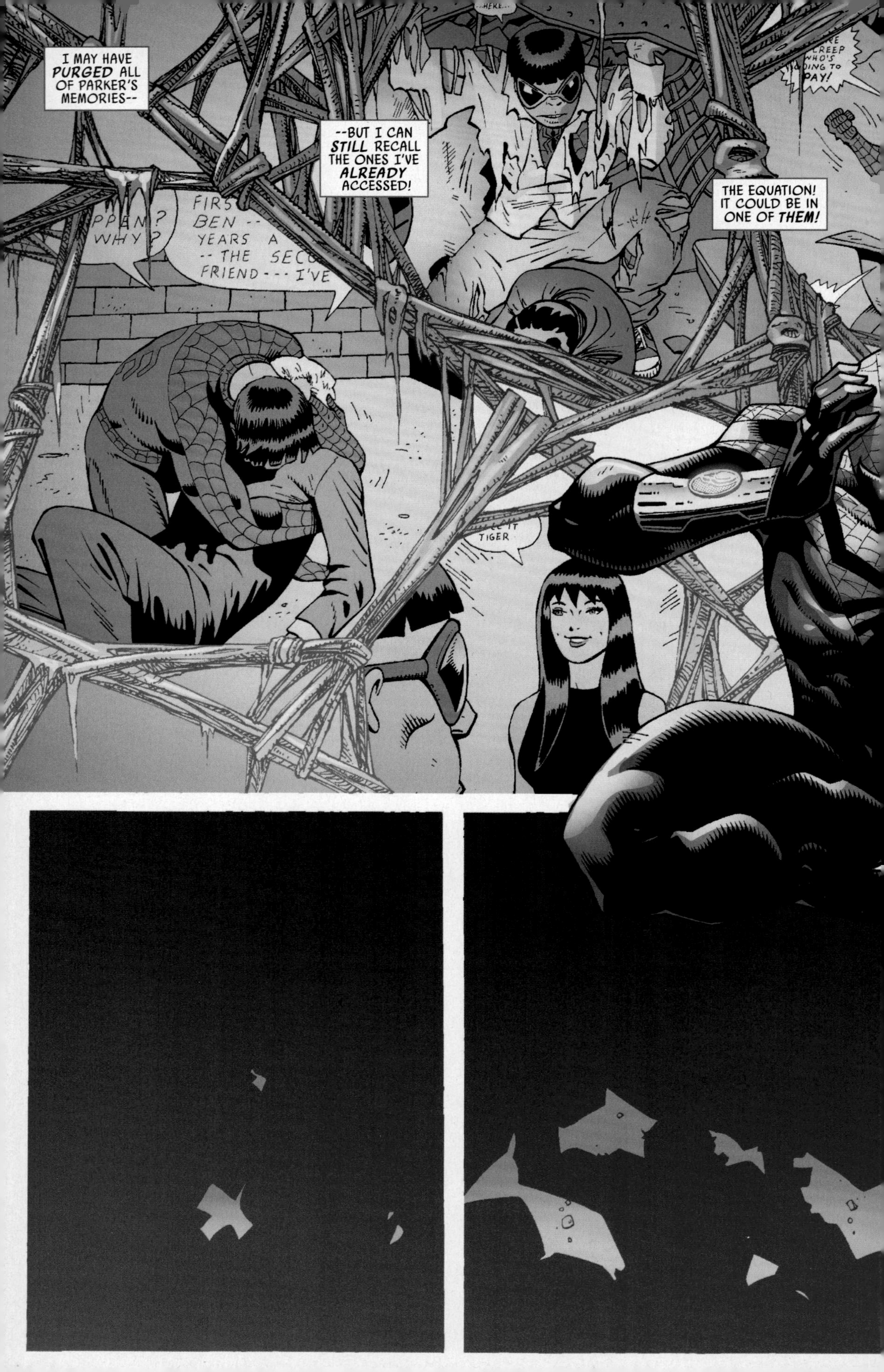
I MAY HAVE PURGED ALL OF PARKER'S MEMORIES--
--BUT I CAN STILL RECALL THE ONES I'VE ALREADY ACCESSED!
THE EQUATION! IT COULD BE IN ONE OF THEM!
TIGER

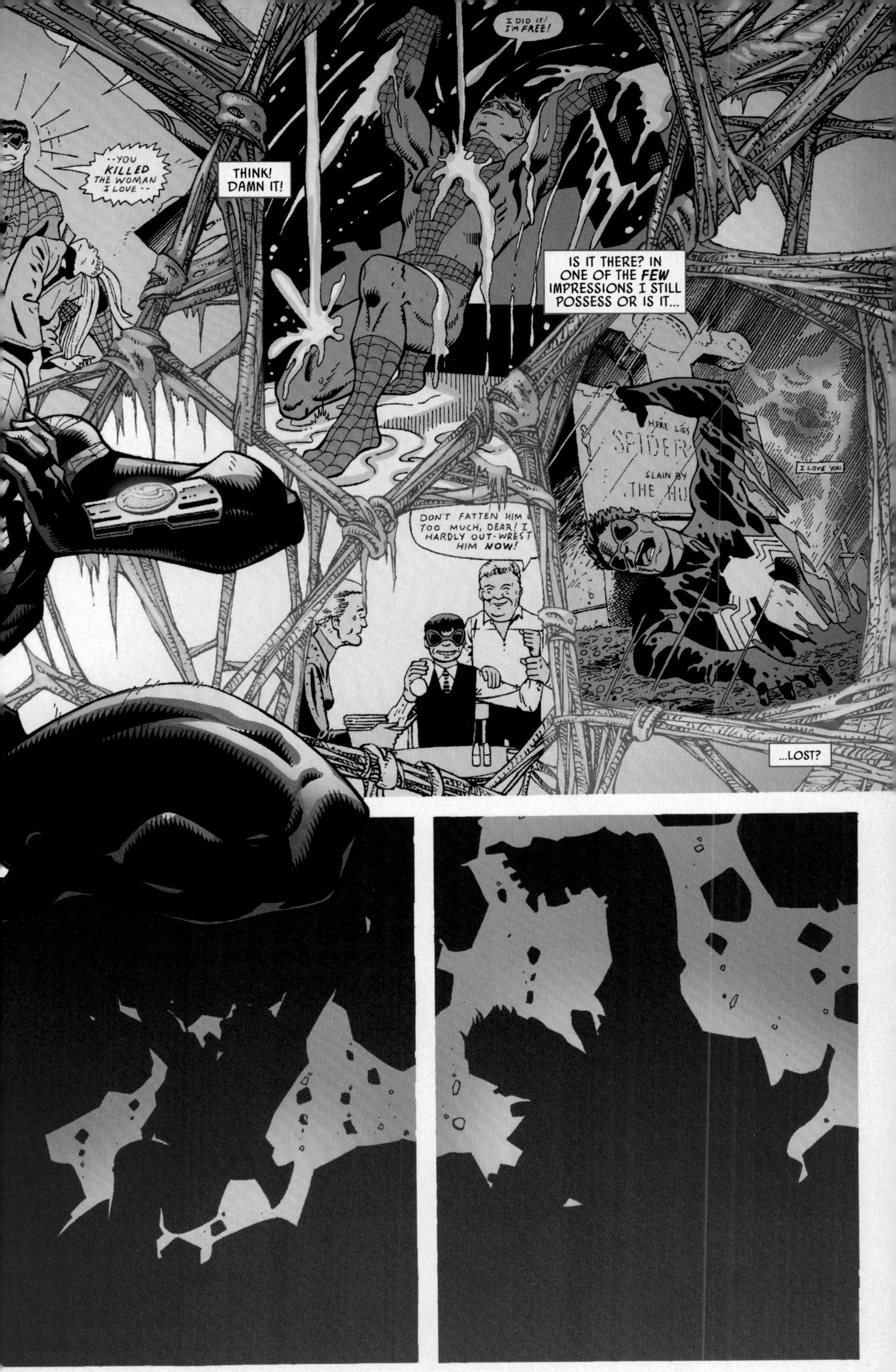
I DID IT! I'M FREE!
--YOU KILLED THE WOMAN I LOVE--
THINK! DAMN IT!
IS IT THERE? IN ONE OF THE FEW IMPRESSIONS I STILL POSSESS OR IS IT...
HERE LIES SPIDER- SLAIN BY THE HU
I LOVE YOU.
DON'T FATTEN HIM UP TOO MUCH, DEAR! I HARDLY OUT-WREST HIM NOW!
...LOST?

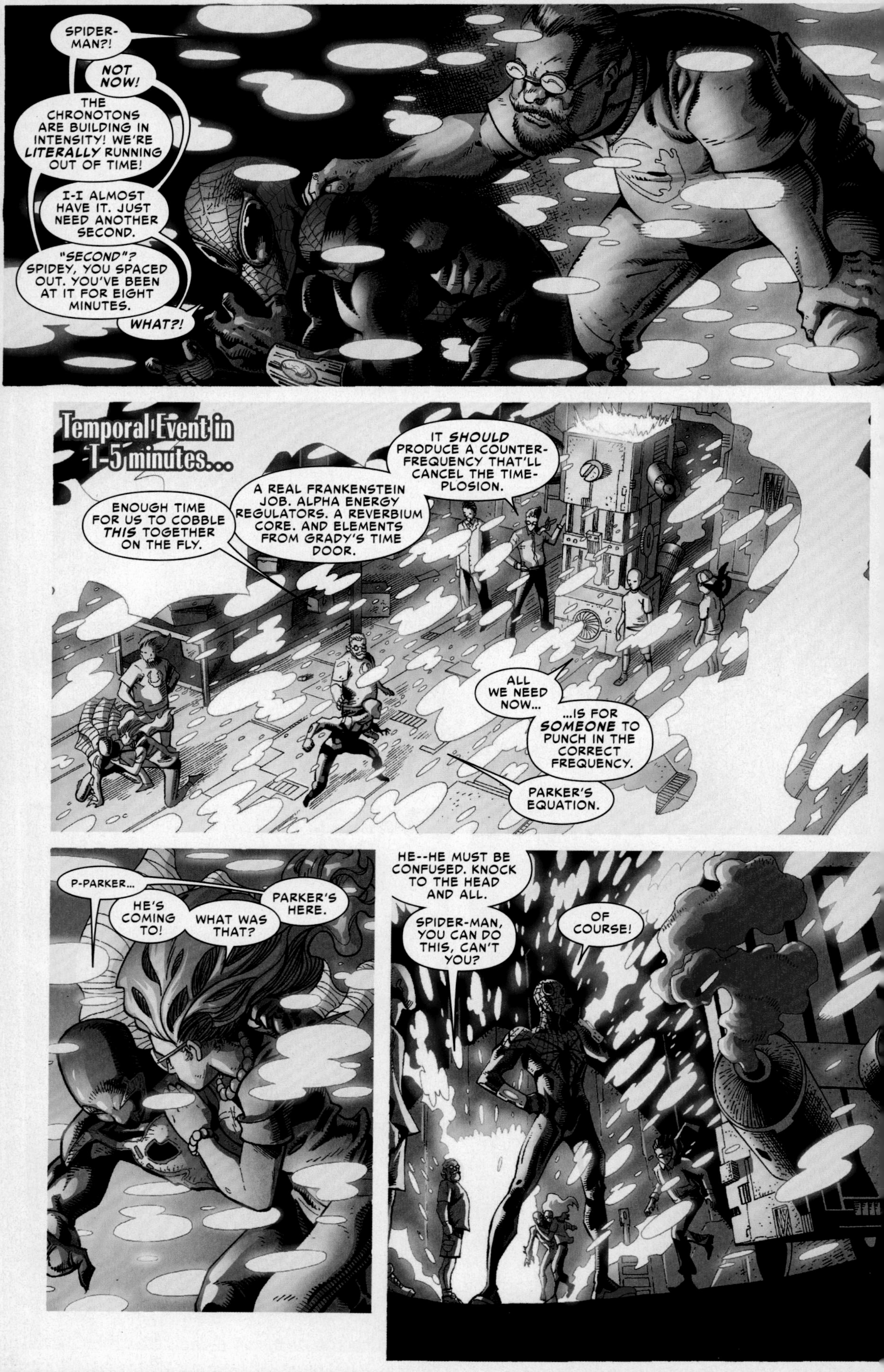
SPIDER-MAN?!
NOT NOW!
THE CHRONOTONS ARE BUILDING IN INTENSITY! WE'RE LITERALLY RUNNING OUT OF TIME!
I-I ALMOST HAVE IT. JUST NEED ANOTHER SECOND.
"SECOND"? SPIDEY, YOU SPACED OUT. YOU'VE BEEN AT IT FOR EIGHT MINUTES.
WHAT?!
Temporal Event in T-5 minutes...
ENOUGH TIME FOR US TO COBBLE THIS TOGETHER ON THE FLY.
A REAL FRANKENSTEIN JOB. ALPHA ENERGY REGULATORS. A REVERBIUM CORE. AND ELEMENTS FROM GRADY'S TIME DOOR.
IT SHOULD PRODUCE A COUNTER-FREQUENCY THAT'LL CANCEL THE TIME-PLOSION.
ALL WE NEED NOW...
...IS FOR SOMEONE TO PUNCH IN THE CORRECT FREQUENCY.
PARKER'S EQUATION.
P-PARKER...
HE'S COMING TO!
WHAT WAS THAT?
PARKER'S HERE.
HE--HE MUST BE CONFUSED. KNOCK TO THE HEAD AND ALL.
SPIDER-MAN, YOU CAN DO THIS, CAN'T YOU?
OF COURSE!

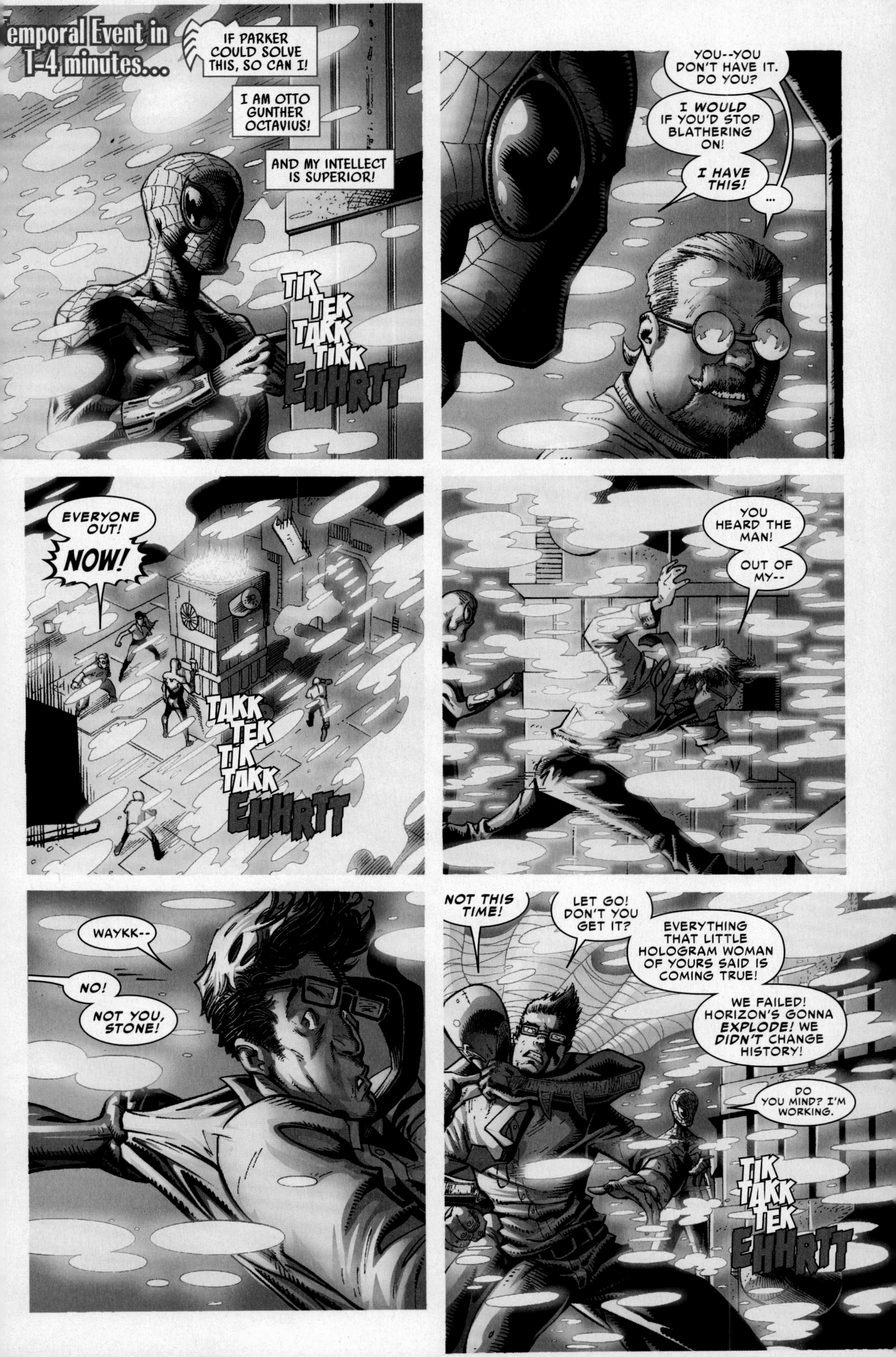
emporal Event in
T-4 minutes...
IF PARKER COULD SOLVE THIS, SO CAN I!
I AM OTTO GUNTHER OCTAVIUS!
AND MY INTELLECT IS SUPERIOR!
TIK TEK TAKK TIKK EHHRTT
YOU--YOU DON'T HAVE IT. DO YOU?
I WOULD IF YOU'D STOP BLATHERING ON!
I HAVE THIS!
...
EVERYONE OUT!
NOW!
TAKK TEK TIK TAKK EHHRTT
YOU HEARD THE MAN!
OUT OF MY--
WAYKK--
NO!
NOT YOU, STONE!
NOT THIS TIME!
LET GO! DON'T YOU GET IT?
EVERYTHING THAT LITTLE HOLOGRAM WOMAN OF YOURS SAID IS COMING TRUE!
WE FAILED! HORIZON'S GONNA EXPLODE! WE DIDN'T CHANGE HISTORY!
DO YOU MIND? I'M WORKING.
TIK TAKK TEK EHHRTT

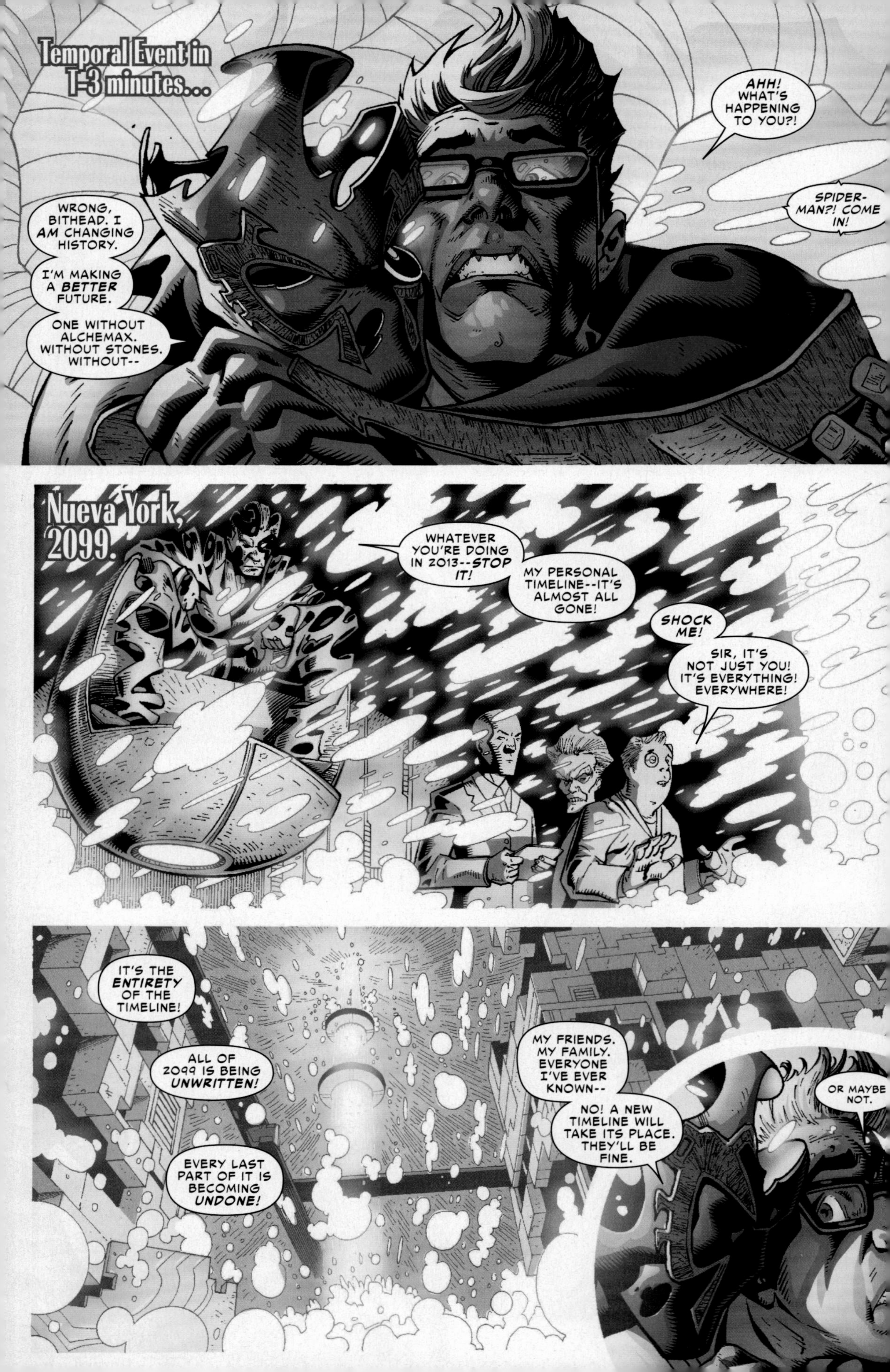

Temporal Event in 1-3 minutes...
AHH! WHAT'S HAPPENING TO YOU?!
SPIDER-MAN?! COME IN!
WRONG, BITHEAD. I AM CHANGING HISTORY.
I'M MAKING A BETTER FUTURE.
ONE WITHOUT ALCHEMAX. WITHOUT STONES. WITHOUT--
Nueva York, 2099.
WHATEVER YOU'RE DOING IN 2013--STOP IT!
MY PERSONAL TIMELINE--IT'S ALMOST ALL GONE!
SHOCK ME!
SIR, IT'S NOT JUST YOU! IT'S EVERYTHING! EVERYWHERE!
IT'S THE ENTIRETY OF THE TIMELINE!
ALL OF 2099 IS BEING UNWRITTEN!
EVERY LAST PART OF IT IS BECOMING UNDONE!
MY FRIENDS. MY FAMILY. EVERYONE I'VE EVER KNOWN--
NO! A NEW TIMELINE WILL TAKE ITS PLACE. THEY'LL BE FINE.
OR MAYBE NOT.

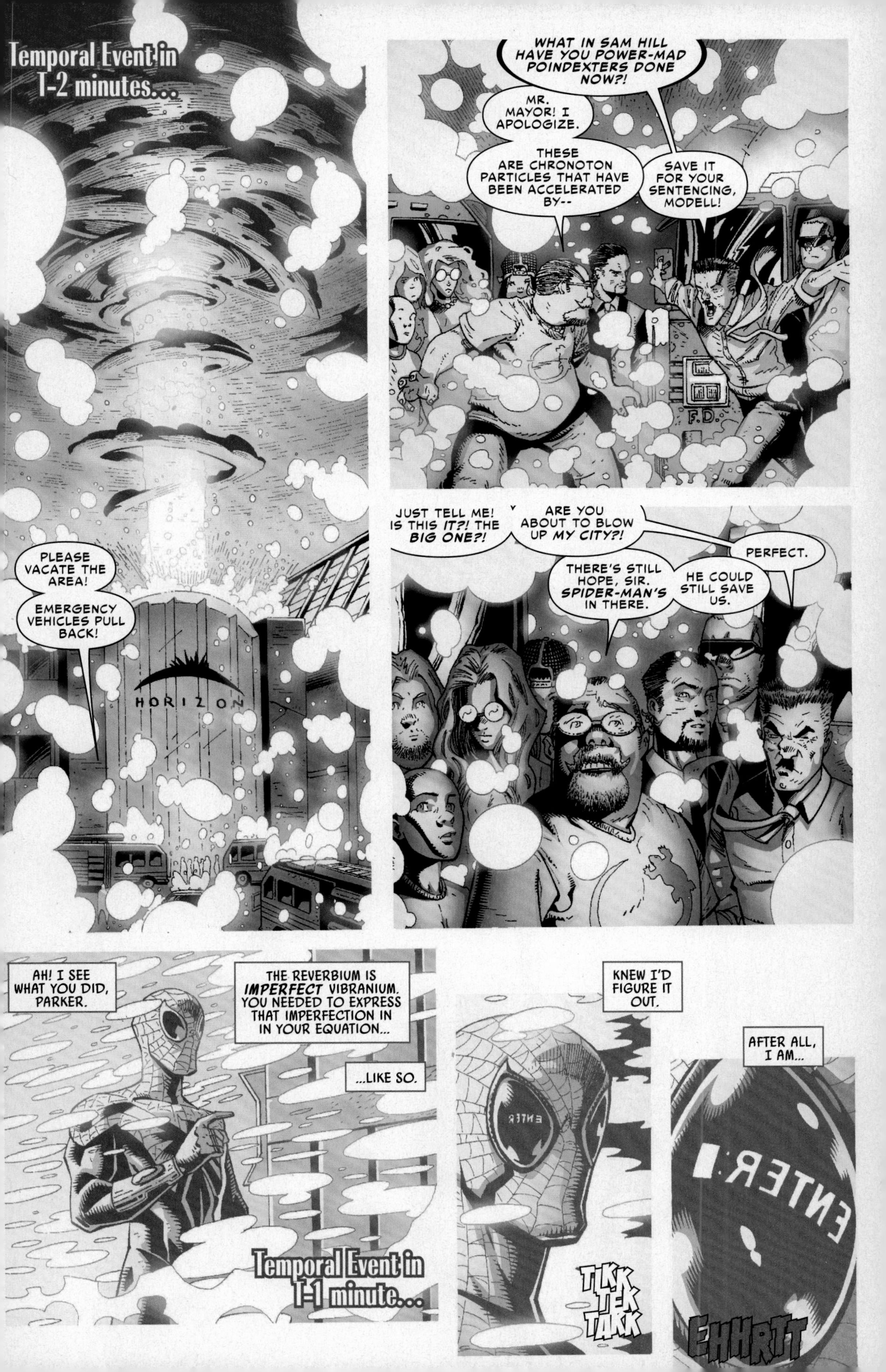

Temporal Event in T-2 minutes...
PLEASE VACATE THE AREA!
EMERGENCY VEHICLES PULL BACK!
HORIZON
WHAT IN SAM HILL HAVE YOU POWER-MAD POINDEXTERS DONE NOW?!
MR. MAYOR! I APOLOGIZE.
THESE ARE CHRONOTON PARTICLES THAT HAVE BEEN ACCELERATED BY--
SAVE IT FOR YOUR SENTENCING, MODELL!
F.D.
JUST TELL ME! IS THIS IT?! THE BIG ONE?!
ARE YOU ABOUT TO BLOW UP MY CITY?!
THERE'S STILL HOPE, SIR. SPIDER-MAN'S IN THERE.
HE COULD STILL SAVE US.
PERFECT.
AH! I SEE WHAT YOU DID, PARKER.
THE REVERBIUM IS IMPERFECT VIBRANIUM. YOU NEEDED TO EXPRESS THAT IMPERFECTION IN IN YOUR EQUATION...
...LIKE SO.
Temporal Event in T-1 minute...
KNEW I'D FIGURE IT OUT.
TIKK TEK TAKK
AFTER ALL, I AM...
ENTER
EHHRTT

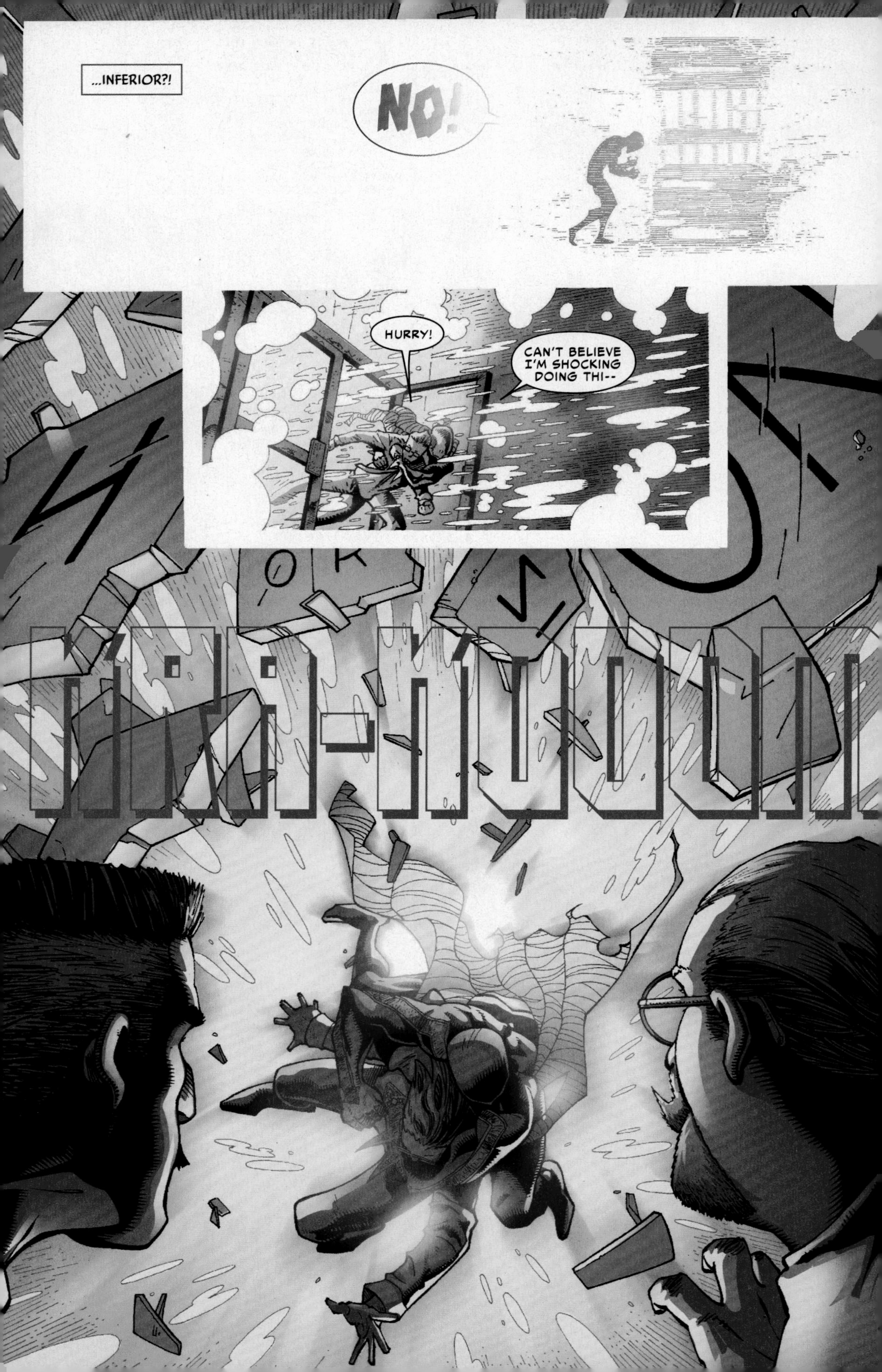
...INFERIOR?!
NO!
HURRY!
CAN'T BELIEVE I'M SHOCKING DOING THI--

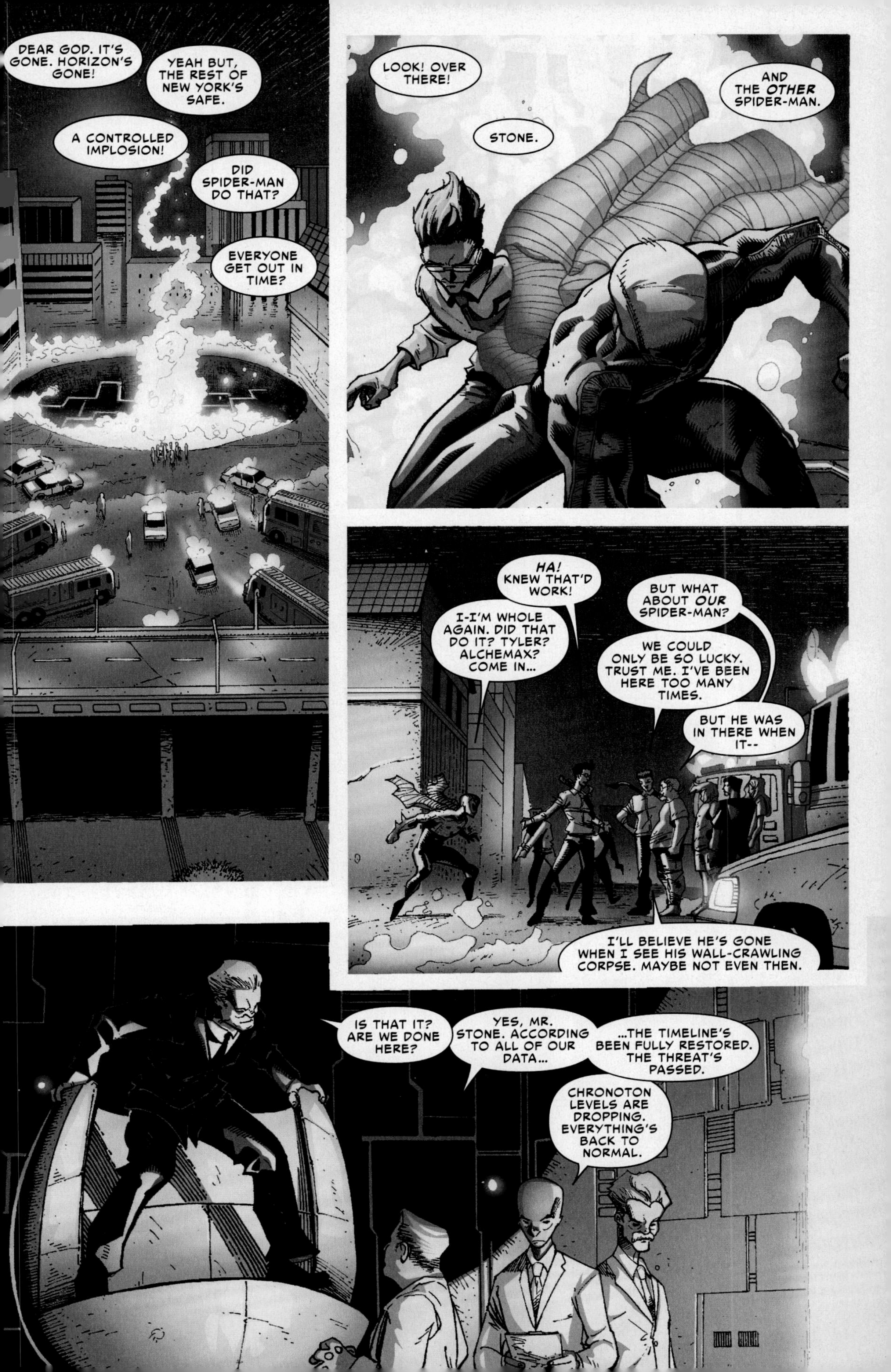
DEAR GOD. IT'S GONE. HORIZON'S GONE!
YEAH BUT, THE REST OF NEW YORK'S SAFE.
A CONTROLLED IMPLOSION!
DID SPIDER-MAN DO THAT?
EVERYONE GET OUT IN TIME?
LOOK! OVER THERE!
STONE.
AND THE *OTHER* SPIDER-MAN.
HA! KNEW THAT'D WORK!
I-I'M WHOLE AGAIN. DID THAT DO IT? TYLER? ALCHEMAX? COME IN...
BUT WHAT ABOUT *OUR* SPIDER-MAN?
WE COULD ONLY BE SO LUCKY. TRUST ME. I'VE BEEN HERE TOO MANY TIMES.
BUT HE WAS IN THERE WHEN IT--
I'LL BELIEVE HE'S GONE WHEN I SEE HIS WALL-CRAWLING CORPSE. MAYBE NOT EVEN THEN.
IS THAT IT? ARE WE DONE HERE?
YES, MR. STONE. ACCORDING TO ALL OF OUR DATA...
...THE TIMELINE'S BEEN FULLY RESTORED. THE THREAT'S PASSED.
CHRONOTON LEVELS ARE DROPPING. EVERYTHING'S BACK TO NORMAL.

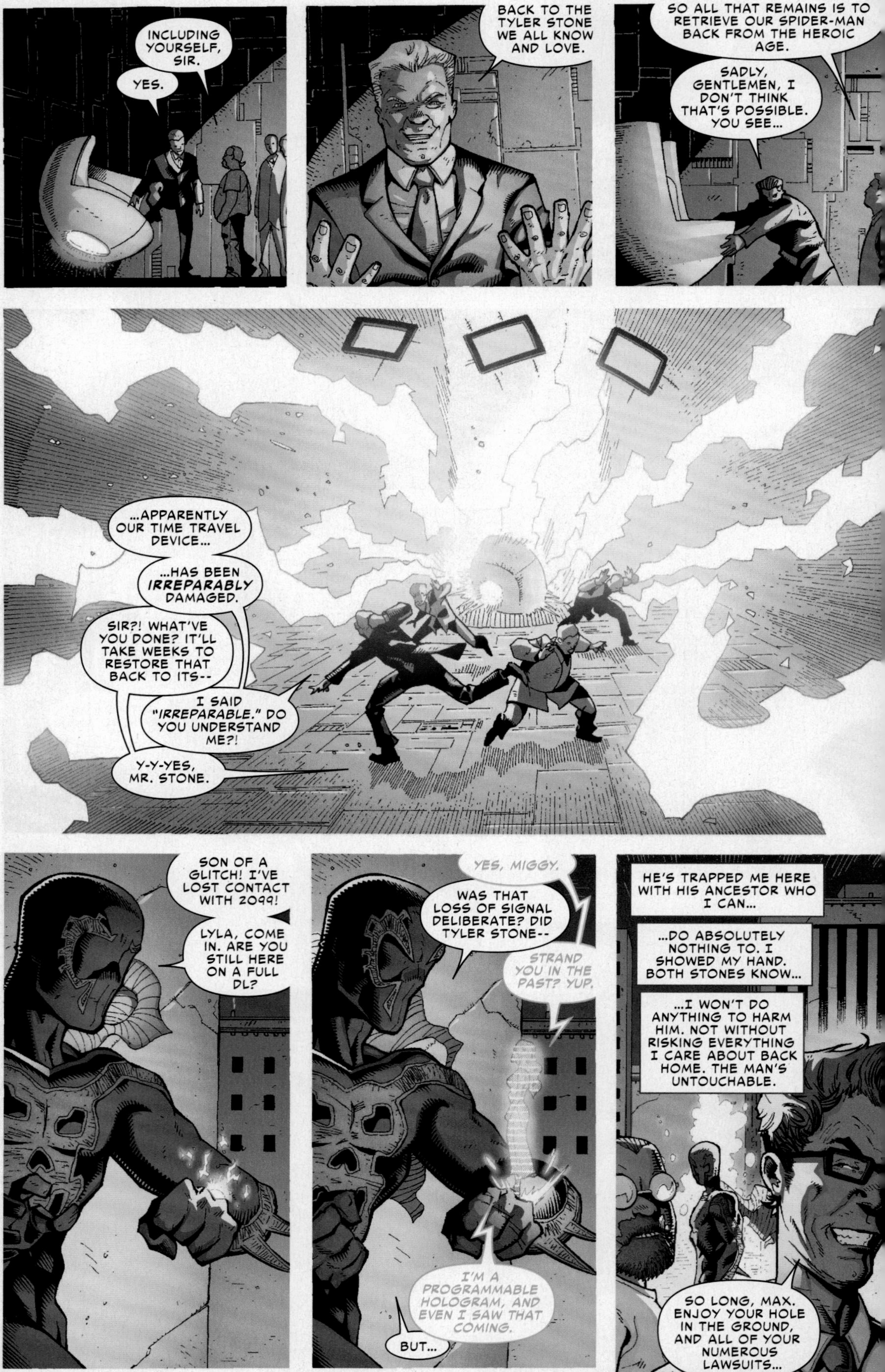
INCLUDING YOURSELF, SIR.
YES.
BACK TO THE TYLER STONE WE ALL KNOW AND LOVE.
SO ALL THAT REMAINS IS TO RETRIEVE OUR SPIDER-MAN BACK FROM THE HEROIC AGE.
SADLY, GENTLEMEN, I DON'T THINK THAT'S POSSIBLE. YOU SEE...
...APPARENTLY OUR TIME TRAVEL DEVICE...
...HAS BEEN IRREPARABLY DAMAGED.
SIR?! WHAT'VE YOU DONE? IT'LL TAKE WEEKS TO RESTORE THAT BACK TO ITS--
I SAID "IRREPARABLE." DO YOU UNDERSTAND ME?!
Y-Y-YES, MR. STONE.
SON OF A GLITCH! I'VE LOST CONTACT WITH 2099!
LYLA, COME IN. ARE YOU STILL HERE ON A FULL DL?
YES, MIGGY.
WAS THAT LOSS OF SIGNAL DELIBERATE? DID TYLER STONE--
STRAND YOU IN THE PAST? YUP.
I'M A PROGRAMMABLE HOLOGRAM, AND EVEN I SAW THAT COMING.
BUT...
HE'S TRAPPED ME HERE WITH HIS ANCESTOR WHO I CAN...
...DO ABSOLUTELY NOTHING TO. I SHOWED MY HAND. BOTH STONES KNOW...
...I WON'T DO ANYTHING TO HARM HIM. NOT WITHOUT RISKING EVERYTHING I CARE ABOUT BACK HOME. THE MAN'S UNTOUCHABLE.
SO LONG, MAX. ENJOY YOUR HOLE IN THE GROUND, AND ALL OF YOUR NUMEROUS LAWSUITS...

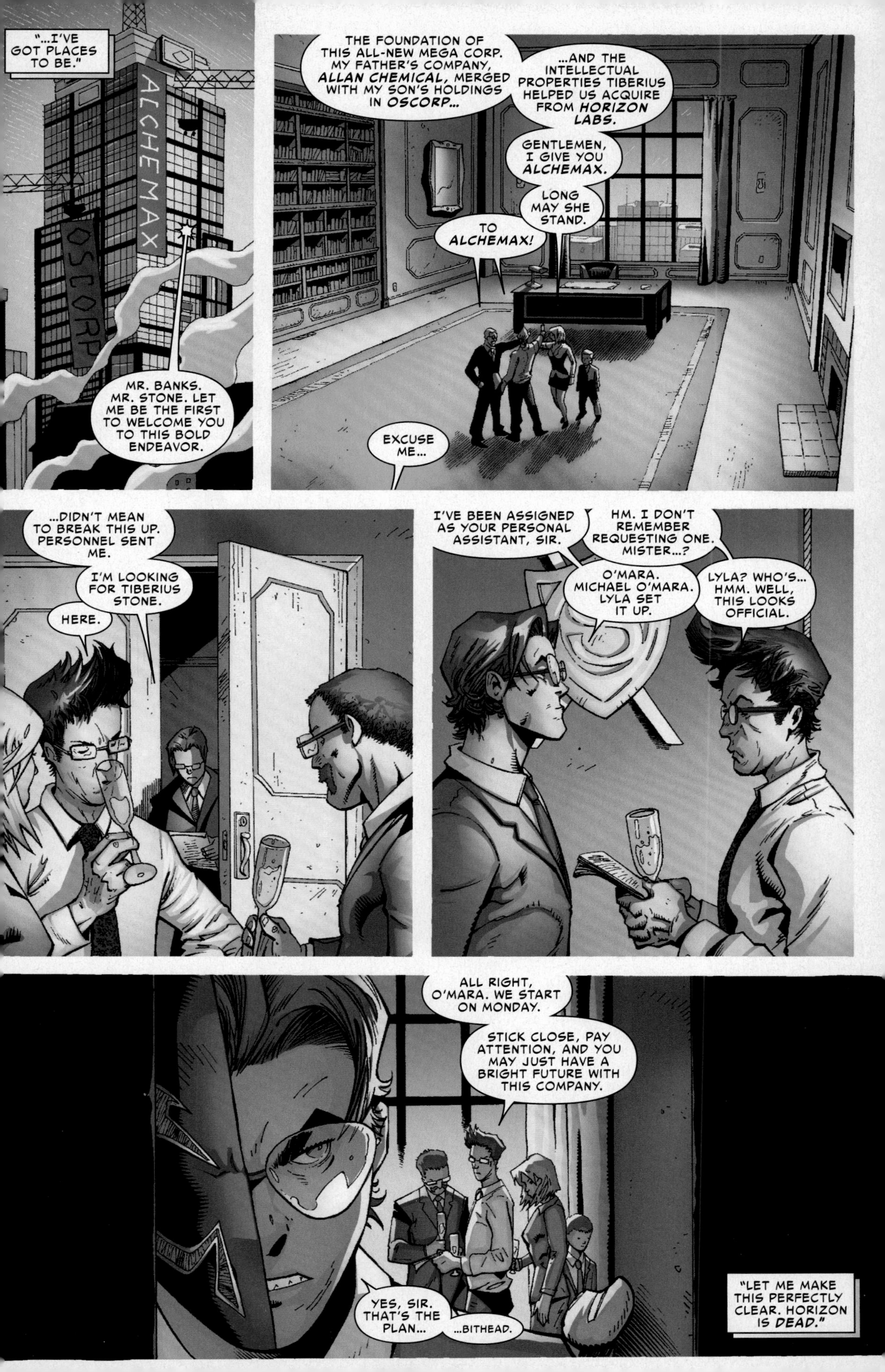
"...I'VE GOT PLACES TO BE."
ALCHEMAX
OSCORP
MR. BANKS. MR. STONE. LET ME BE THE FIRST TO WELCOME YOU TO THIS BOLD ENDEAVOR.
THE FOUNDATION OF THIS ALL-NEW MEGA CORP. MY FATHER'S COMPANY, ALLAN CHEMICAL, MERGED WITH MY SON'S HOLDINGS IN OSCORP...
...AND THE INTELLECTUAL PROPERTIES TIBERIUS HELPED US ACQUIRE FROM HORIZON LABS.
GENTLEMEN, I GIVE YOU ALCHEMAX.
LONG MAY SHE STAND.
TO ALCHEMAX!
EXCUSE ME...
...DIDN'T MEAN TO BREAK THIS UP. PERSONNEL SENT ME.
I'M LOOKING FOR TIBERIUS STONE.
HERE.
I'VE BEEN ASSIGNED AS YOUR PERSONAL ASSISTANT, SIR.
HM. I DON'T REMEMBER REQUESTING ONE. MISTER...?
O'MARA. MICHAEL O'MARA. LYLA SET IT UP.
LYLA? WHO'S... HMM. WELL, THIS LOOKS OFFICIAL.
ALL RIGHT, O'MARA. WE START ON MONDAY.
STICK CLOSE, PAY ATTENTION, AND YOU MAY JUST HAVE A BRIGHT FUTURE WITH THIS COMPANY.
YES, SIR. THAT'S THE PLAN...
...BITHEAD.
"LET ME MAKE THIS PERFECTLY CLEAR. HORIZON IS DEAD."

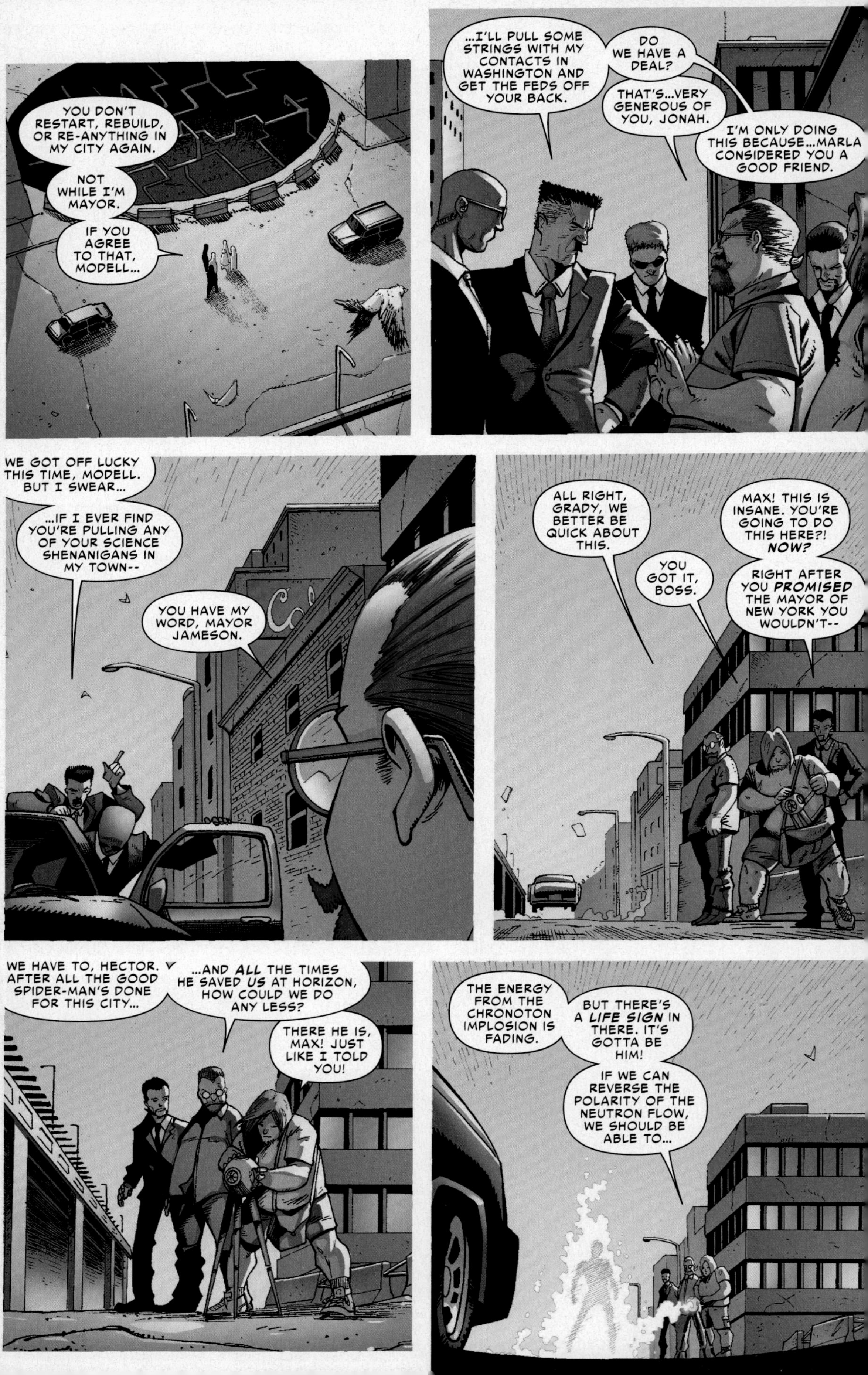
YOU DON'T RESTART, REBUILD, OR RE-ANYTHING IN MY CITY AGAIN.
NOT WHILE I'M MAYOR.
IF YOU AGREE TO THAT, MODELL...
...I'LL PULL SOME STRINGS WITH MY CONTACTS IN WASHINGTON AND GET THE FEDS OFF YOUR BACK.
DO WE HAVE A DEAL?
THAT'S...VERY GENEROUS OF YOU, JONAH.
I'M ONLY DOING THIS BECAUSE...MARLA CONSIDERED YOU A GOOD FRIEND.
WE GOT OFF LUCKY THIS TIME, MODELL. BUT I SWEAR...
...IF I EVER FIND YOU'RE PULLING ANY OF YOUR SCIENCE SHENANIGANS IN MY TOWN--
YOU HAVE MY WORD, MAYOR JAMESON.
ALL RIGHT, GRADY, WE BETTER BE QUICK ABOUT THIS.
YOU GOT IT, BOSS.
MAX! THIS IS INSANE. YOU'RE GOING TO DO THIS HERE?! NOW?
RIGHT AFTER YOU PROMISED THE MAYOR OF NEW YORK YOU WOULDN'T--
WE HAVE TO, HECTOR. AFTER ALL THE GOOD SPIDER-MAN'S DONE FOR THIS CITY...
...AND ALL THE TIMES HE SAVED US AT HORIZON, HOW COULD WE DO ANY LESS?
THERE HE IS, MAX! JUST LIKE I TOLD YOU!
THE ENERGY FROM THE CHRONOTON IMPLOSION IS FADING.
BUT THERE'S A LIFE SIGN IN THERE. IT'S GOTTA BE HIM!
IF WE CAN REVERSE THE POLARITY OF THE NEUTRON FLOW, WE SHOULD BE ABLE TO...

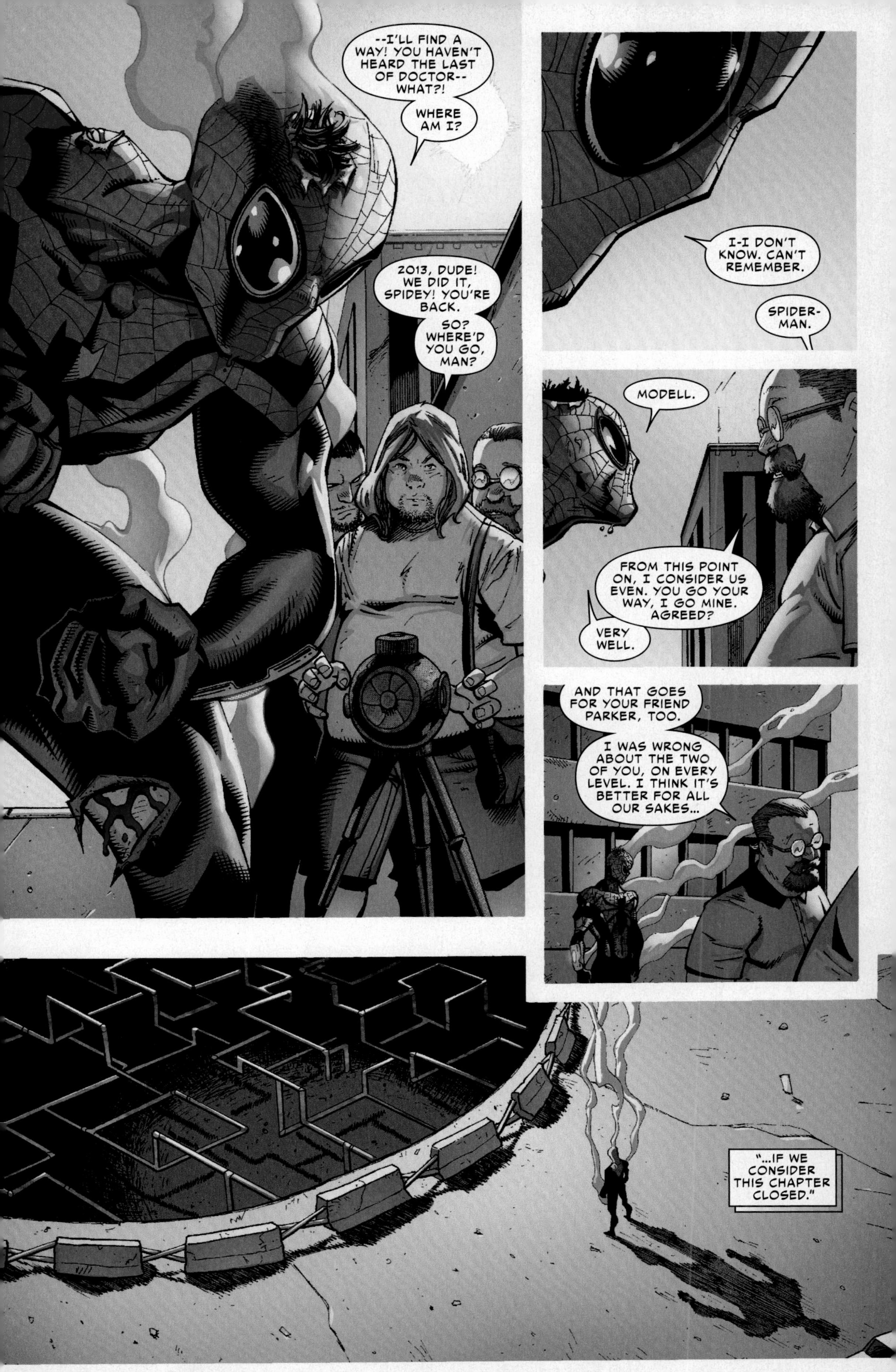
--I'LL FIND A WAY! YOU HAVEN'T HEARD THE LAST OF DOCTOR-- WHAT?!
WHERE AM I?
2013, DUDE! WE DID IT, SPIDEY! YOU'RE BACK.
SO? WHERE'D YOU GO, MAN?
I-I DON'T KNOW. CAN'T REMEMBER.
SPIDER-MAN.
MODELL.
FROM THIS POINT ON, I CONSIDER US EVEN. YOU GO YOUR WAY, I GO MINE. AGREED?
VERY WELL.
AND THAT GOES FOR YOUR FRIEND PARKER, TOO.
I WAS WRONG ABOUT THE TWO OF YOU, ON EVERY LEVEL. I THINK IT'S BETTER FOR ALL OUR SAKES...
"...IF WE CONSIDER THIS CHAPTER CLOSED."

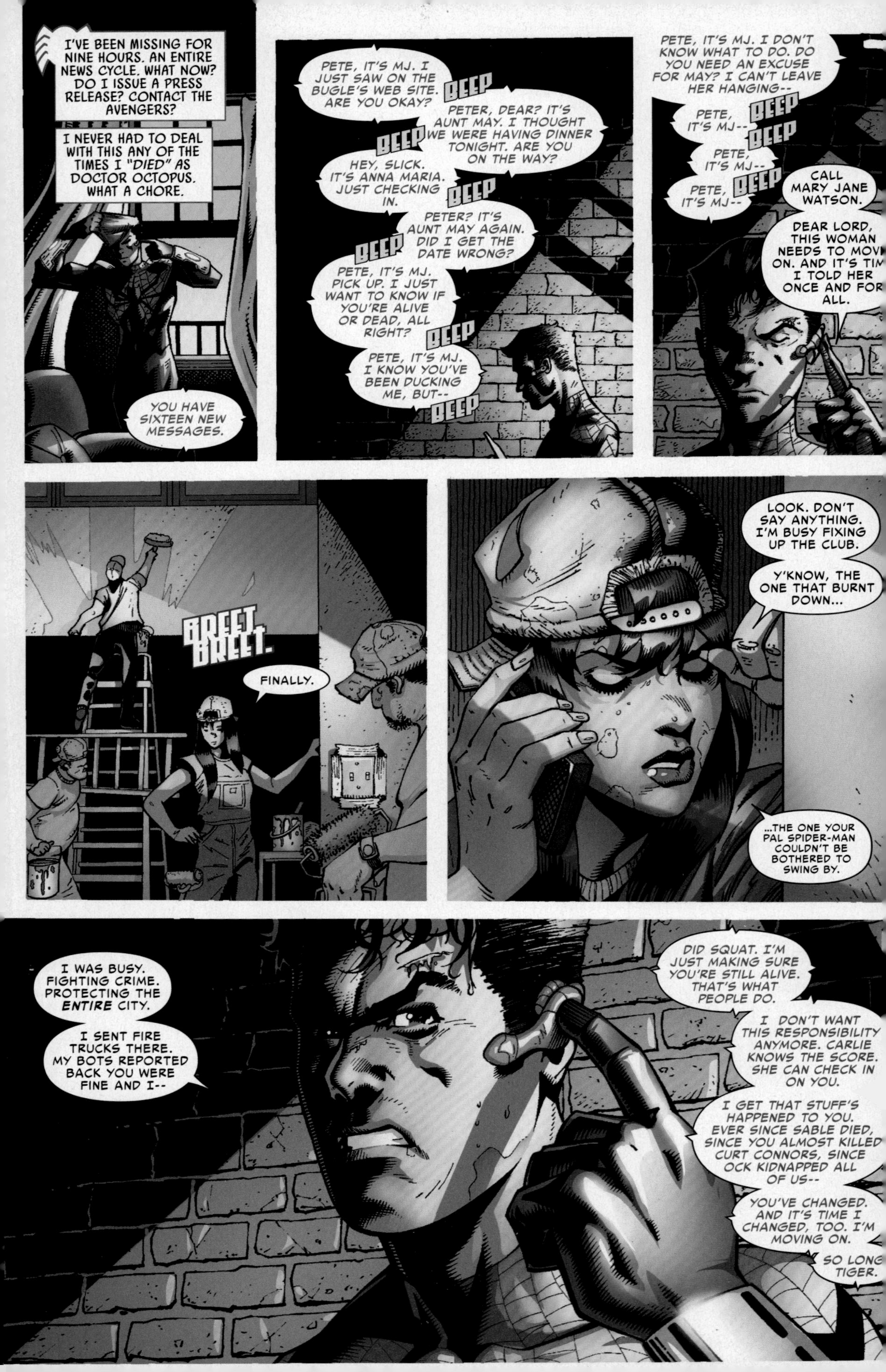

I'VE BEEN MISSING FOR NINE HOURS. AN ENTIRE NEWS CYCLE. WHAT NOW? DO I ISSUE A PRESS RELEASE? CONTACT THE AVENGERS?
I NEVER HAD TO DEAL WITH THIS ANY OF THE TIMES I "DIED" AS DOCTOR OCTOPUS. WHAT A CHORE.
YOU HAVE SIXTEEN NEW MESSAGES.
PETE, IT'S MJ. I JUST SAW ON THE BUGLE'S WEB SITE. ARE YOU OKAY?
BEEP
PETER, DEAR? IT'S AUNT MAY. I THOUGHT WE WERE HAVING DINNER TONIGHT. ARE YOU ON THE WAY?
BEEP
HEY, SLICK. IT'S ANNA MARIA. JUST CHECKING IN.
BEEP
PETER? IT'S AUNT MAY AGAIN. DID I GET THE DATE WRONG?
BEEP
PETE, IT'S MJ. PICK UP. I JUST WANT TO KNOW IF YOU'RE ALIVE OR DEAD, ALL RIGHT?
BEEP
PETE, IT'S MJ. I KNOW YOU'VE BEEN DUCKING ME, BUT--
BEEP
PETE, IT'S MJ. I DON'T KNOW WHAT TO DO. DO YOU NEED AN EXCUSE FOR MAY? I CAN'T LEAVE HER HANGING--
PETE, IT'S MJ--
BEEP
PETE, IT'S MJ--
BEEP
PETE, IT'S MJ--
BEEP
CALL MARY JANE WATSON.
DEAR LORD, THIS WOMAN NEEDS TO MOVE ON. AND IT'S TIME I TOLD HER ONCE AND FOR ALL.
BREET BREET.
FINALLY.
LOOK. DON'T SAY ANYTHING. I'M BUSY FIXING UP THE CLUB.
Y'KNOW, THE ONE THAT BURNT DOWN...
...THE ONE YOUR PAL SPIDER-MAN COULDN'T BE BOTHERED TO SWING BY.
I WAS BUSY. FIGHTING CRIME. PROTECTING THE ENTIRE CITY.
I SENT FIRE TRUCKS THERE. MY BOTS REPORTED BACK YOU WERE FINE AND I--
DID SQUAT. I'M JUST MAKING SURE YOU'RE STILL ALIVE. THAT'S WHAT PEOPLE DO.
I DON'T WANT THIS RESPONSIBILITY ANYMORE. CARLIE KNOWS THE SCORE. SHE CAN CHECK IN ON YOU.
I GET THAT STUFF'S HAPPENED TO YOU. EVER SINCE SABLE DIED, SINCE YOU ALMOST KILLED CURT CONNORS, SINCE OCK KIDNAPPED ALL OF US--
YOU'VE CHANGED. AND IT'S TIME I CHANGED, TOO. I'M MOVING ON.
SO LONG TIGER.

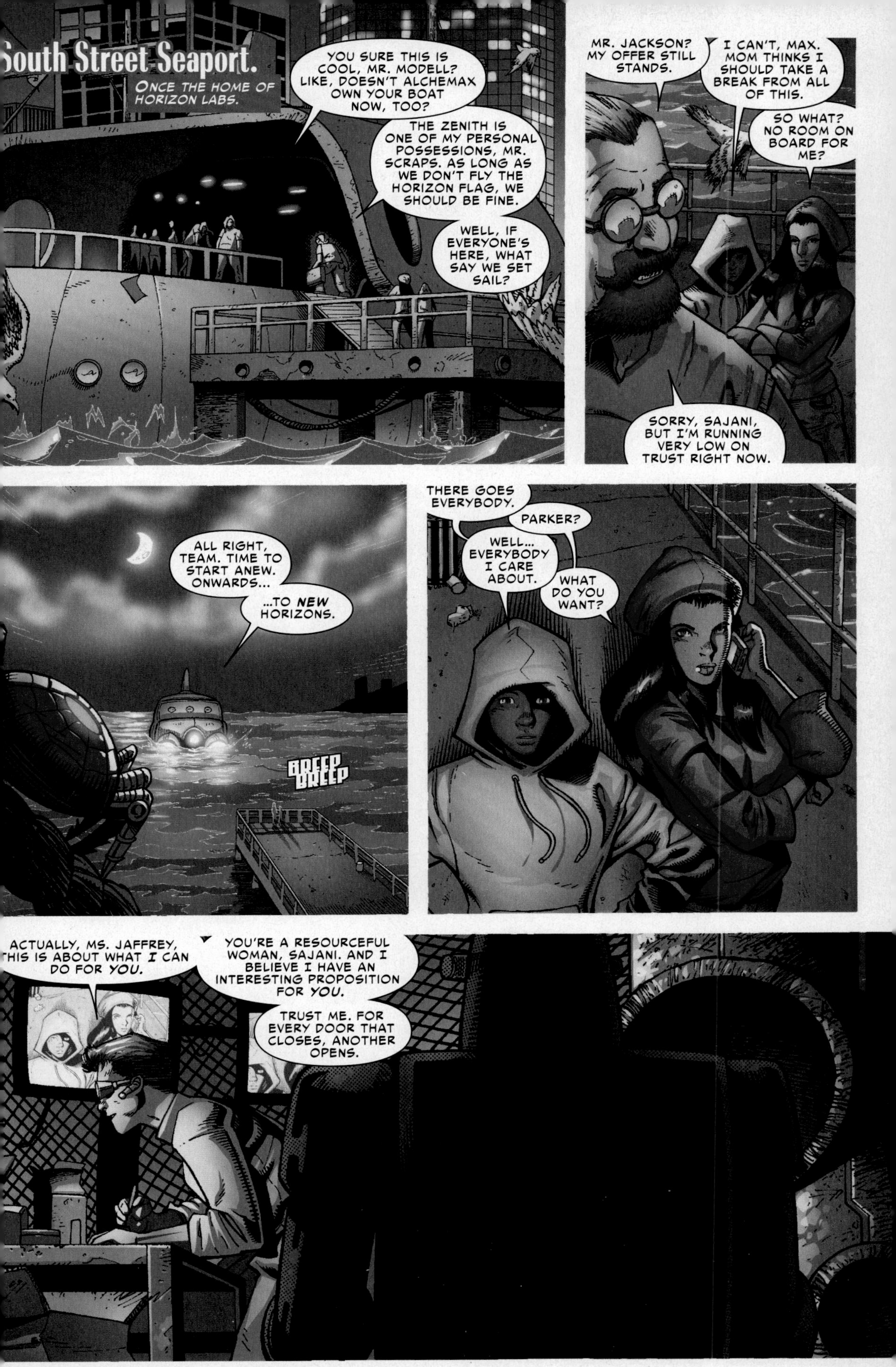
South Street Seaport.
ONCE THE HOME OF HORIZON LABS.
YOU SURE THIS IS COOL, MR. MODELL? LIKE, DOESN'T ALCHEMAX OWN YOUR BOAT NOW, TOO?
THE ZENITH IS ONE OF MY PERSONAL POSSESSIONS, MR. SCRAPS. AS LONG AS WE DON'T FLY THE HORIZON FLAG, WE SHOULD BE FINE.
WELL, IF EVERYONE'S HERE, WHAT SAY WE SET SAIL?
MR. JACKSON? MY OFFER STILL STANDS.
I CAN'T, MAX. MOM THINKS I SHOULD TAKE A BREAK FROM ALL OF THIS.
SO WHAT? NO ROOM ON BOARD FOR ME?
SORRY, SAJANI, BUT I'M RUNNING VERY LOW ON TRUST RIGHT NOW.
ALL RIGHT, TEAM. TIME TO START ANEW. ONWARDS...
...TO NEW HORIZONS.
BREEP BREEP
THERE GOES EVERYBODY.
PARKER?
WELL... EVERYBODY I CARE ABOUT.
WHAT DO YOU WANT?
ACTUALLY, MS. JAFFREY, THIS IS ABOUT WHAT I CAN DO FOR YOU.
YOU'RE A RESOURCEFUL WOMAN, SAJANI. AND I BELIEVE I HAVE AN INTERESTING PROPOSITION FOR YOU.
TRUST ME. FOR EVERY DOOR THAT CLOSES, ANOTHER OPENS.

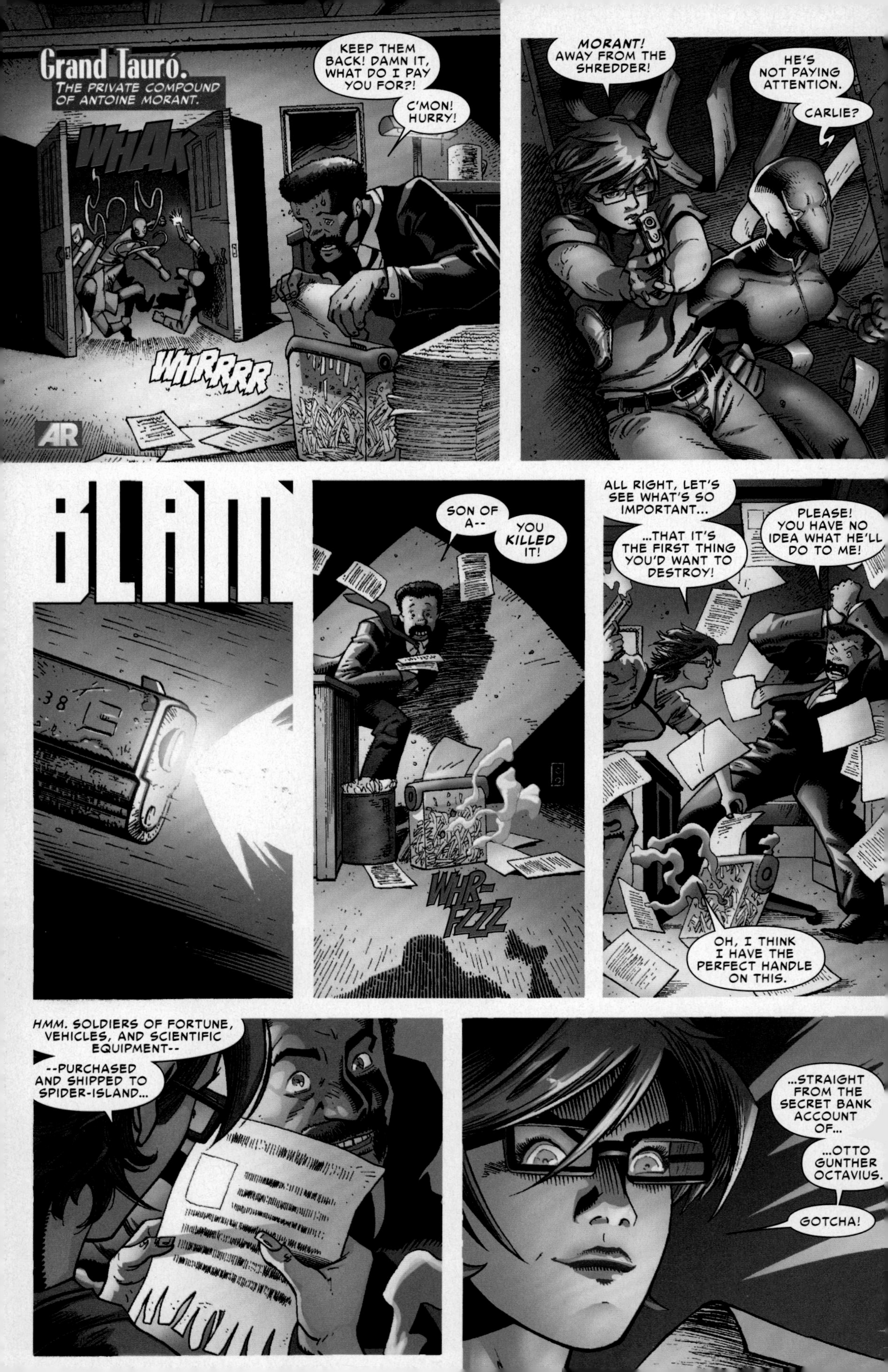
Grand Tauró.
THE PRIVATE COMPOUND OF ANTOINE MORANT.
KEEP THEM BACK! DAMN IT, WHAT DO I PAY YOU FOR?!
C'MON! HURRY!
WHAK
WHRRRR
MORANT! AWAY FROM THE SHREDDER!
HE'S NOT PAYING ATTENTION.
CARLIE?
BLAM
SON OF A--
YOU KILLED IT!
WHR-FZZZ
ALL RIGHT, LET'S SEE WHAT'S SO IMPORTANT...
...THAT IT'S THE FIRST THING YOU'D WANT TO DESTROY!
PLEASE! YOU HAVE NO IDEA WHAT HE'LL DO TO ME!
OH, I THINK I HAVE THE PERFECT HANDLE ON THIS.
HMM. SOLDIERS OF FORTUNE, VEHICLES, AND SCIENTIFIC EQUIPMENT--
--PURCHASED AND SHIPPED TO SPIDER-ISLAND...
...STRAIGHT FROM THE SECRET BANK ACCOUNT OF...
...OTTO GUNTHER OCTAVIUS.
GOTCHA!

20

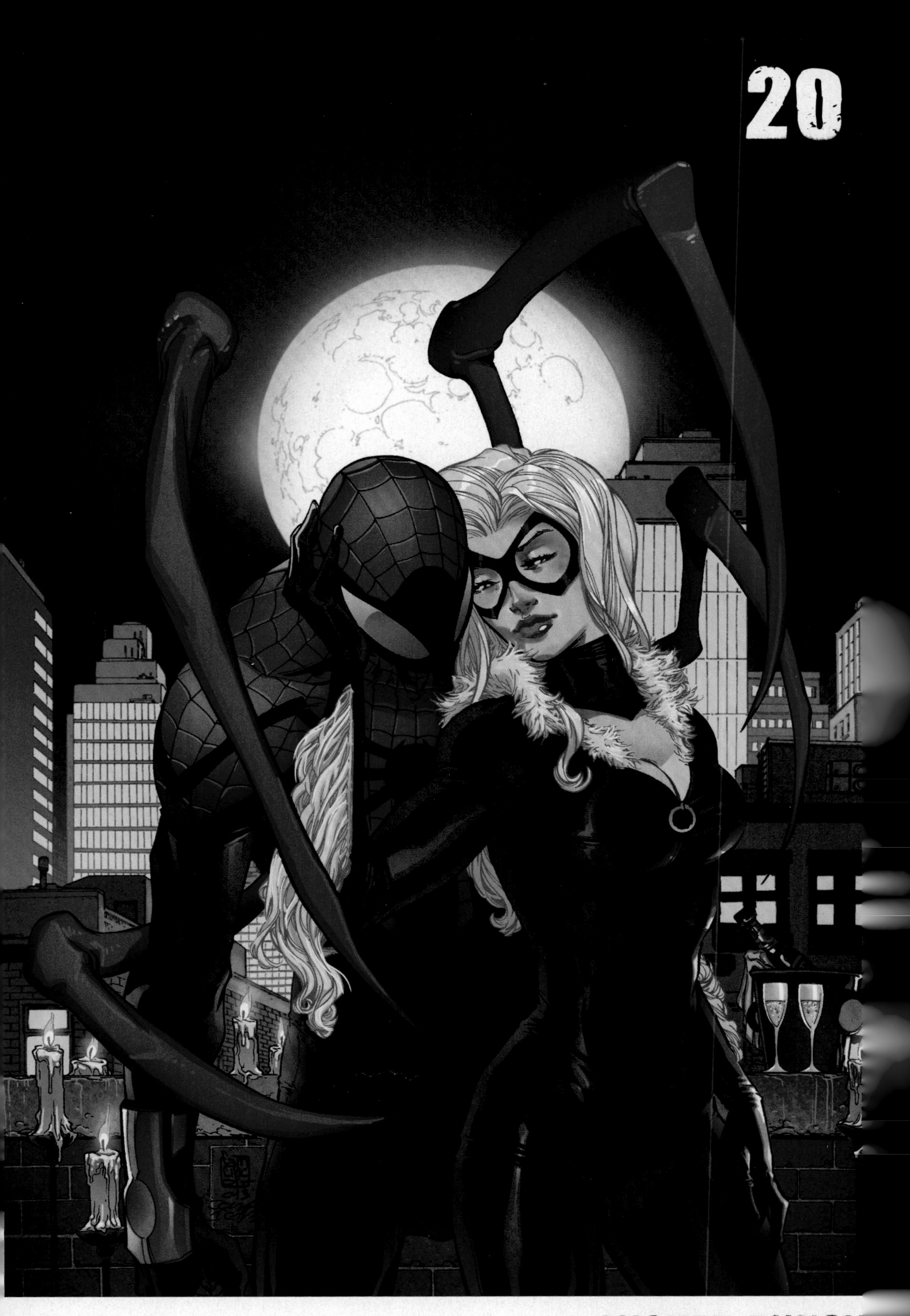

SUCKER PUNCH

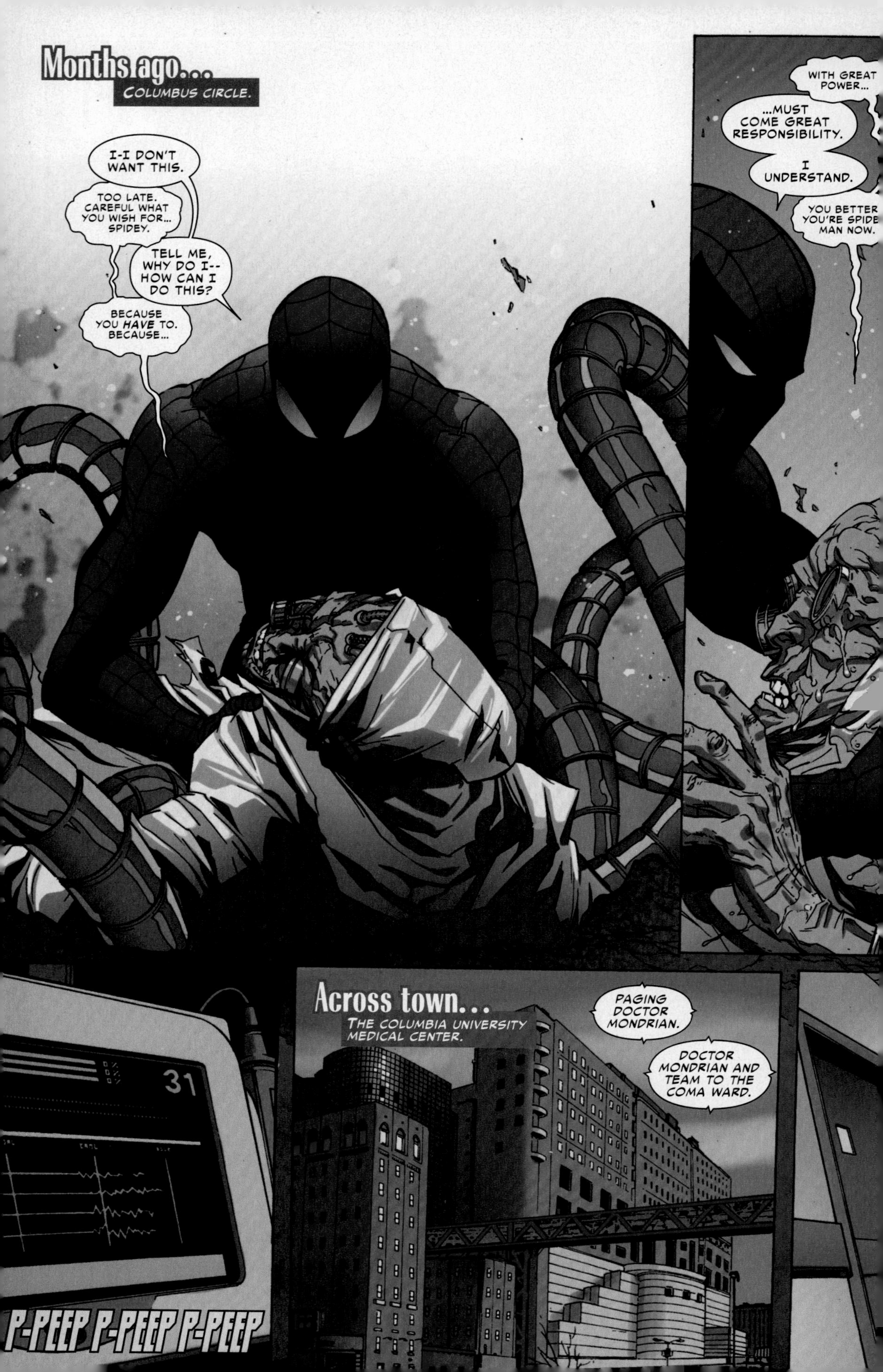
Months ago...
COLUMBUS CIRCLE.
I-I DON'T WANT THIS.
TOO LATE. CAREFUL WHAT YOU WISH FOR... SPIDEY.
TELL ME, WHY DO I-- HOW CAN I DO THIS?
BECAUSE YOU HAVE TO. BECAUSE...
WITH GREAT POWER...
...MUST COME GREAT RESPONSIBILITY.
I UNDERSTAND.
YOU BETTER YOU'RE SPIDE MAN NOW.
31
P-PEEP P-PEEP P-PEEP
Across town...
THE COLUMBIA UNIVERSITY MEDICAL CENTER.
PAGING DOCTOR MONDRIAN.
DOCTOR MONDRIAN AND TEAM TO THE COMA WARD.

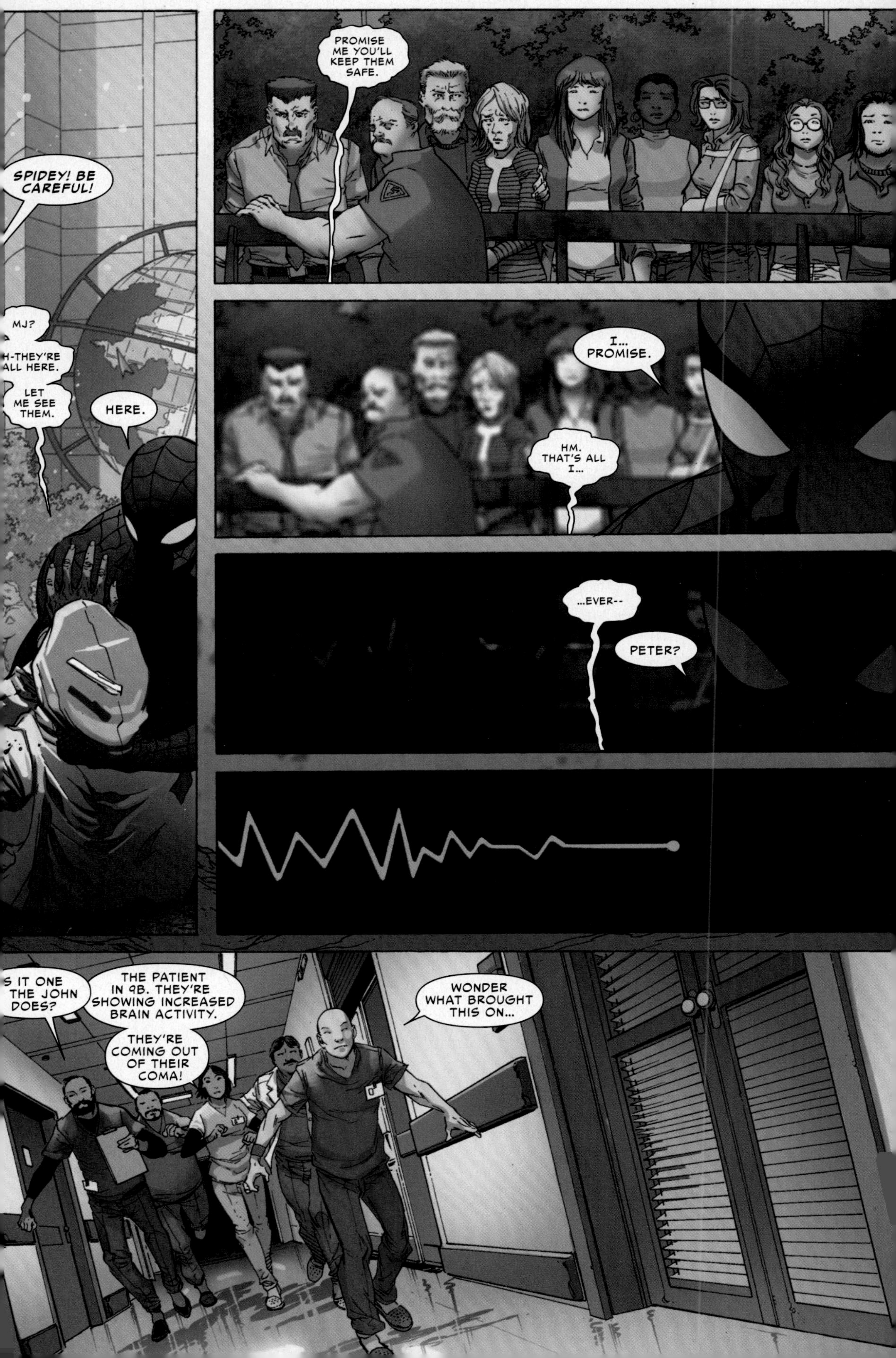

SPIDEY! BE CAREFUL!
PROMISE ME YOU'LL KEEP THEM SAFE.
MJ?
H-THEY'RE ALL HERE.
LET ME SEE THEM.
HERE.
I... PROMISE.
HM. THAT'S ALL I...
...EVER--
PETER?
S IT ONE THE JOHN DOES?
THE PATIENT IN 9B. THEY'RE SHOWING INCREASED BRAIN ACTIVITY.
THEY'RE COMING OUT OF THEIR COMA!
WONDER WHAT BROUGHT THIS ON...

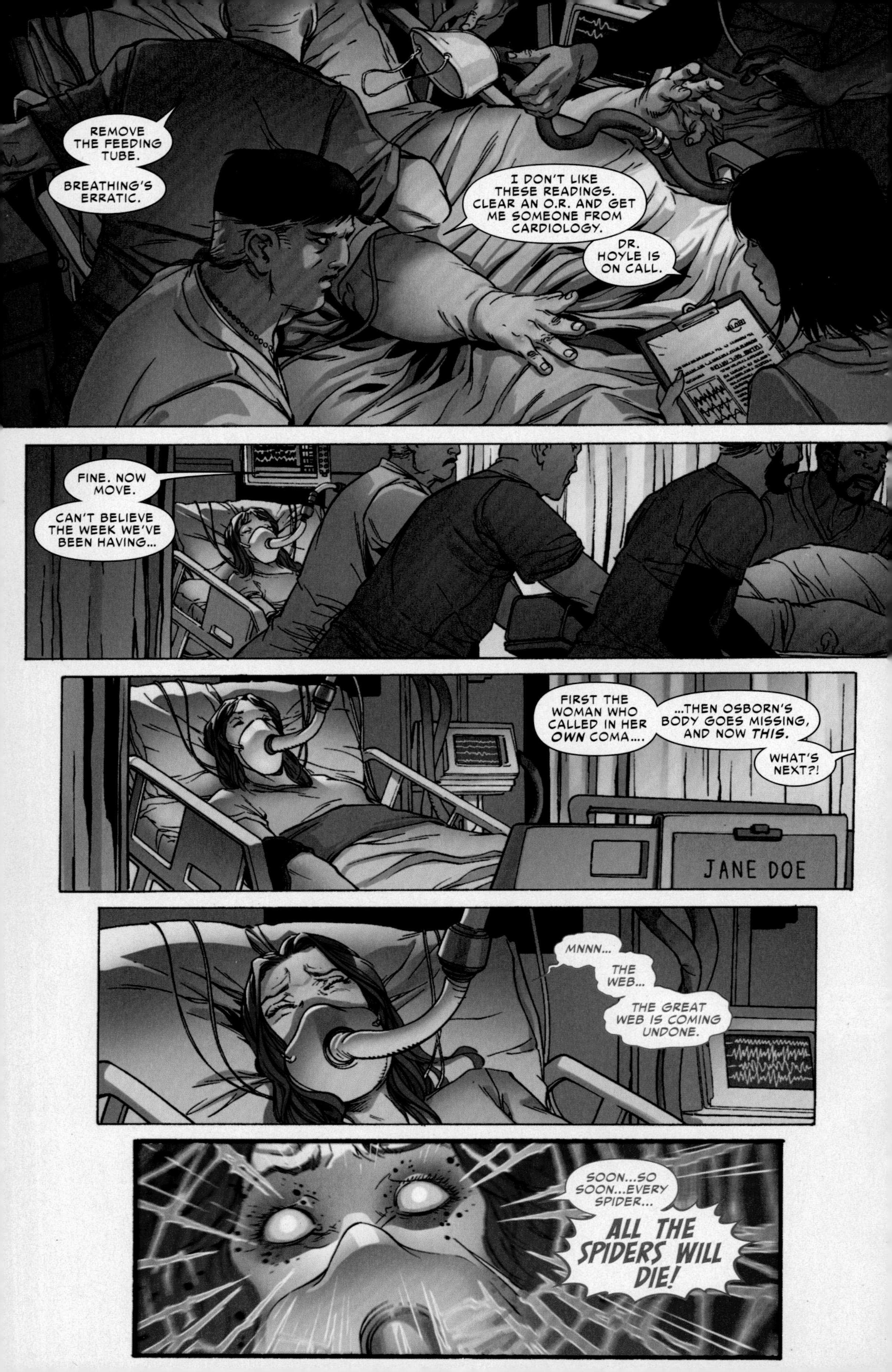
REMOVE THE FEEDING TUBE.
BREATHING'S ERRATIC.
I DON'T LIKE THESE READINGS. CLEAR AN O.R. AND GET ME SOMEONE FROM CARDIOLOGY.
DR. HOYLE IS ON CALL.
FINE. NOW MOVE.
CAN'T BELIEVE THE WEEK WE'VE BEEN HAVING...
FIRST THE WOMAN WHO CALLED IN HER OWN COMA....
...THEN OSBORN'S BODY GOES MISSING, AND NOW THIS.
WHAT'S NEXT?!
JANE DOE
MNNN...
THE WEB...
THE GREAT WEB IS COMING UNDONE.
SOON...SO SOON...EVERY SPIDER...
ALL THE SPIDERS WILL DIE!

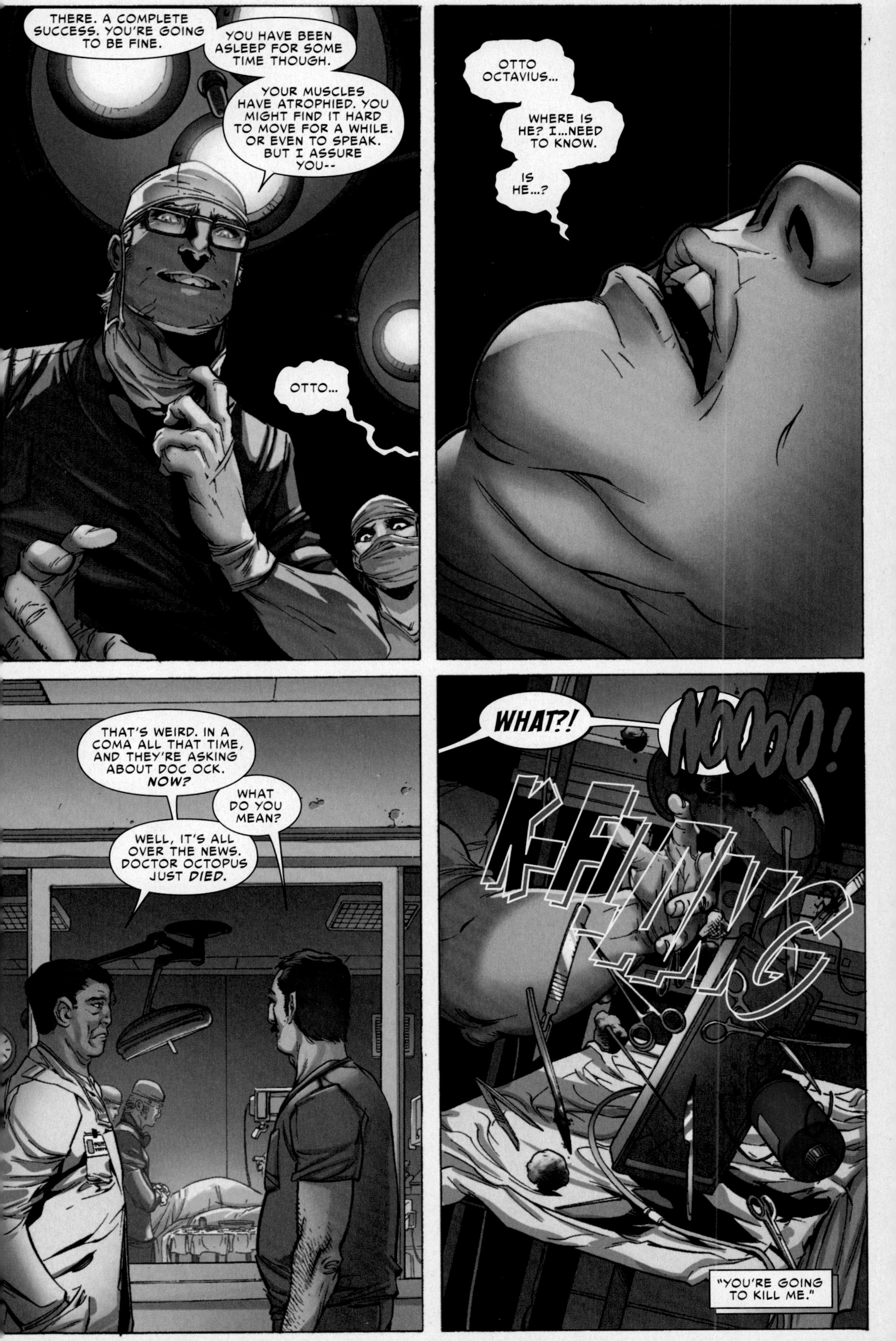
THERE. A COMPLETE SUCCESS. YOU'RE GOING TO BE FINE.
YOU HAVE BEEN ASLEEP FOR SOME TIME THOUGH.
YOUR MUSCLES HAVE ATROPHIED. YOU MIGHT FIND IT HARD TO MOVE FOR A WHILE. OR EVEN TO SPEAK. BUT I ASSURE YOU--
OTTO...
OTTO OCTAVIUS...
WHERE IS HE? I...NEED TO KNOW.
IS HE...?
THAT'S WEIRD. IN A COMA ALL THAT TIME, AND THEY'RE ASKING ABOUT DOC OCK. *NOW?*
WHAT DO YOU MEAN?
WELL, IT'S ALL OVER THE NEWS. DOCTOR OCTOPUS JUST *DIED*.
WHAT?!
NOOOO!
K-KLANG
"YOU'RE GOING TO KILL ME."

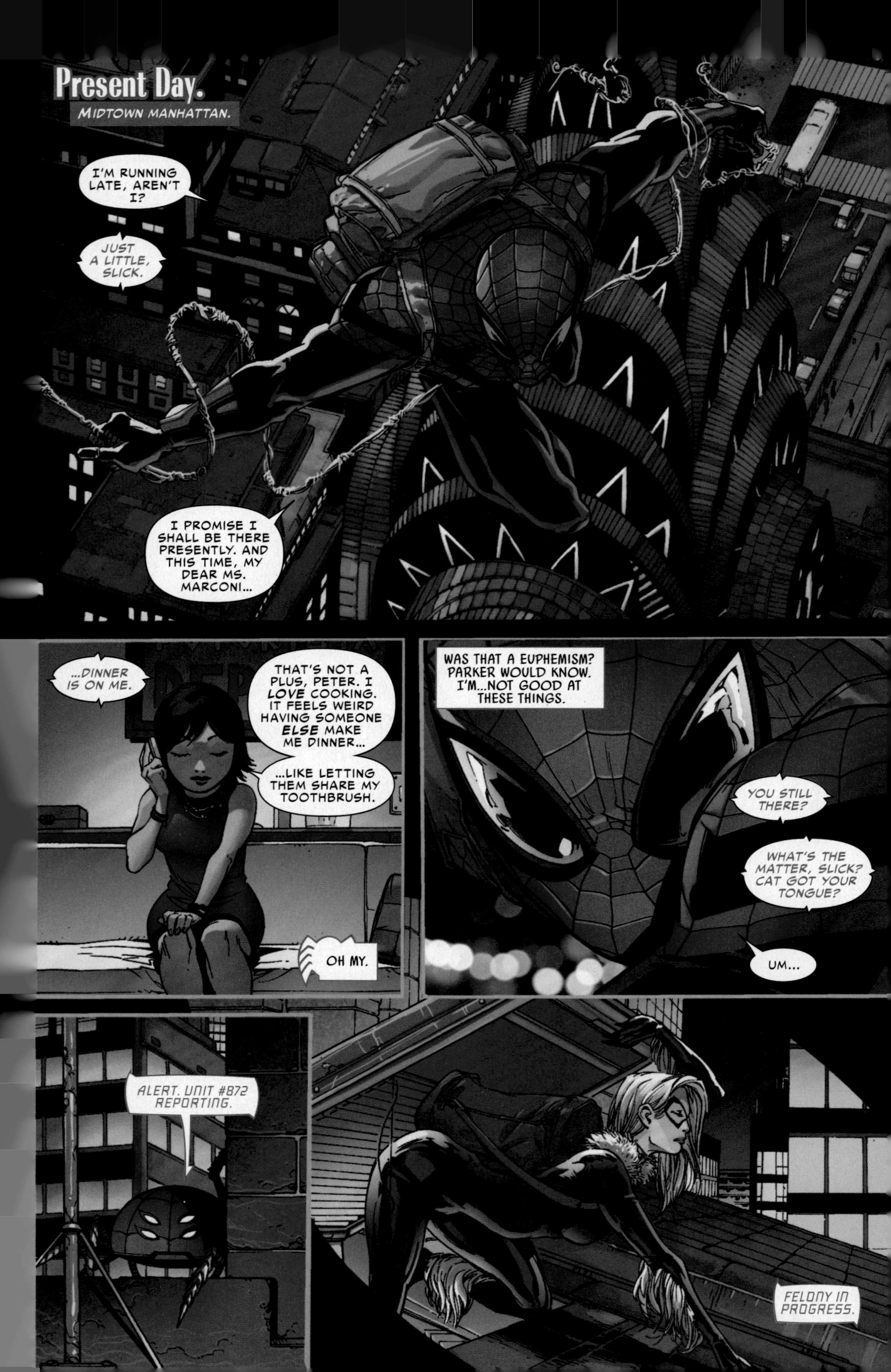
Present Day.
MIDTOWN MANHATTAN.
I'M RUNNING LATE, AREN'T I?
JUST A LITTLE, SLICK.
I PROMISE I SHALL BE THERE PRESENTLY. AND THIS TIME, MY DEAR MS. MARCONI...
...DINNER IS ON ME.
THAT'S NOT A PLUS, PETER. I LOVE COOKING. IT FEELS WEIRD HAVING SOMEONE ELSE MAKE ME DINNER...
...LIKE LETTING THEM SHARE MY TOOTHBRUSH.
OH MY.
WAS THAT A EUPHEMISM? PARKER WOULD KNOW. I'M...NOT GOOD AT THESE THINGS.
YOU STILL THERE?
WHAT'S THE MATTER, SLICK? CAT GOT YOUR TONGUE?
UM...
ALERT. UNIT #872 REPORTING.
FELONY IN PROGRESS.

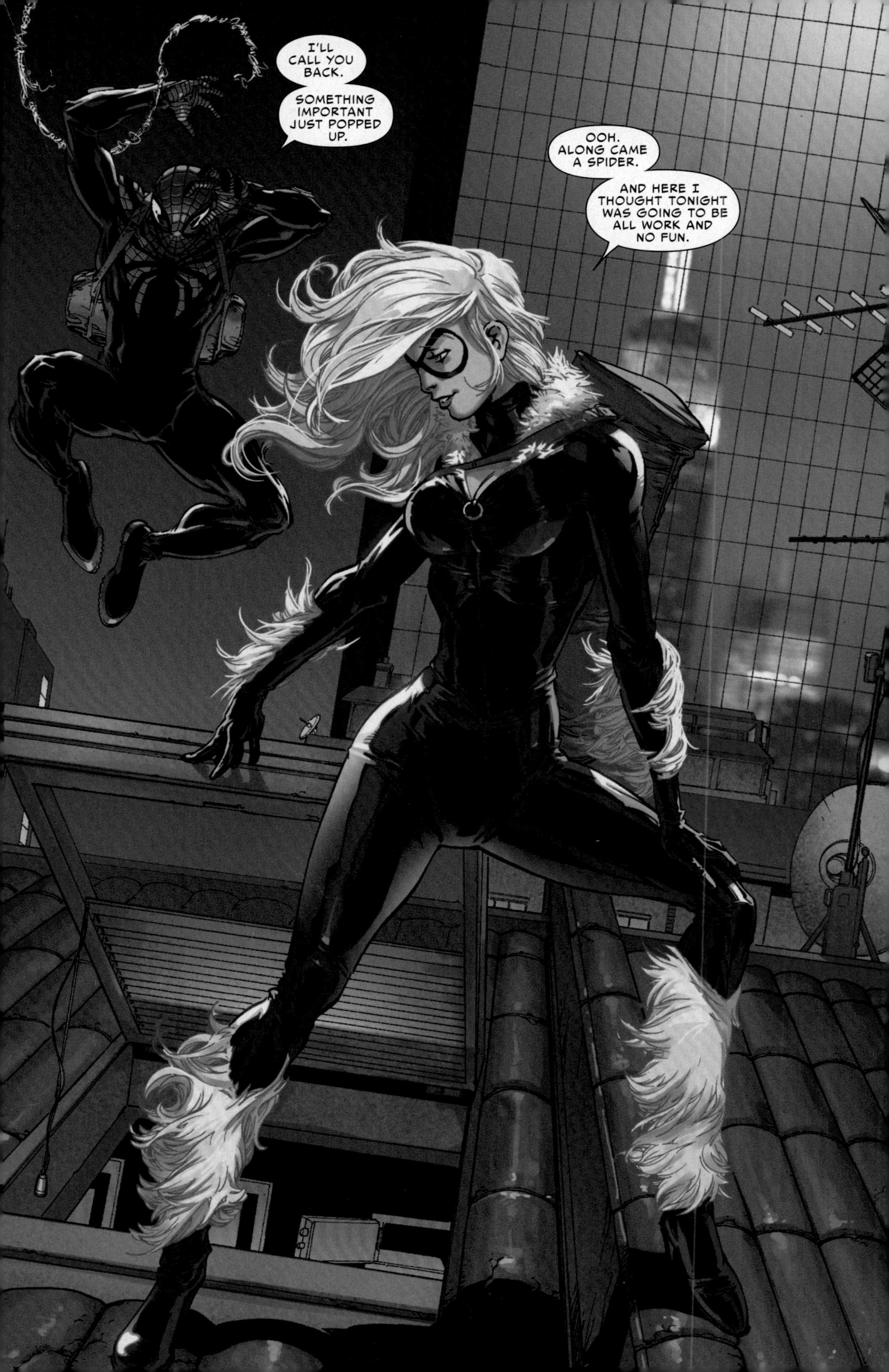
I'LL CALL YOU BACK.
SOMETHING IMPORTANT JUST POPPED UP.
OOH. ALONG CAME A SPIDER.
AND HERE I THOUGHT TONIGHT WAS GOING TO BE ALL WORK AND NO FUN.

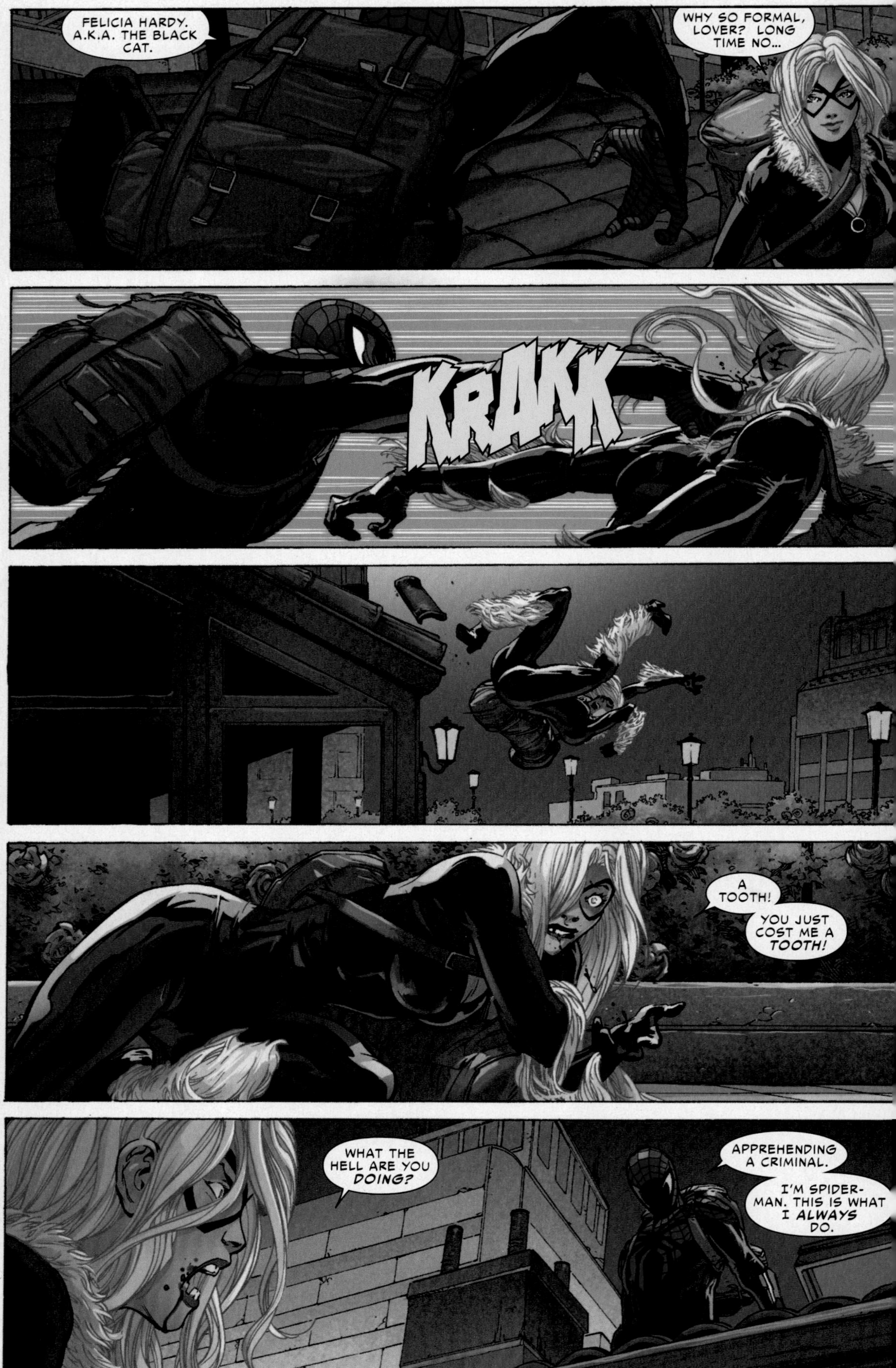
FELICIA HARDY. A.K.A. THE BLACK CAT.
WHY SO FORMAL, LOVER? LONG TIME NO...
KRAKK
A TOOTH!
YOU JUST COST ME A *TOOTH!*
WHAT THE HELL ARE YOU *DOING?*
APPREHENDING A CRIMINAL.
I'M SPIDER-MAN. THIS IS WHAT I *ALWAYS* DO.

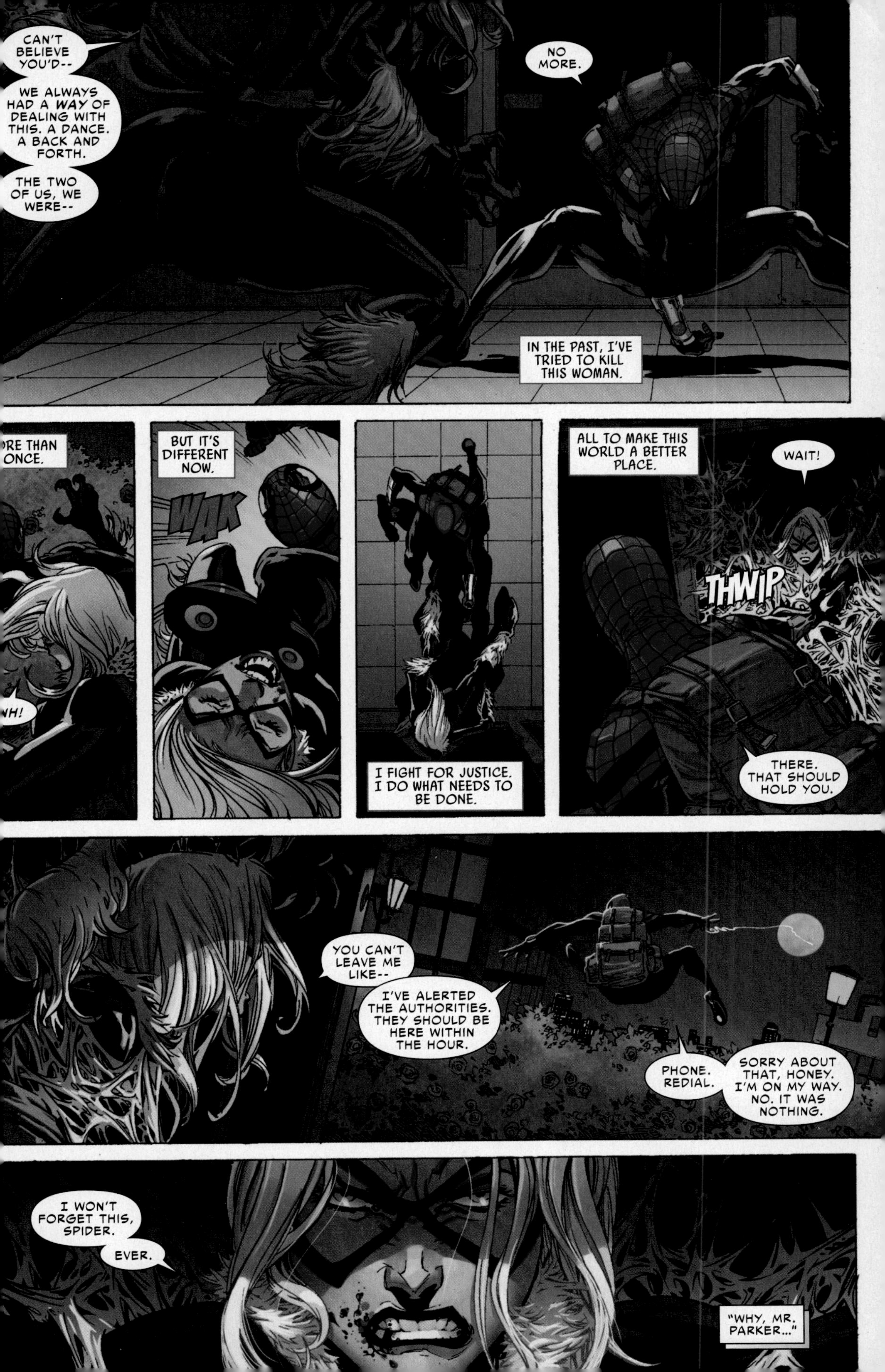
CAN'T BELIEVE YOU'D--
WE ALWAYS HAD A WAY OF DEALING WITH THIS. A DANCE. A BACK AND FORTH.
THE TWO OF US, WE WERE--
NO MORE.
IN THE PAST, I'VE TRIED TO KILL THIS WOMAN.
RE THAN ONCE.
NH!
BUT IT'S DIFFERENT NOW.
WAK
I FIGHT FOR JUSTICE. I DO WHAT NEEDS TO BE DONE.
ALL TO MAKE THIS WORLD A BETTER PLACE.
WAIT!
THWIP
THERE. THAT SHOULD HOLD YOU.
YOU CAN'T LEAVE ME LIKE--
I'VE ALERTED THE AUTHORITIES. THEY SHOULD BE HERE WITHIN THE HOUR.
PHONE. REDIAL.
SORRY ABOUT THAT, HONEY. I'M ON MY WAY. NO. IT WAS NOTHING.
I WON'T FORGET THIS, SPIDER.
EVER.
"WHY, MR. PARKER..."

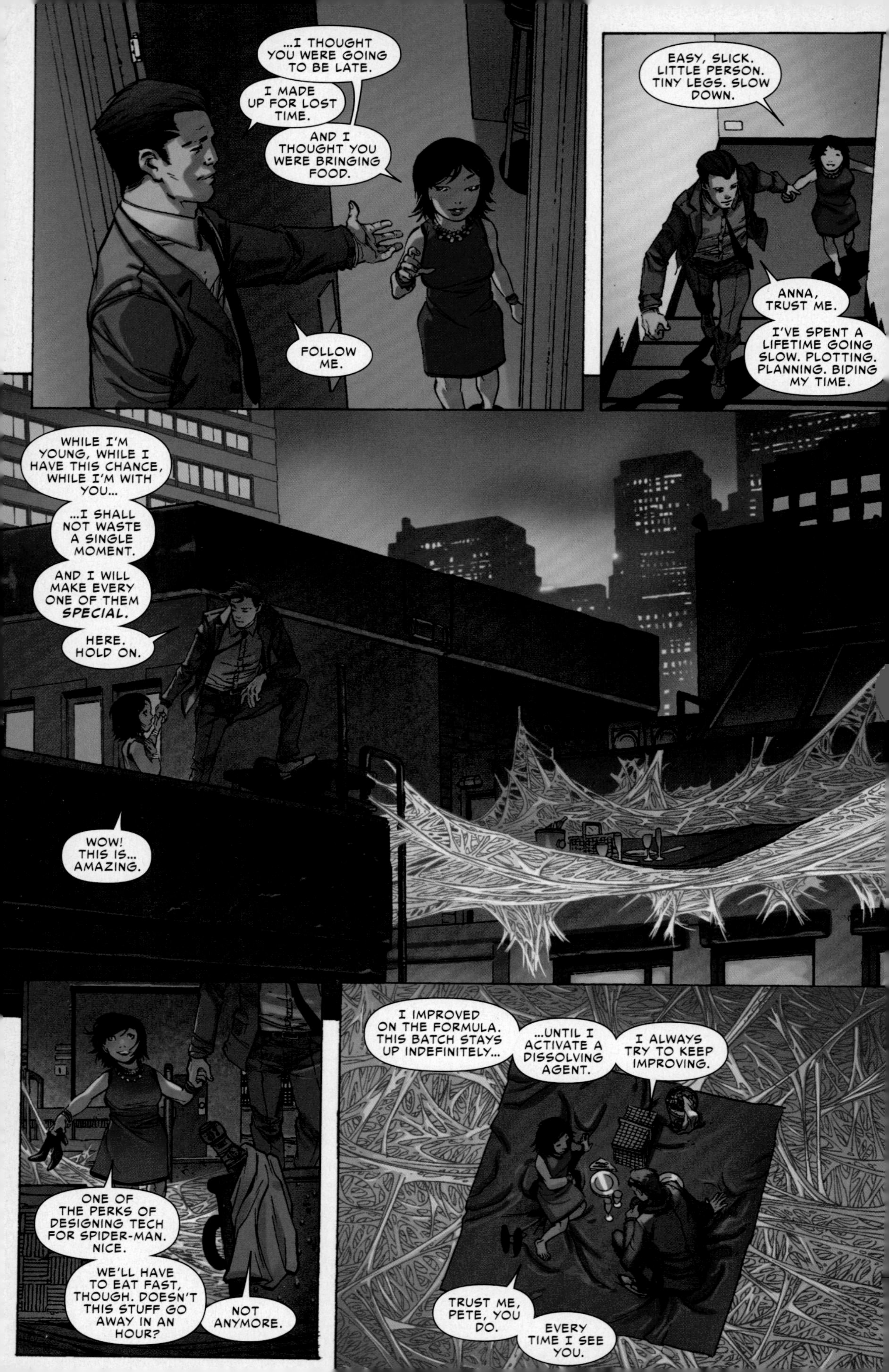
...I THOUGHT YOU WERE GOING TO BE LATE.
I MADE UP FOR LOST TIME.
AND I THOUGHT YOU WERE BRINGING FOOD.
FOLLOW ME.
EASY, SLICK. LITTLE PERSON. TINY LEGS. SLOW DOWN.
ANNA, TRUST ME.
I'VE SPENT A LIFETIME GOING SLOW. PLOTTING. PLANNING. BIDING MY TIME.
WHILE I'M YOUNG, WHILE I HAVE THIS CHANCE, WHILE I'M WITH YOU...
...I SHALL NOT WASTE A SINGLE MOMENT.
AND I WILL MAKE EVERY ONE OF THEM *SPECIAL.*
HERE. HOLD ON.
WOW! THIS IS... AMAZING.
ONE OF THE PERKS OF DESIGNING TECH FOR SPIDER-MAN. NICE.
WE'LL HAVE TO EAT FAST, THOUGH. DOESN'T THIS STUFF GO AWAY IN AN HOUR?
NOT ANYMORE.
I IMPROVED ON THE FORMULA. THIS BATCH STAYS UP INDEFINITELY...
...UNTIL I ACTIVATE A DISSOLVING AGENT.
I ALWAYS TRY TO KEEP IMPROVING.
TRUST ME, PETE, YOU DO.
EVERY TIME I SEE YOU.

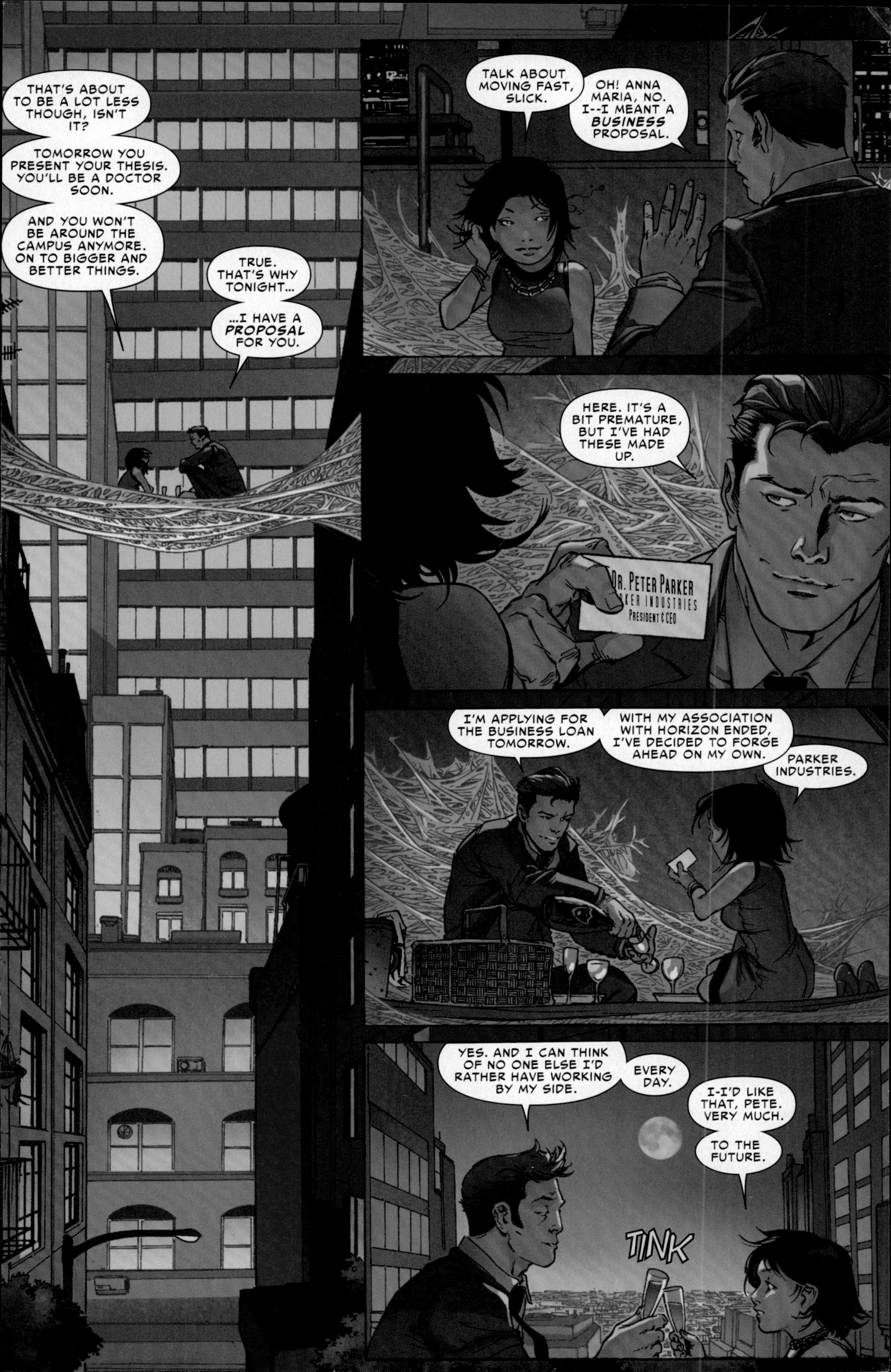
THAT'S ABOUT TO BE A LOT LESS THOUGH, ISN'T IT?
TOMORROW YOU PRESENT YOUR THESIS. YOU'LL BE A DOCTOR SOON.
AND YOU WON'T BE AROUND THE CAMPUS ANYMORE. ON TO BIGGER AND BETTER THINGS.
TRUE. THAT'S WHY TONIGHT...
...I HAVE A PROPOSAL FOR YOU.
TALK ABOUT MOVING FAST, SLICK.
OH! ANNA MARIA, NO. I--I MEANT A BUSINESS PROPOSAL.
HERE. IT'S A BIT PREMATURE, BUT I'VE HAD THESE MADE UP.
DR. PETER PARKER
PARKER INDUSTRIES
President & CEO
I'M APPLYING FOR THE BUSINESS LOAN TOMORROW.
WITH MY ASSOCIATION WITH HORIZON ENDED, I'VE DECIDED TO FORGE AHEAD ON MY OWN.
PARKER INDUSTRIES.
YES. AND I CAN THINK OF NO ONE ELSE I'D RATHER HAVE WORKING BY MY SIDE.
EVERY DAY.
I-I'D LIKE THAT, PETE. VERY MUCH.
TO THE FUTURE.
TINK

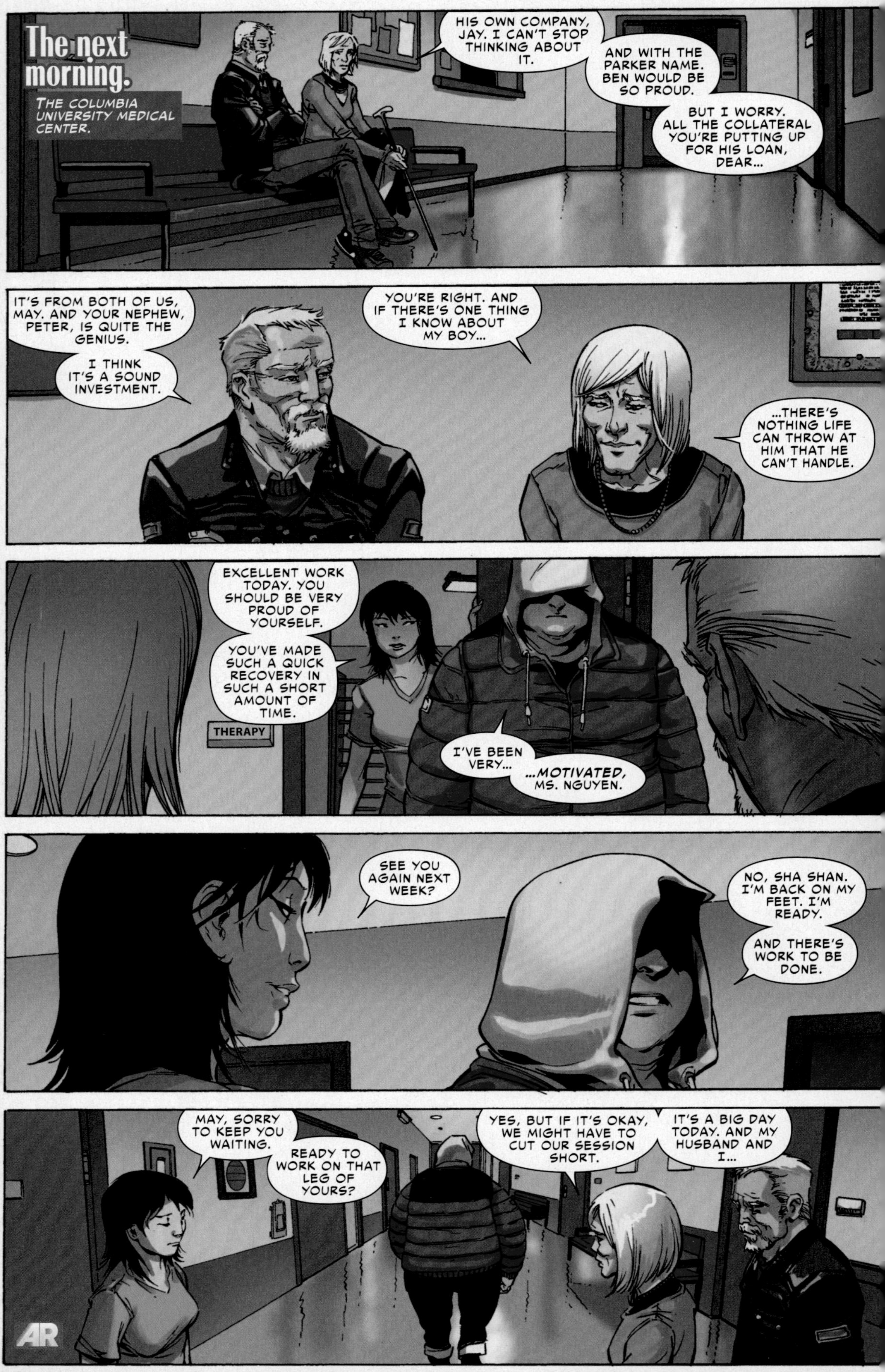
The next morning.
THE COLUMBIA UNIVERSITY MEDICAL CENTER.
HIS OWN COMPANY, JAY. I CAN'T STOP THINKING ABOUT IT.
AND WITH THE PARKER NAME. BEN WOULD BE SO PROUD.
BUT I WORRY. ALL THE COLLATERAL YOU'RE PUTTING UP FOR HIS LOAN, DEAR...
IT'S FROM BOTH OF US, MAY. AND YOUR NEPHEW, PETER, IS QUITE THE GENIUS.
I THINK IT'S A SOUND INVESTMENT.
YOU'RE RIGHT. AND IF THERE'S ONE THING I KNOW ABOUT MY BOY...
...THERE'S NOTHING LIFE CAN THROW AT HIM THAT HE CAN'T HANDLE.
EXCELLENT WORK TODAY. YOU SHOULD BE VERY PROUD OF YOURSELF.
YOU'VE MADE SUCH A QUICK RECOVERY IN SUCH A SHORT AMOUNT OF TIME.
THERAPY
I'VE BEEN VERY...
...*MOTIVATED,* MS. NGUYEN.
SEE YOU AGAIN NEXT WEEK?
NO, SHA SHAN. I'M BACK ON MY FEET. I'M READY.
AND THERE'S WORK TO BE DONE.
MAY, SORRY TO KEEP YOU WAITING.
READY TO WORK ON THAT LEG OF YOURS?
YES, BUT IF IT'S OKAY, WE MIGHT HAVE TO CUT OUR SESSION SHORT.
IT'S A BIG DAY TODAY. AND MY HUSBAND AND I...
AR

"...HAVE A *VERY* SPECIAL APPOINTMENT TO KEEP."

...BUT YOU WON'T REGRET IT. PARKER INDUSTRIES IS GOING TO CHANGE THE WORLD.

AND PAY YOU BACK TENFOLD. AT LEAST.

NEW YORK CITY BANK

THANK YOU AGAIN, JAY. I KNOW THIS A SIZEABLE LOAN...

PETER, PLEASE. THAT'S NOT HOW I RAISED YOU. PRIDE GOETH BEFORE A FALL.

...AY, FOR AS LONG AS I'VE ...NOWN HIM, PETER'S BEEN ...UNASSUMING AND SOFT-SPOKEN.

IF HE HAS THIS MUCH CONFIDENCE ABOUT THIS, I'LL TAKE IT AS A GOOD OMEN.

GOOD MAN. NOW, MS. JAFFREY...

...MY FUTURE VICE PRESIDENT. READY TO SHARE THE RISK--AND THE REWARDS?

PARKER, YOU ARE ONE ARROGANT LITTLE TWIT.

BUT I'VE SEEN YOUR WORK. YOU'RE ALMOST AS GOOD AS ME. HERE WE GO.

UGH. EVERY NUT I'VE SQUIRRELED AWAY. OKAY, YOUR TURN.

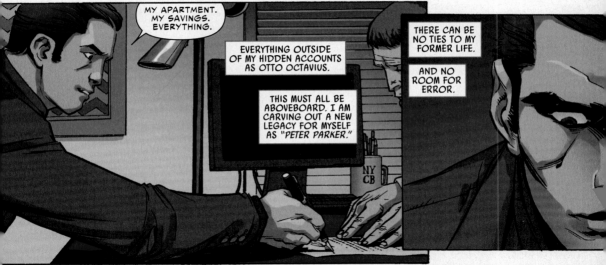

MY APARTMENT. MY SAVINGS. EVERYTHING.

EVERYTHING OUTSIDE OF MY HIDDEN ACCOUNTS AS OTTO OCTAVIUS.

THERE CAN BE NO TIES TO MY FORMER LIFE.

AND NO ROOM FOR ERROR.

THIS MUST ALL BE ABOVEBOARD. I AM CARVING OUT A NEW LEGACY FOR MYSELF AS "PETER PARKER."

NY CB

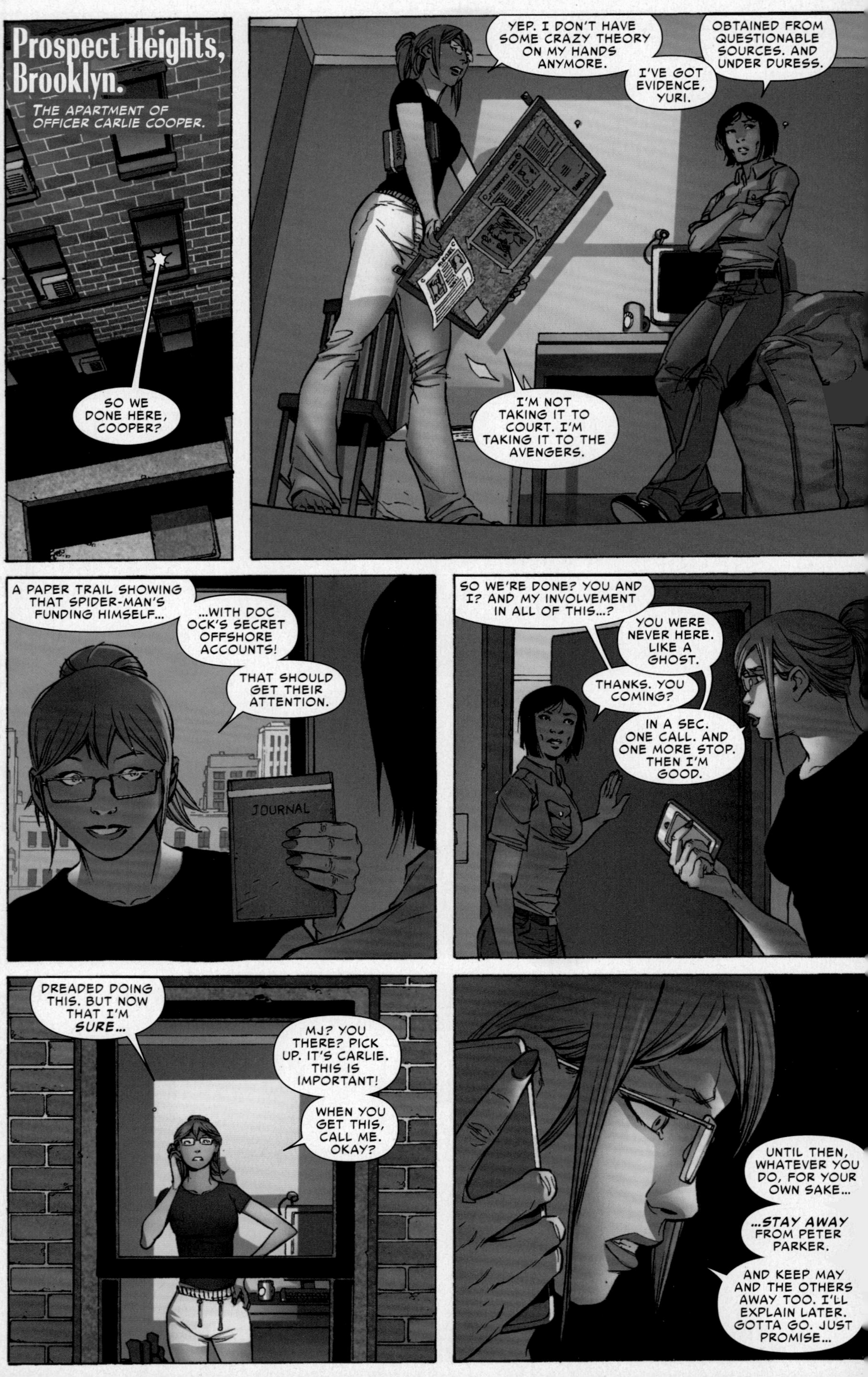
Prospect Heights, Brooklyn.
THE APARTMENT OF OFFICER CARLIE COOPER.
SO WE DONE HERE, COOPER?
YEP. I DON'T HAVE SOME CRAZY THEORY ON MY HANDS ANYMORE.
I'VE GOT EVIDENCE, YURI.
OBTAINED FROM QUESTIONABLE SOURCES. AND UNDER DURESS.
I'M NOT TAKING IT TO COURT. I'M TAKING IT TO THE AVENGERS.
A PAPER TRAIL SHOWING THAT SPIDER-MAN'S FUNDING HIMSELF...
...WITH DOC OCK'S SECRET OFFSHORE ACCOUNTS!
THAT SHOULD GET THEIR ATTENTION.
JOURNAL
SO WE'RE DONE? YOU AND I? AND MY INVOLVEMENT IN ALL OF THIS...?
YOU WERE NEVER HERE. LIKE A GHOST.
THANKS. YOU COMING?
IN A SEC. ONE CALL. AND ONE MORE STOP. THEN I'M GOOD.
DREADED DOING THIS. BUT NOW THAT I'M *SURE*...
MJ? YOU THERE? PICK UP. IT'S CARLIE. THIS IS IMPORTANT!
WHEN YOU GET THIS, CALL ME. OKAY?
UNTIL THEN, WHATEVER YOU DO, FOR YOUR OWN SAKE...
...*STAY AWAY* FROM PETER PARKER.
AND KEEP MAY AND THE OTHERS AWAY TOO. I'LL EXPLAIN LATER. GOTTA GO. JUST PROMISE...

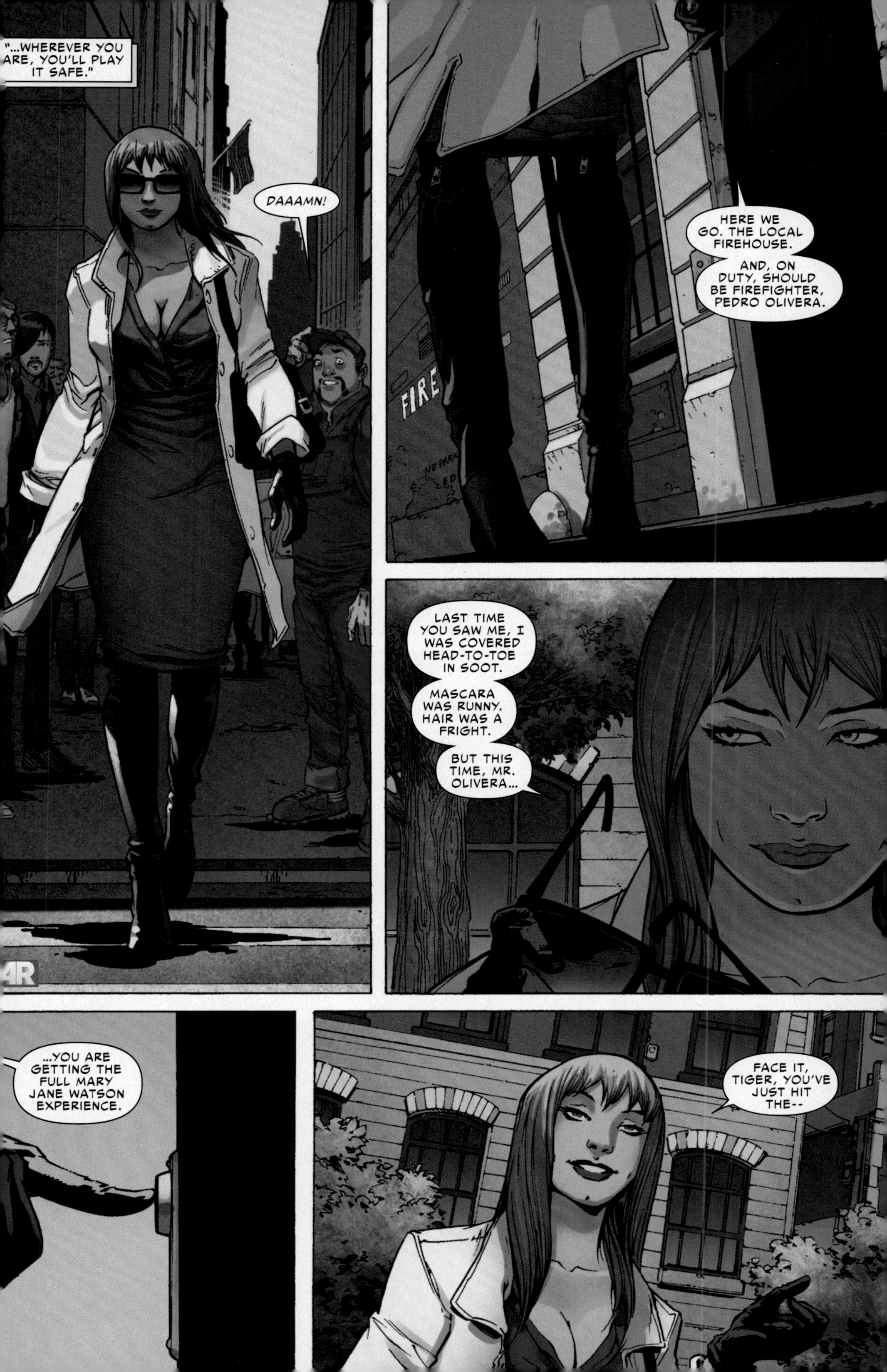
"...WHEREVER YOU ARE, YOU'LL PLAY IT SAFE."
DAAAMN!
HERE WE GO. THE LOCAL FIREHOUSE.
AND, ON DUTY, SHOULD BE FIREFIGHTER, PEDRO OLIVERA.
FIRE
LAST TIME YOU SAW ME, I WAS COVERED HEAD-TO-TOE IN SOOT.
MASCARA WAS RUNNY. HAIR WAS A FRIGHT.
BUT THIS TIME, MR. OLIVERA...
...YOU ARE GETTING THE FULL MARY JANE WATSON EXPERIENCE.
FACE IT, TIGER, YOU'VE JUST HIT THE--

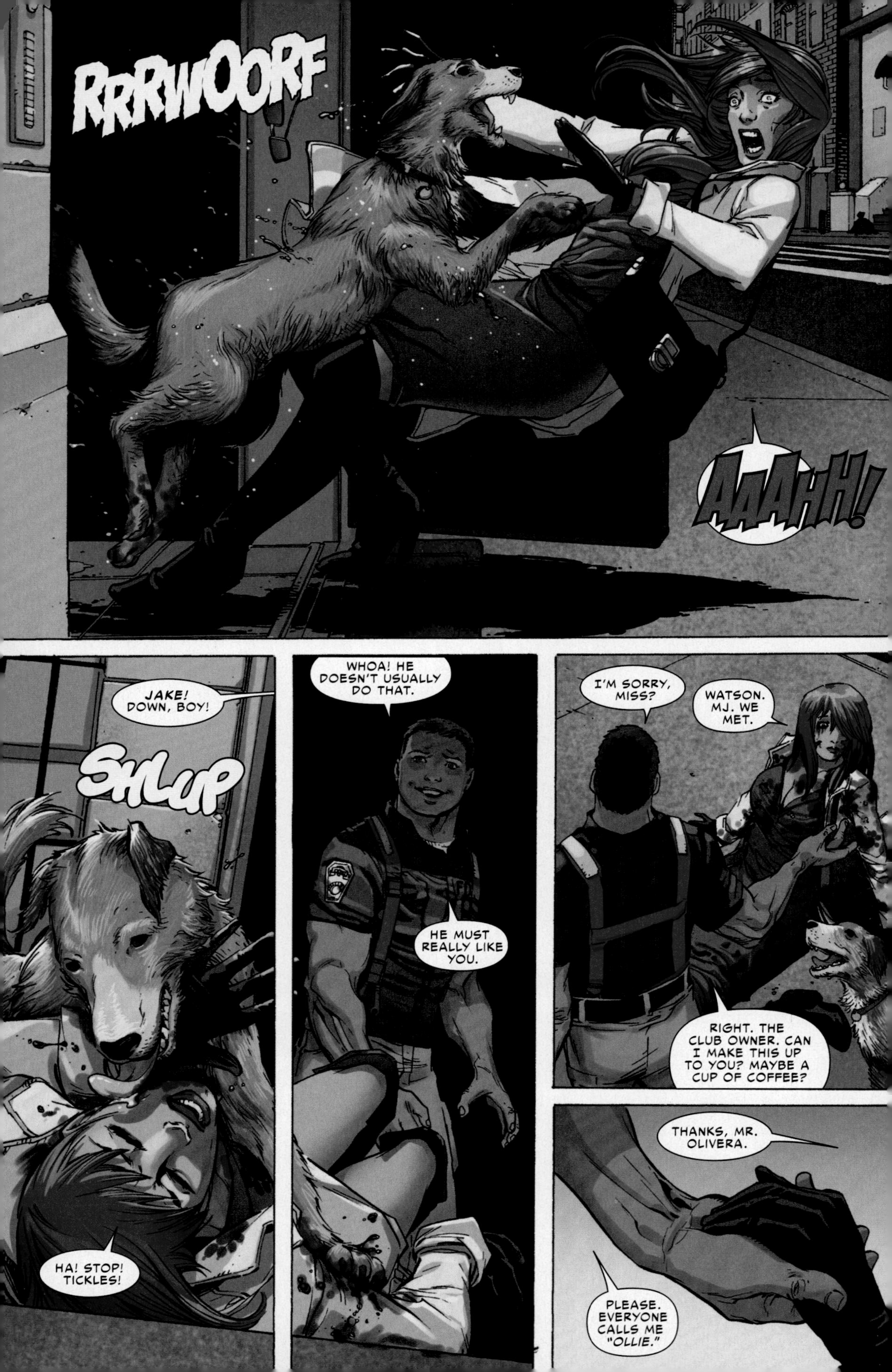
RRRWOORF
AAAHH!
JAKE! DOWN, BOY!
SHLUP
HA! STOP! TICKLES!
WHOA! HE DOESN'T USUALLY DO THAT.
HE MUST REALLY LIKE YOU.
I'M SORRY, MISS?
WATSON. MJ. WE MET.
RIGHT. THE CLUB OWNER. CAN I MAKE THIS UP TO YOU? MAYBE A CUP OF COFFEE?
THANKS, MR. OLIVERA.
PLEASE. EVERYONE CALLS ME "OLLIE."

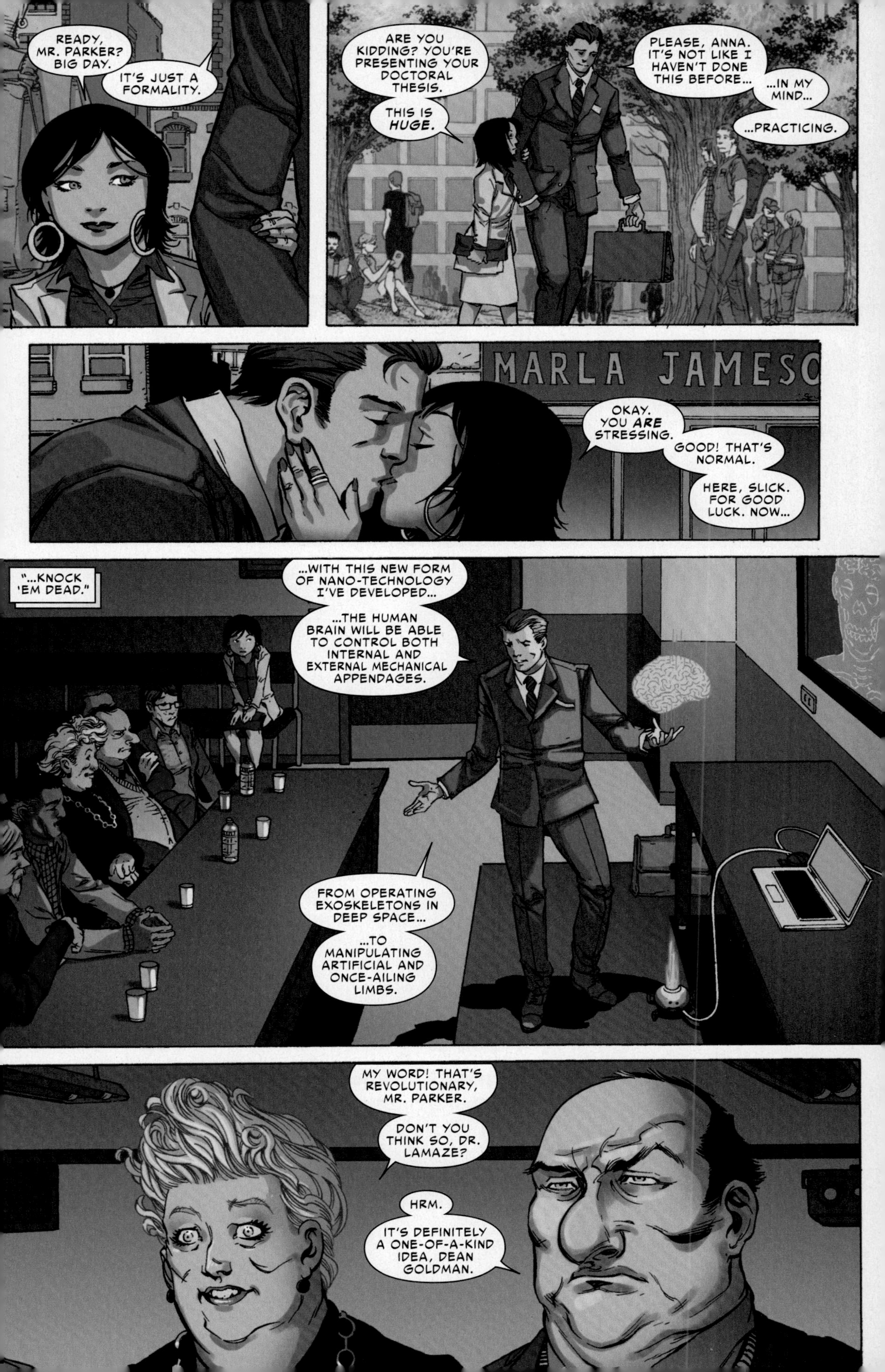
READY, MR. PARKER? BIG DAY.
IT'S JUST A FORMALITY.
ARE YOU KIDDING? YOU'RE PRESENTING YOUR DOCTORAL THESIS.
THIS IS HUGE.
PLEASE, ANNA. IT'S NOT LIKE I HAVEN'T DONE THIS BEFORE...
...IN MY MIND...
...PRACTICING.
MARLA JAMESO
OKAY. YOU ARE STRESSING.
GOOD! THAT'S NORMAL.
HERE, SLICK. FOR GOOD LUCK. NOW...
"...KNOCK 'EM DEAD."
...WITH THIS NEW FORM OF NANO-TECHNOLOGY I'VE DEVELOPED...
...THE HUMAN BRAIN WILL BE ABLE TO CONTROL BOTH INTERNAL AND EXTERNAL MECHANICAL APPENDAGES.
FROM OPERATING EXOSKELETONS IN DEEP SPACE...
...TO MANIPULATING ARTIFICIAL AND ONCE-AILING LIMBS.
MY WORD! THAT'S REVOLUTIONARY, MR. PARKER.
DON'T YOU THINK SO, DR. LAMAZE?
HRM.
IT'S DEFINITELY A ONE-OF-A-KIND IDEA, DEAN GOLDMAN.

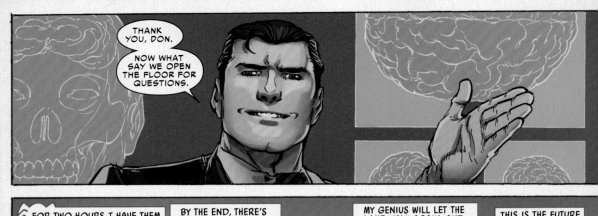

THANK YOU, DON.

NOW WHAT SAY WE OPEN THE FLOOR FOR QUESTIONS.

FOR TWO HOURS I HAVE THEM IN THE PALM OF MY HAND.

BY THE END, THERE'S NO DOUBT. THEY ARE WITNESSING GREATNESS.

MY GENIUS WILL LET THE LAME WALK AGAIN, AND EXTEND MANKIND'S GRASP OUT INTO THE HEAVENS ITSELF.

THIS IS THE FUTURE FOR DR. PETER PARKER. AND IT IS ONLY FITTING...

...IT BEGINS WITH A ROUND OF APPLAU--

OH, STOP THAT. WE'RE NOT DONE HERE.

I HAVE ONE LAST QUESTION FOR OUR MR. PARKER.

DO YOU TAKE ME FOR A FOOL, PARKER?

WHAT?!

WHAT ARE YOU ON ABOUT, LAMAZE?

YOU THOUGHT I WOULDN'T RECOGNIZE THE BASIC CONCEPTS, THEORIES, OR DESIGNS?!

THIS ISN'T YOUR WORK AT ALL, PETER!

YOU, SIR, HAVE STOLEN THE LIFE'S WORK OF MY GOOD FRIEND--

--THE LATE DR. OTTO OCTAVIUS!

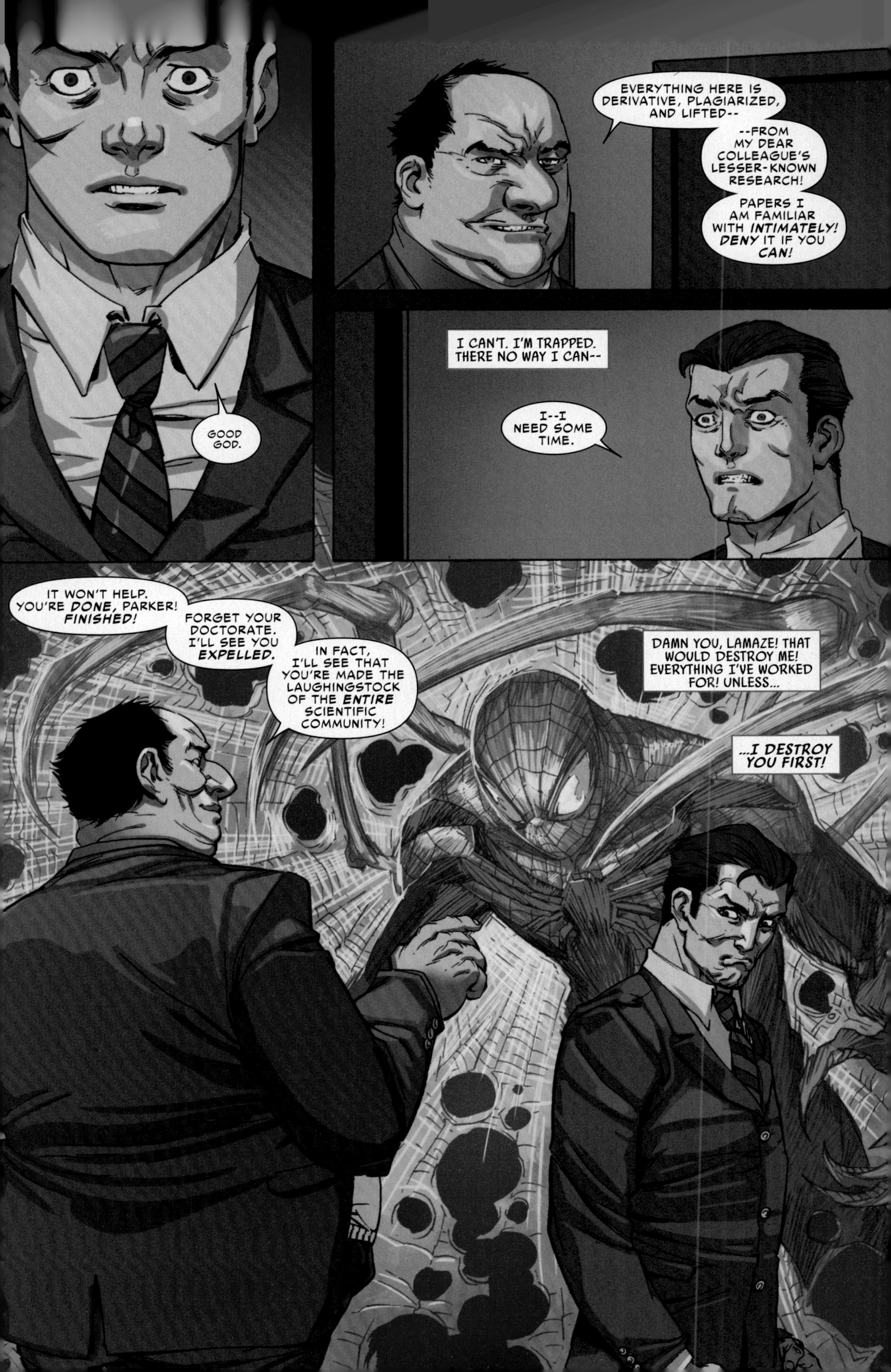
EVERYTHING HERE IS DERIVATIVE, PLAGIARIZED, AND LIFTED--
--FROM MY DEAR COLLEAGUE'S LESSER-KNOWN RESEARCH!
PAPERS I AM FAMILIAR WITH INTIMATELY! DENY IT IF YOU CAN!
GOOD GOD.
I CAN'T. I'M TRAPPED. THERE NO WAY I CAN--
I--I NEED SOME TIME.
IT WON'T HELP. YOU'RE DONE, PARKER! FINISHED!
FORGET YOUR DOCTORATE. I'LL SEE YOU EXPELLED.
IN FACT, I'LL SEE THAT YOU'RE MADE THE LAUGHINGSTOCK OF THE ENTIRE SCIENTIFIC COMMUNITY!
DAMN YOU, LAMAZE! THAT WOULD DESTROY ME! EVERYTHING I'VE WORKED FOR! UNLESS...
...I DESTROY YOU FIRST!

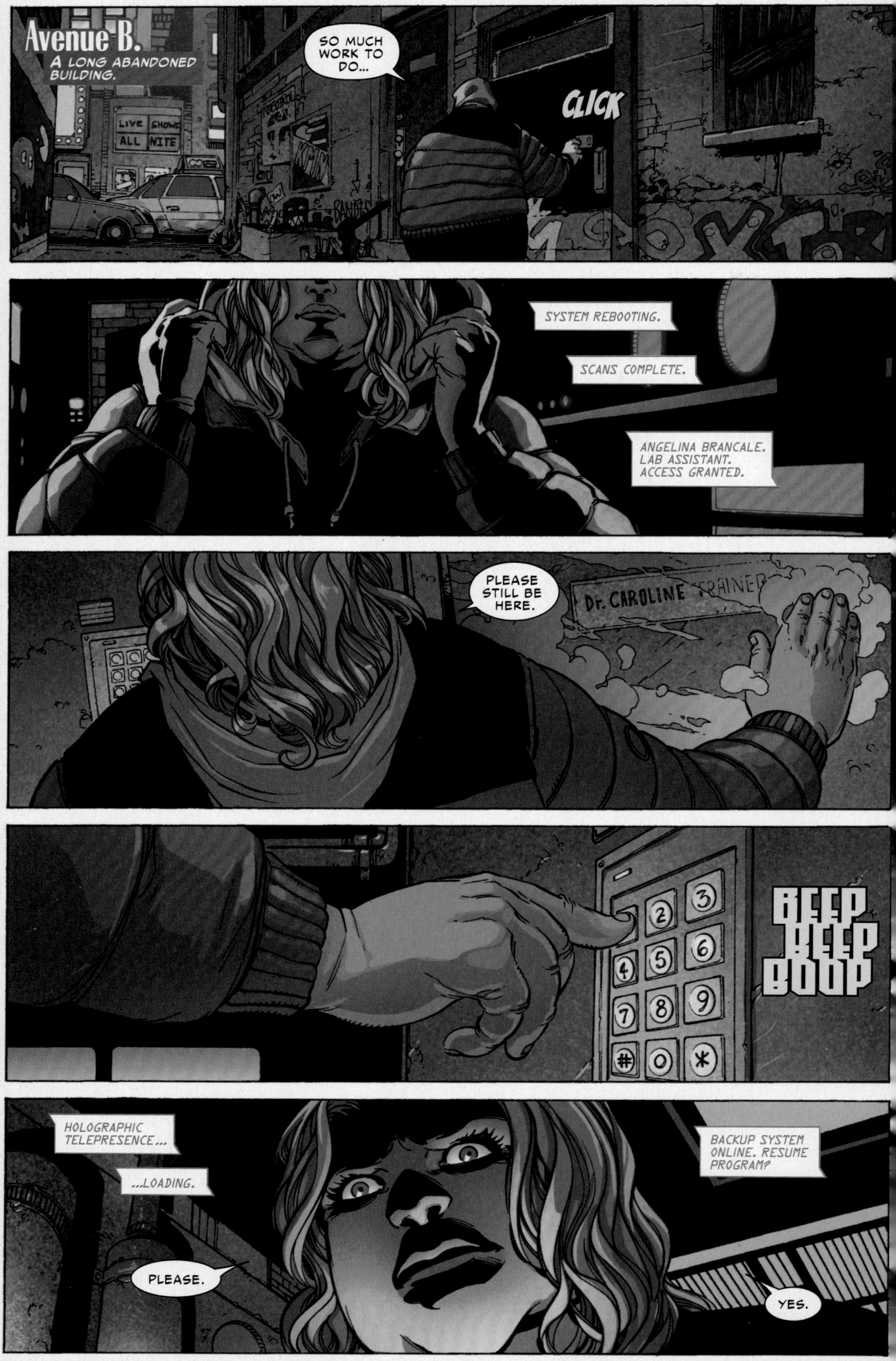
Avenue B.
A LONG ABANDONED BUILDING.
SO MUCH WORK TO DO...
CLICK
LIVE SHOWS ALL NITE
SYSTEM REBOOTING.
SCANS COMPLETE.
ANGELINA BRANCALE. LAB ASSISTANT. ACCESS GRANTED.
PLEASE STILL BE HERE.
Dr. CAROLINE TRAINER
BEEP BEEP BOOP
HOLOGRAPHIC TELEPRESENCE...
...LOADING.
BACKUP SYSTEM ONLINE. RESUME PROGRAM?
PLEASE.
YES.

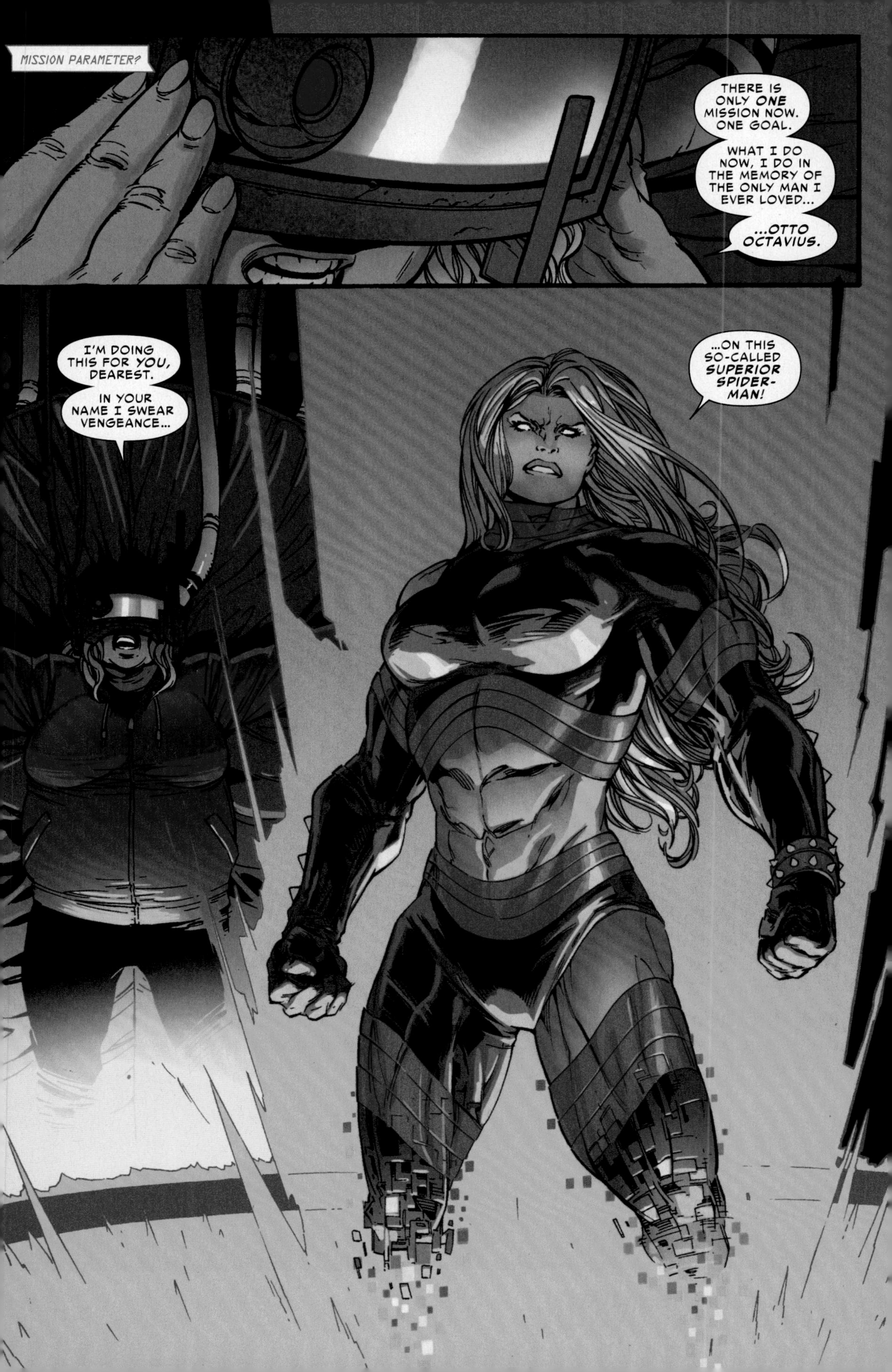

MISSION PARAMETER?
THERE IS ONLY ONE MISSION NOW. ONE GOAL.
WHAT I DO NOW, I DO IN THE MEMORY OF THE ONLY MAN I EVER LOVED...
...OTTO OCTAVIUS.
I'M DOING THIS FOR YOU, DEAREST.
IN YOUR NAME I SWEAR VENGEANCE...
...ON THIS SO-CALLED SUPERIOR SPIDER-MAN!

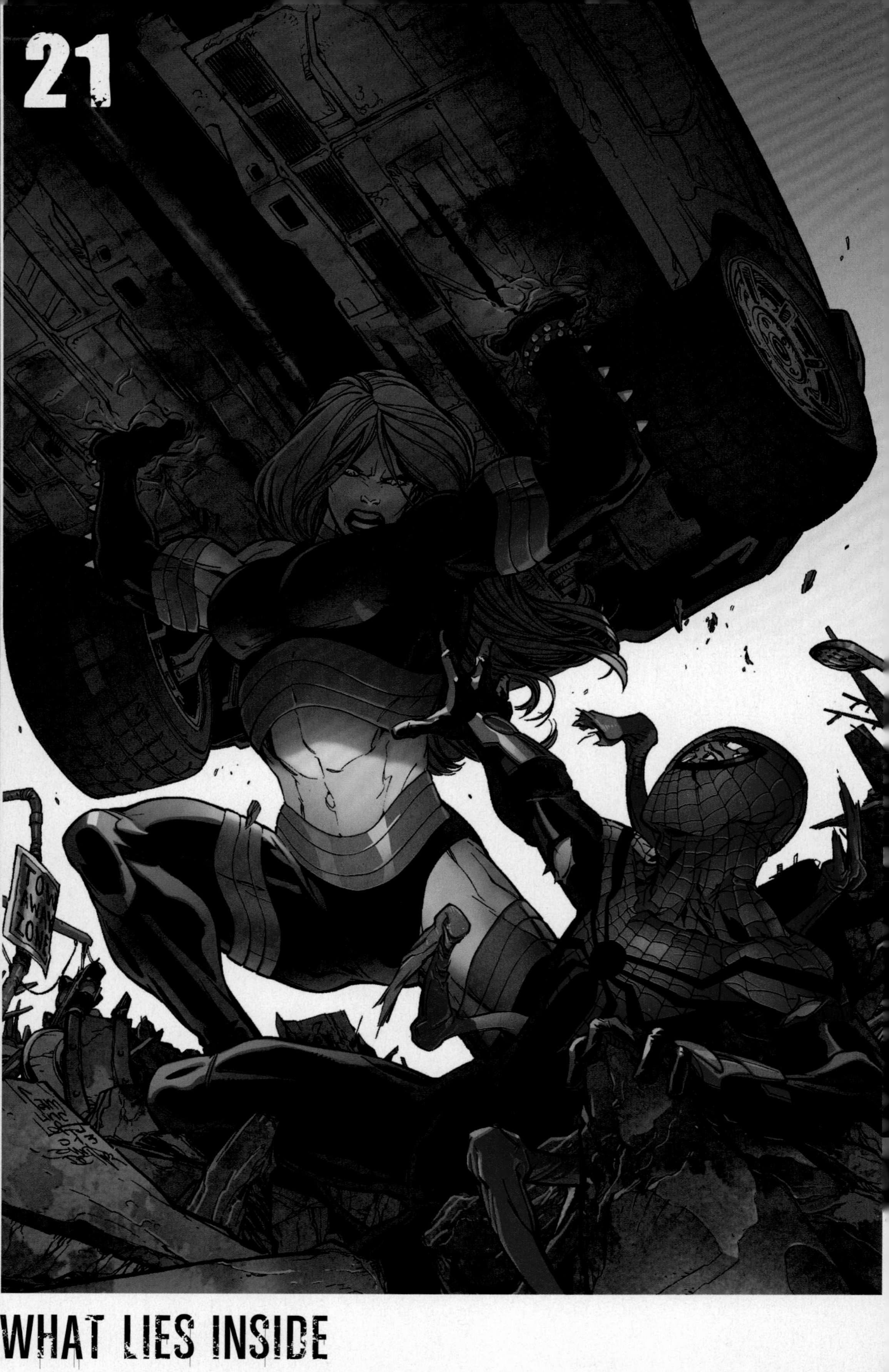
21
TOW AWAY ZONE

WHAT LIES INSIDE

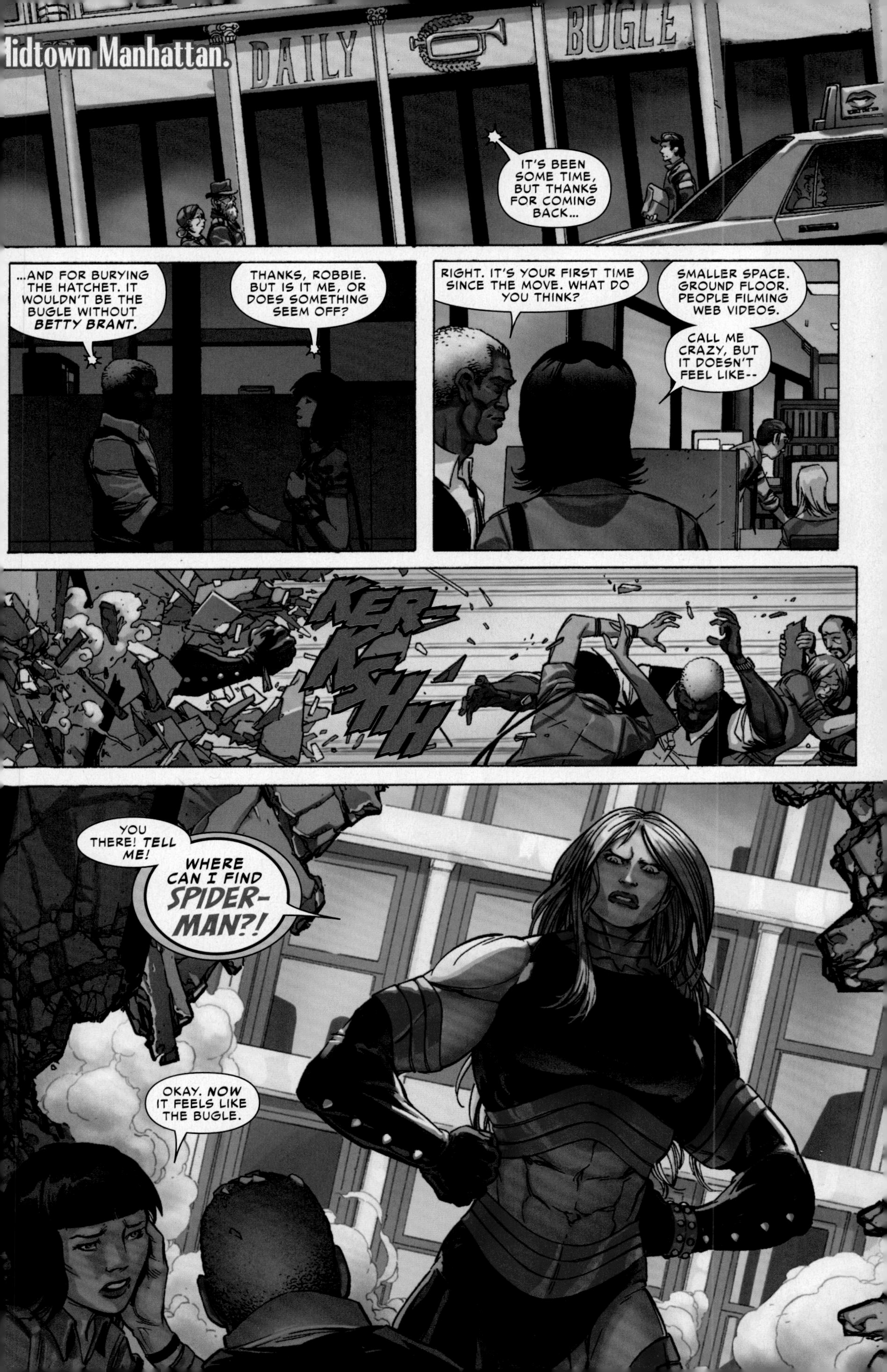

lidtown Manhattan.
DAILY BUGLE
IT'S BEEN SOME TIME, BUT THANKS FOR COMING BACK...
...AND FOR BURYING THE HATCHET. IT WOULDN'T BE THE BUGLE WITHOUT BETTY BRANT.
THANKS, ROBBIE. BUT IS IT ME, OR DOES SOMETHING SEEM OFF?
RIGHT. IT'S YOUR FIRST TIME SINCE THE MOVE. WHAT DO YOU THINK?
SMALLER SPACE. GROUND FLOOR. PEOPLE FILMING WEB VIDEOS.
CALL ME CRAZY, BUT IT DOESN'T FEEL LIKE--
KER-KSHH
YOU THERE! TELL ME!
WHERE CAN I FIND SPIDER-MAN?!
OKAY. NOW IT FEELS LIKE THE BUGLE.

THE WALL-CRAWLER IS ALWAYS HANGING AROUND HERE.

HOW DO YOU CONTACT HIM?! BRING HIM HERE! NOW!

ROBBIE? HELP ME OUT. I'M A LITTLE RUSTY.

SHE'S ANGELINA BRANCALE. STUNNER. USED TO BE DOC OCK'S GIRLFRIEND.

DON'T JUST STAND THERE, PEOPLE. SOMEBODY BETTER BE FILMING THIS.

TALK!

MS. BRANCALE, YOU'VE BEEN AWAY FOR A WHILE. THINGS HAVE CHANGED.

WE'RE NOT ON GOOD TERMS WITH SPIDER-MAN. BUT DON'T WORRY...

...IF YOU'RE A CRIMINAL IN THIS TOWN, HE'LL FIND YOU.

FINAL DAILY BUGLE
NEW YORK'S FINEST DAILY NEWSPAPER
HOBGOBLIN UMASKED

FINAL DAILY BUGLE
NEW YORK'S FINEST DAILY NEWSPAPER
BLACK CAT CAPTURED

AND HOW EXACTLY DOES HE GO ABOUT DOING THAT?

THE MAN'S GOT EYES EVERYWHERE.

THOUSANDS OF THOSE SURVEILLANCE DRONES ACROSS THE CITY.

IT'S WORSE THAN THE N.S.A.

WE'RE DOING AN EXPOSÉ ON IT THIS WEEK.

SO ALL ONE HAS TO DO IS COMMIT A CRIME IN FRONT OF ONE OF THOSE CAMERAS.

LIKE THAT ONE OVER THERE.

OHHH. THIS IS NOT GOOD.

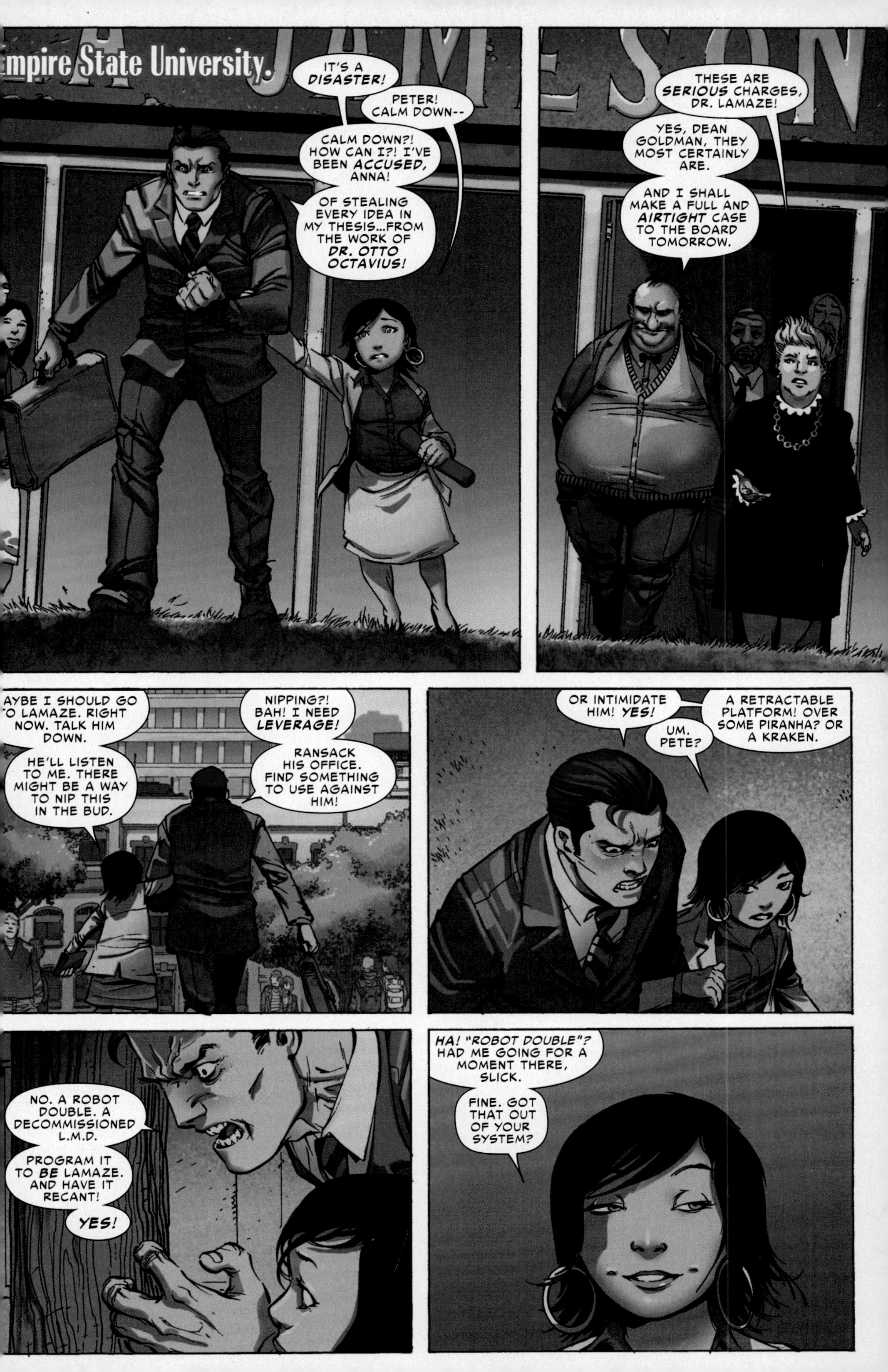
mpire State University.
IT'S A DISASTER!
PETER! CALM DOWN--
CALM DOWN?! HOW CAN I?! I'VE BEEN ACCUSED, ANNA!
OF STEALING EVERY IDEA IN MY THESIS...FROM THE WORK OF DR. OTTO OCTAVIUS!
THESE ARE SERIOUS CHARGES, DR. LAMAZE!
YES, DEAN GOLDMAN, THEY MOST CERTAINLY ARE.
AND I SHALL MAKE A FULL AND AIRTIGHT CASE TO THE BOARD TOMORROW.
AYBE I SHOULD GO O LAMAZE. RIGHT NOW. TALK HIM DOWN.
HE'LL LISTEN TO ME. THERE MIGHT BE A WAY TO NIP THIS IN THE BUD.
NIPPING?! BAH! I NEED LEVERAGE!
RANSACK HIS OFFICE. FIND SOMETHING TO USE AGAINST HIM!
OR INTIMIDATE HIM! YES!
A RETRACTABLE PLATFORM! OVER SOME PIRANHA? OR A KRAKEN.
UM. PETE?
NO. A ROBOT DOUBLE. A DECOMMISSIONED L.M.D.
PROGRAM IT TO BE LAMAZE. AND HAVE IT RECANT!
YES!
HA! "ROBOT DOUBLE"? HAD ME GOING FOR A MOMENT THERE, SLICK.
FINE. GOT THAT OUT OF YOUR SYSTEM?

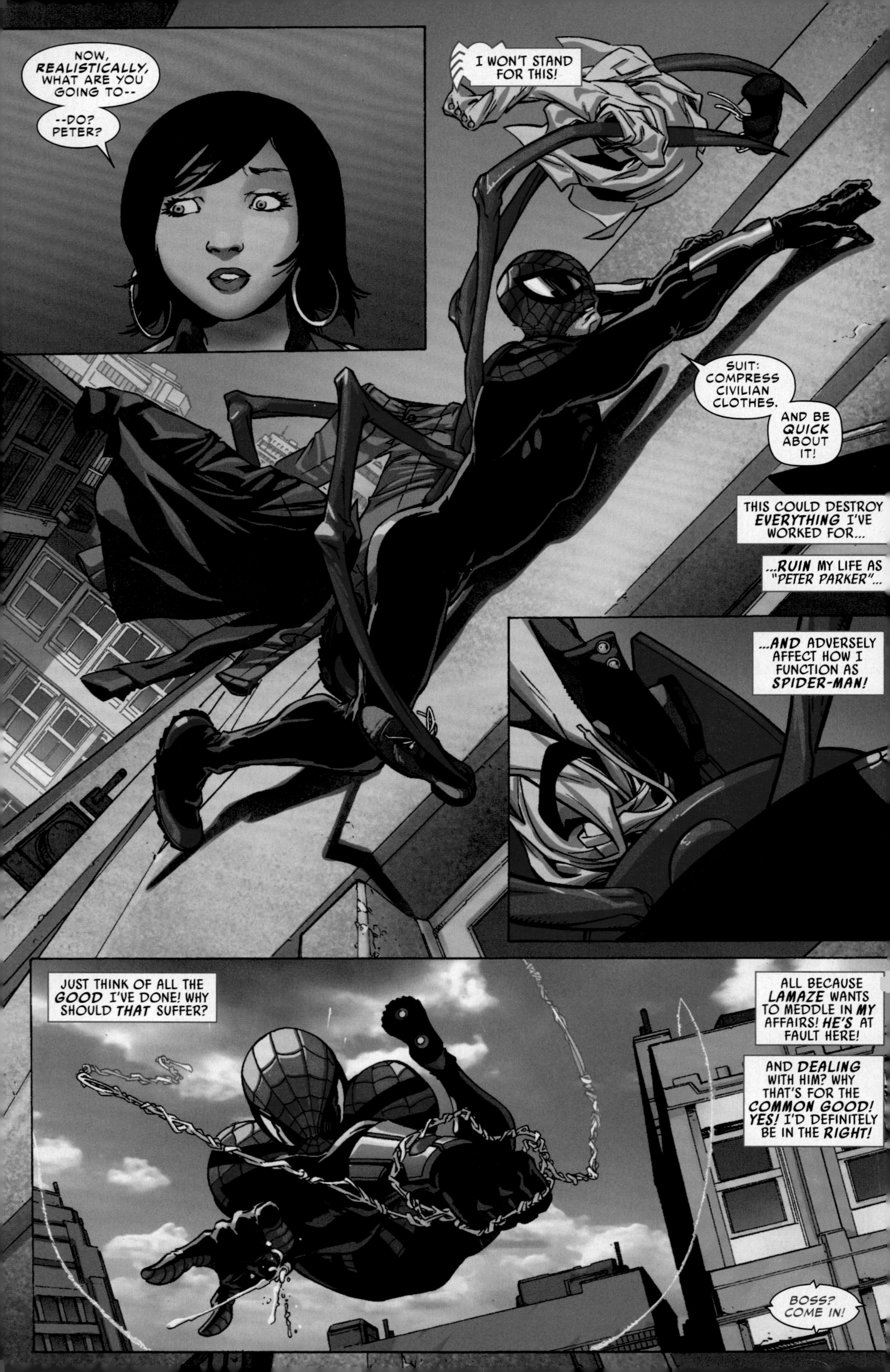
NOW, REALISTICALLY, WHAT ARE YOU GOING TO--
--DO? PETER?
I WON'T STAND FOR THIS!
SUIT: COMPRESS CIVILIAN CLOTHES.
AND BE QUICK ABOUT IT!
THIS COULD DESTROY EVERYTHING I'VE WORKED FOR...
...RUIN MY LIFE AS "PETER PARKER"...
...AND ADVERSELY AFFECT HOW I FUNCTION AS SPIDER-MAN!
JUST THINK OF ALL THE GOOD I'VE DONE! WHY SHOULD THAT SUFFER?
ALL BECAUSE LAMAZE WANTS TO MEDDLE IN MY AFFAIRS! HE'S AT FAULT HERE!
AND DEALING WITH HIM? WHY THAT'S FOR THE COMMON GOOD! YES! I'D DEFINITELY BE IN THE RIGHT!
BOSS? COME IN!

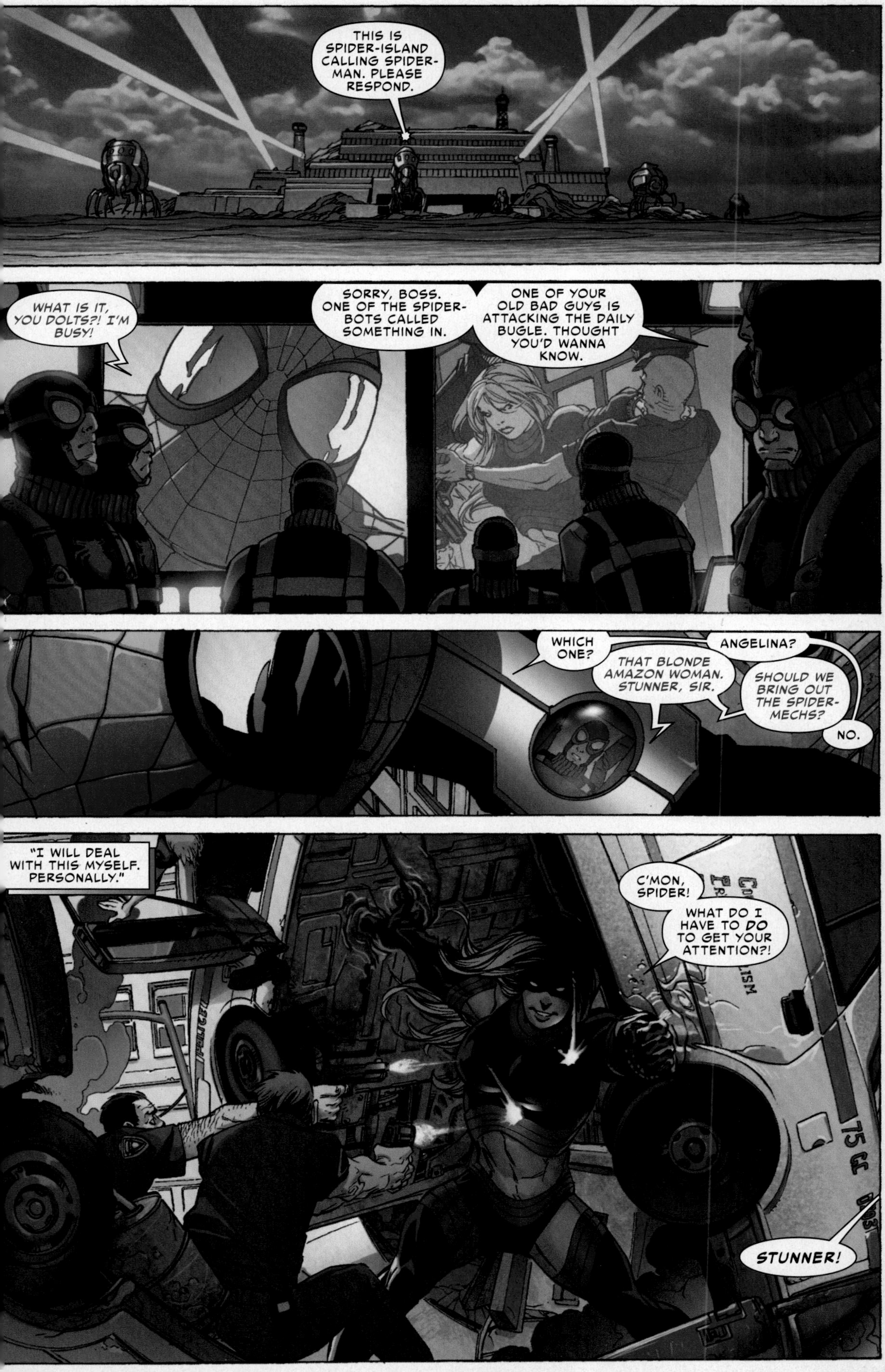
THIS IS SPIDER-ISLAND CALLING SPIDER-MAN. PLEASE RESPOND.
WHAT IS IT, YOU DOLTS?! I'M BUSY!
SORRY, BOSS. ONE OF THE SPIDER-BOTS CALLED SOMETHING IN.
ONE OF YOUR OLD BAD GUYS IS ATTACKING THE DAILY BUGLE. THOUGHT YOU'D WANNA KNOW.
WHICH ONE?
THAT BLONDE AMAZON WOMAN. STUNNER, SIR.
ANGELINA?
SHOULD WE BRING OUT THE SPIDER-MECHS?
NO.
"I WILL DEAL WITH THIS MYSELF. PERSONALLY."
C'MON, SPIDER!
WHAT DO I HAVE TO *DO* TO GET YOUR ATTENTION?!
STUNNER!

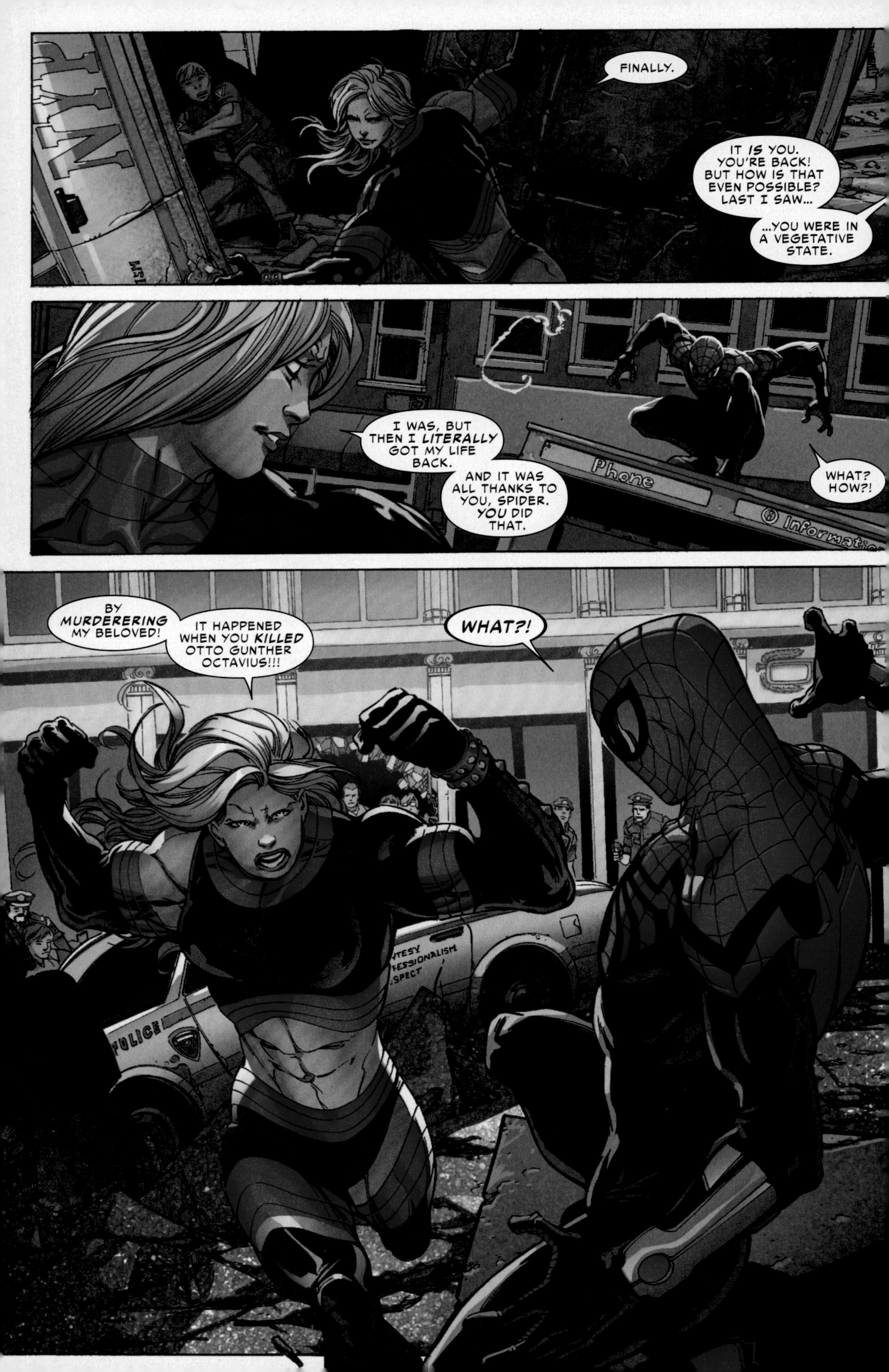
FINALLY.
IT IS YOU. YOU'RE BACK! BUT HOW IS THAT EVEN POSSIBLE? LAST I SAW...
...YOU WERE IN A VEGETATIVE STATE.
I WAS, BUT THEN I LITERALLY GOT MY LIFE BACK.
AND IT WAS ALL THANKS TO YOU, SPIDER. YOU DID THAT.
WHAT? HOW?!
BY MURDERERING MY BELOVED!
IT HAPPENED WHEN YOU KILLED OTTO GUNTHER OCTAVIUS!!!
WHAT?!
Phone
Informatio
POLICE

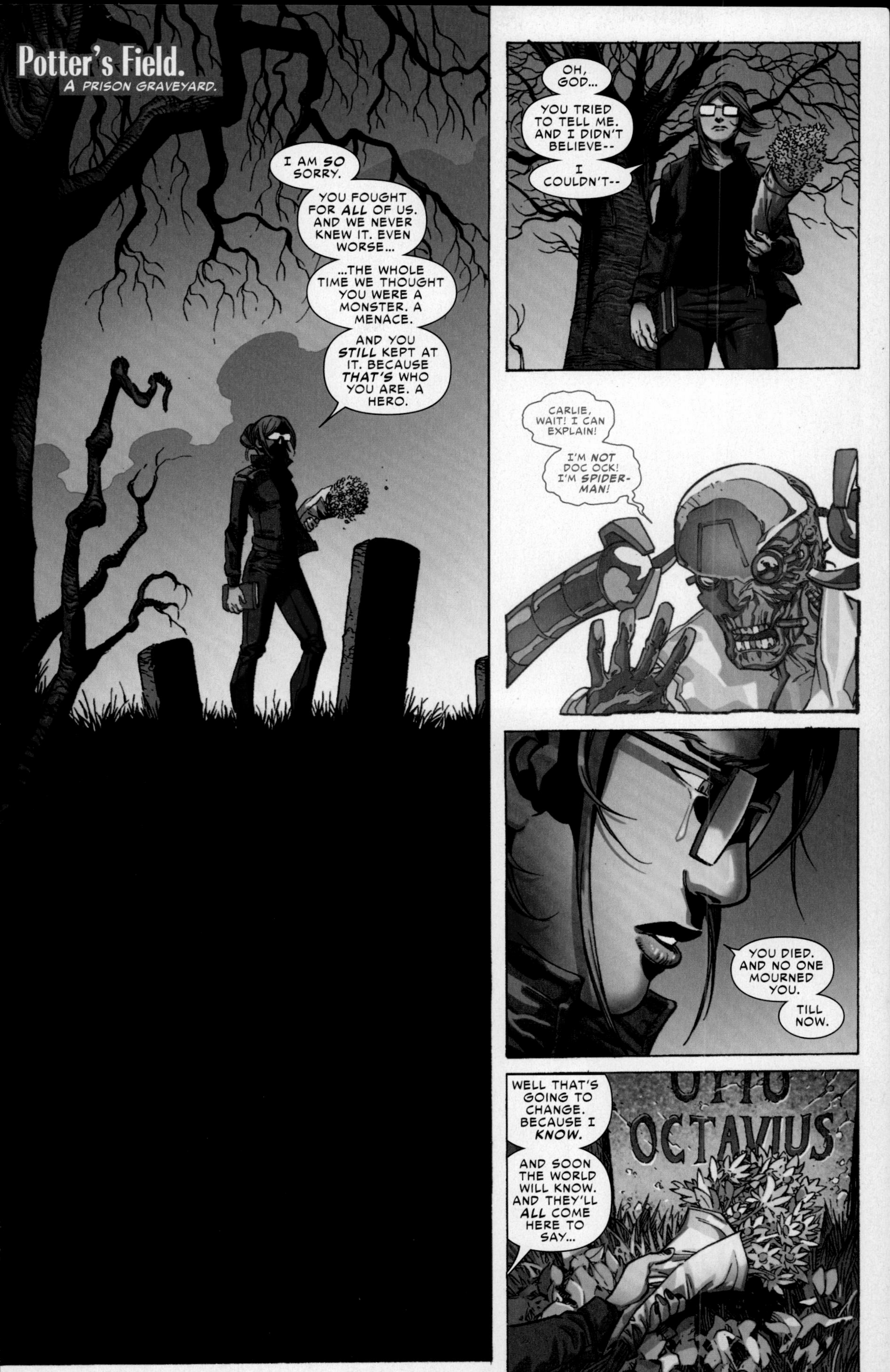
Potter's Field.
A PRISON GRAVEYARD.
I AM SO SORRY.
YOU FOUGHT FOR ALL OF US. AND WE NEVER KNEW IT. EVEN WORSE...
...THE WHOLE TIME WE THOUGHT YOU WERE A MONSTER. A MENACE.
AND YOU STILL KEPT AT IT. BECAUSE THAT'S WHO YOU ARE. A HERO.
OH, GOD...
YOU TRIED TO TELL ME. AND I DIDN'T BELIEVE--
I COULDN'T--
CARLIE, WAIT! I CAN EXPLAIN!
I'M NOT DOC OCK! I'M SPIDER-MAN!
YOU DIED. AND NO ONE MOURNED YOU.
TILL NOW.
WELL THAT'S GOING TO CHANGE. BECAUSE I KNOW.
AND SOON THE WORLD WILL KNOW. AND THEY'LL ALL COME HERE TO SAY...
OCTAVIUS

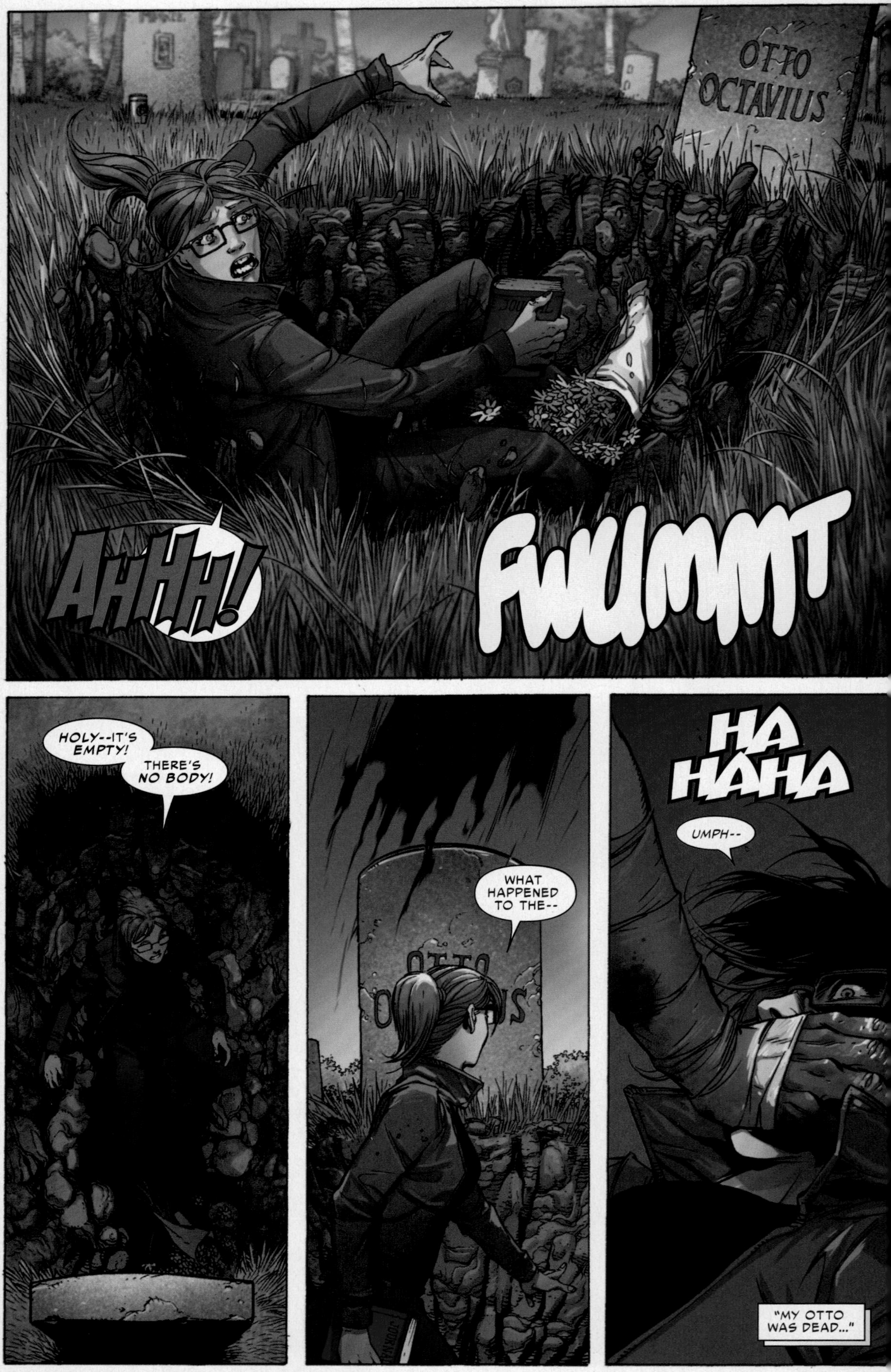
OTTO OCTAVIUS
AHHH!
FWUMMT
HOLY--IT'S EMPTY!
THERE'S NO BODY!
WHAT HAPPENED TO THE--
HA HAHA
UMPH--
"MY OTTO WAS DEAD..."

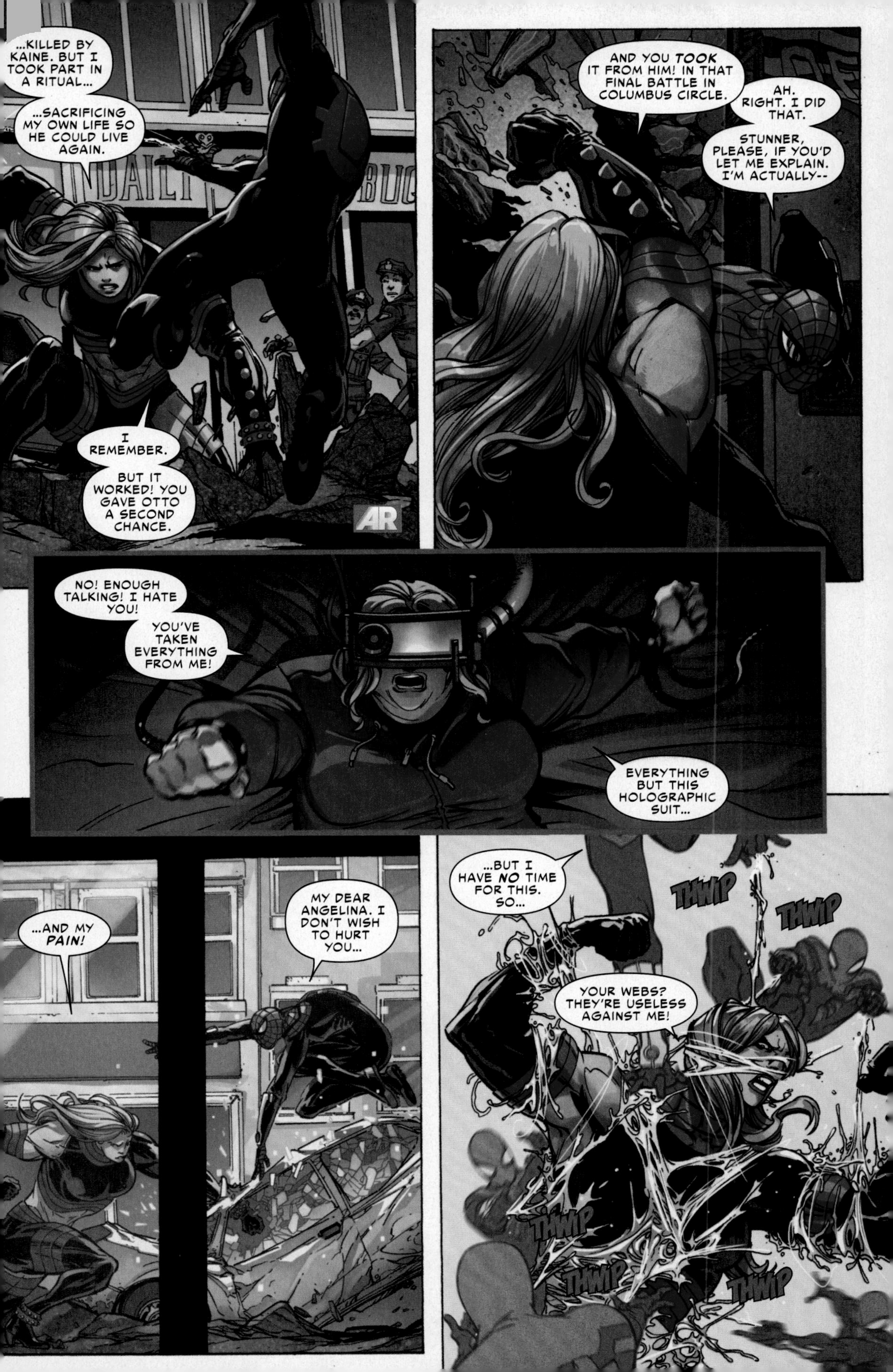
...KILLED BY KAINE. BUT I TOOK PART IN A RITUAL...
...SACRIFICING MY OWN LIFE SO HE COULD LIVE AGAIN.
I REMEMBER.
BUT IT WORKED! YOU GAVE OTTO A SECOND CHANCE.
AND YOU *TOOK* IT FROM HIM! IN THAT FINAL BATTLE IN COLUMBUS CIRCLE.
AH. RIGHT. I DID THAT.
STUNNER, PLEASE, IF YOU'D LET ME EXPLAIN. I'M ACTUALLY--
NO! ENOUGH TALKING! I HATE YOU!
YOU'VE TAKEN EVERYTHING FROM ME!
EVERYTHING BUT THIS HOLOGRAPHIC SUIT...
...AND MY *PAIN!*
MY DEAR ANGELINA. I DON'T WISH TO HURT YOU...
...BUT I HAVE **NO** TIME FOR THIS. SO...
THWIP
THWIP
YOUR WEBS? THEY'RE USELESS AGAINST ME!
THWIP
THWIP
THWIP

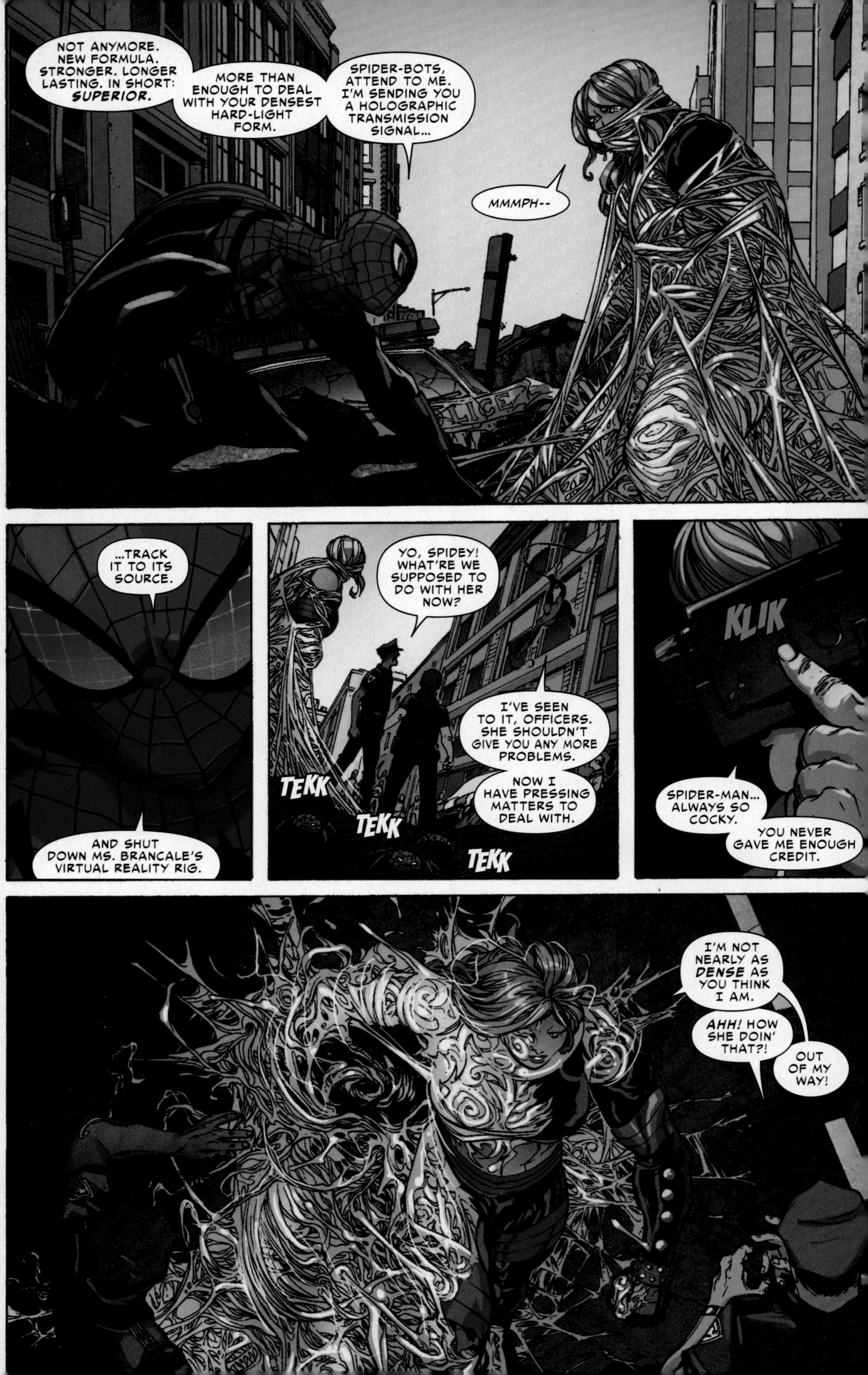
NOT ANYMORE. NEW FORMULA. STRONGER. LONGER LASTING. IN SHORT: SUPERIOR.
MORE THAN ENOUGH TO DEAL WITH YOUR DENSEST HARD-LIGHT FORM.
SPIDER-BOTS, ATTEND TO ME. I'M SENDING YOU A HOLOGRAPHIC TRANSMISSION SIGNAL...
MMMPH--
...TRACK IT TO ITS SOURCE.
AND SHUT DOWN MS. BRANCALE'S VIRTUAL REALITY RIG.
YO, SPIDEY! WHAT'RE WE SUPPOSED TO DO WITH HER NOW?
I'VE SEEN TO IT, OFFICERS. SHE SHOULDN'T GIVE YOU ANY MORE PROBLEMS.
NOW I HAVE PRESSING MATTERS TO DEAL WITH.
TEKK
TEKK
TEKK
KLIK
SPIDER-MAN... ALWAYS SO COCKY.
YOU NEVER GAVE ME ENOUGH CREDIT.
I'M NOT NEARLY AS DENSE AS YOU THINK I AM.
AHH! HOW SHE DOIN' THAT?!
OUT OF MY WAY!

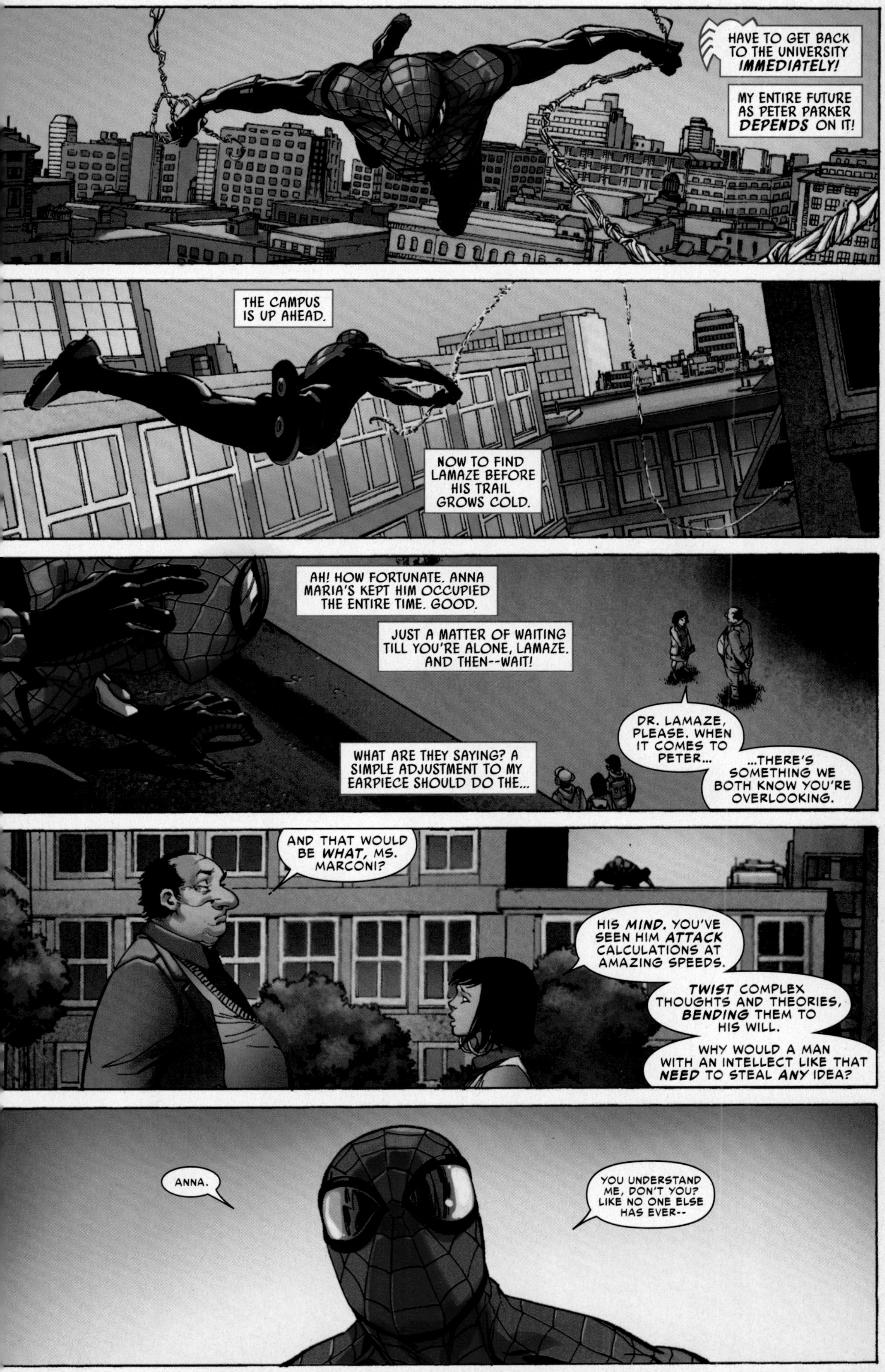
HAVE TO GET BACK TO THE UNIVERSITY IMMEDIATELY!
MY ENTIRE FUTURE AS PETER PARKER DEPENDS ON IT!
THE CAMPUS IS UP AHEAD.
NOW TO FIND LAMAZE BEFORE HIS TRAIL GROWS COLD.
AH! HOW FORTUNATE. ANNA MARIA'S KEPT HIM OCCUPIED THE ENTIRE TIME. GOOD.
JUST A MATTER OF WAITING TILL YOU'RE ALONE, LAMAZE. AND THEN--WAIT!
WHAT ARE THEY SAYING? A SIMPLE ADJUSTMENT TO MY EARPIECE SHOULD DO THE...
DR. LAMAZE, PLEASE. WHEN IT COMES TO PETER...
...THERE'S SOMETHING WE BOTH KNOW YOU'RE OVERLOOKING.
AND THAT WOULD BE WHAT, MS. MARCONI?
HIS MIND. YOU'VE SEEN HIM ATTACK CALCULATIONS AT AMAZING SPEEDS.
TWIST COMPLEX THOUGHTS AND THEORIES, BENDING THEM TO HIS WILL.
WHY WOULD A MAN WITH AN INTELLECT LIKE THAT NEED TO STEAL ANY IDEA?
ANNA.
YOU UNDERSTAND ME, DON'T YOU? LIKE NO ONE ELSE HAS EVER--

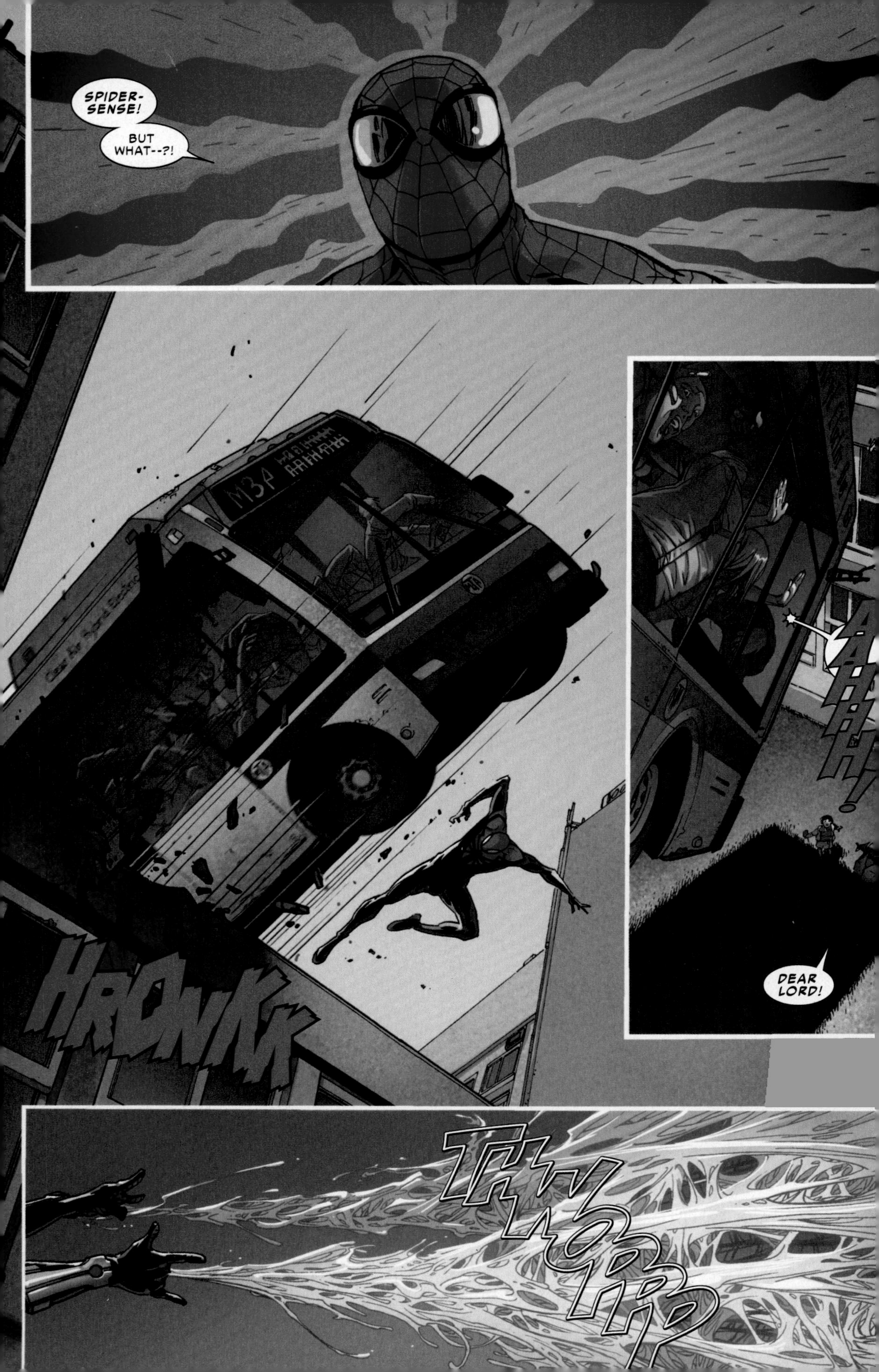
SPIDER-SENSE!
BUT WHAT--?!
M3A
HRONK
AAHHH!
DEAR LORD!
THWOOMP

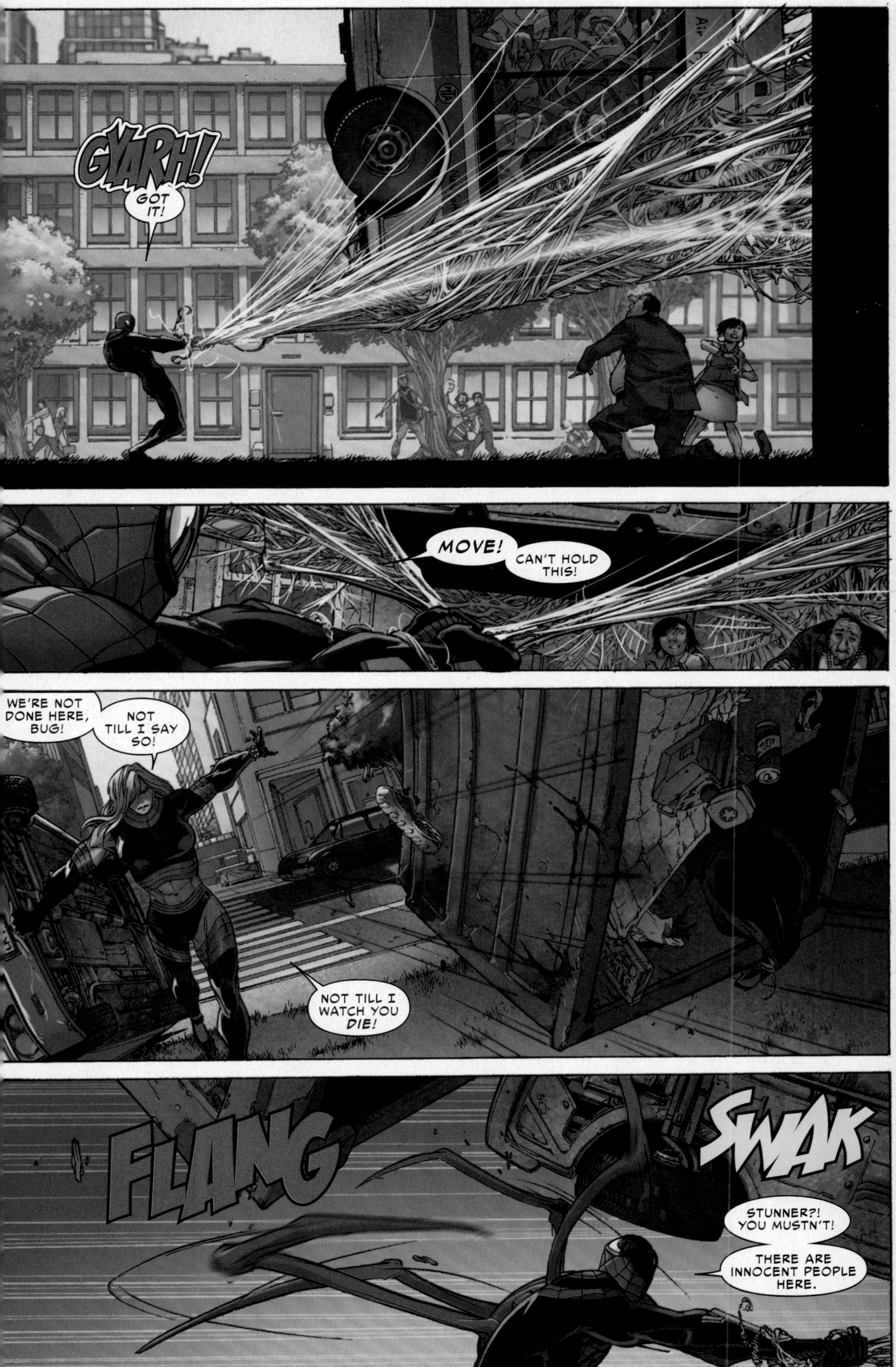
GYARH!
GOT IT!
MOVE!
CAN'T HOLD THIS!
WE'RE NOT DONE HERE, BUG!
NOT TILL I SAY SO!
NOT TILL I WATCH YOU DIE!
FLANG
SWAK
STUNNER?! YOU MUSTN'T!
THERE ARE INNOCENT PEOPLE HERE.

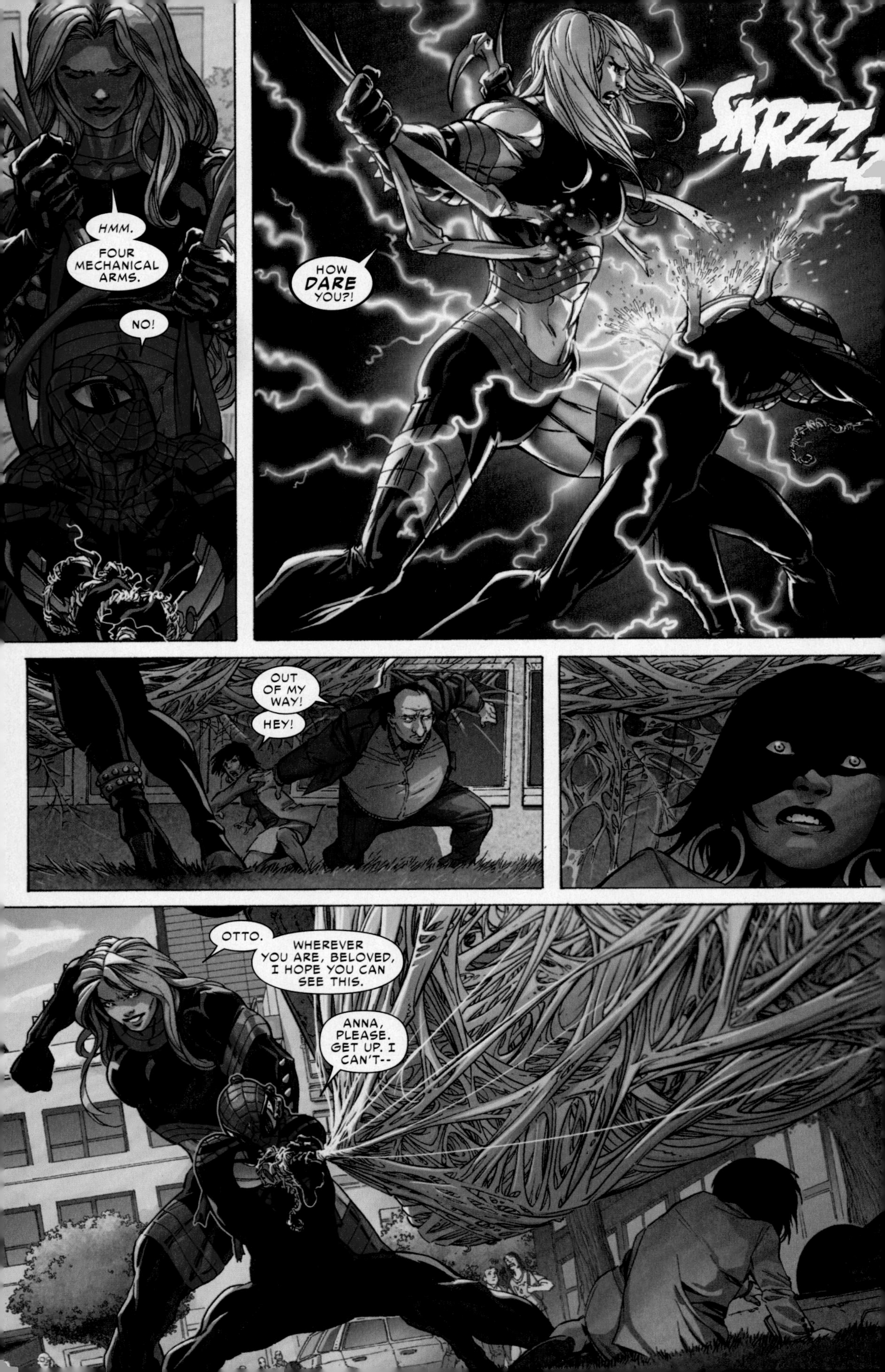
HMM.
FOUR MECHANICAL ARMS.
NO!
HOW DARE YOU?!
SKRZZ
OUT OF MY WAY!
HEY!
OTTO.
WHEREVER YOU ARE, BELOVED, I HOPE YOU CAN SEE THIS.
ANNA, PLEASE. GET UP. I CAN'T--

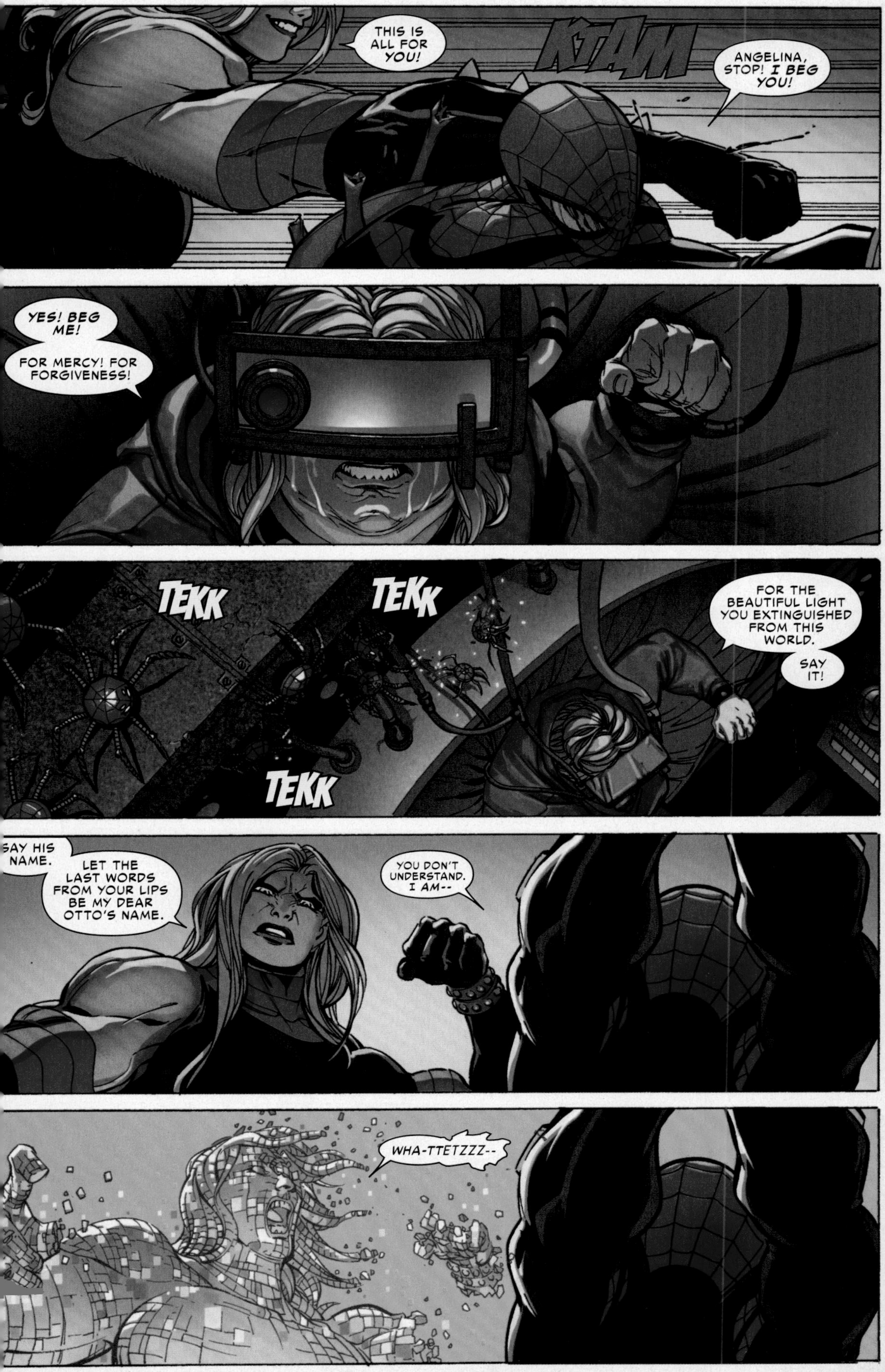
THIS IS ALL FOR YOU!
KTAM
ANGELINA, STOP! I BEG YOU!
YES! BEG ME!
FOR MERCY! FOR FORGIVENESS!
TEKK
TEKK
TEKK
FOR THE BEAUTIFUL LIGHT YOU EXTINGUISHED FROM THIS WORLD.
SAY IT!
SAY HIS NAME.
LET THE LAST WORDS FROM YOUR LIPS BE MY DEAR OTTO'S NAME.
YOU DON'T UNDERSTAND. I AM--
WHA-TTETZZZ--

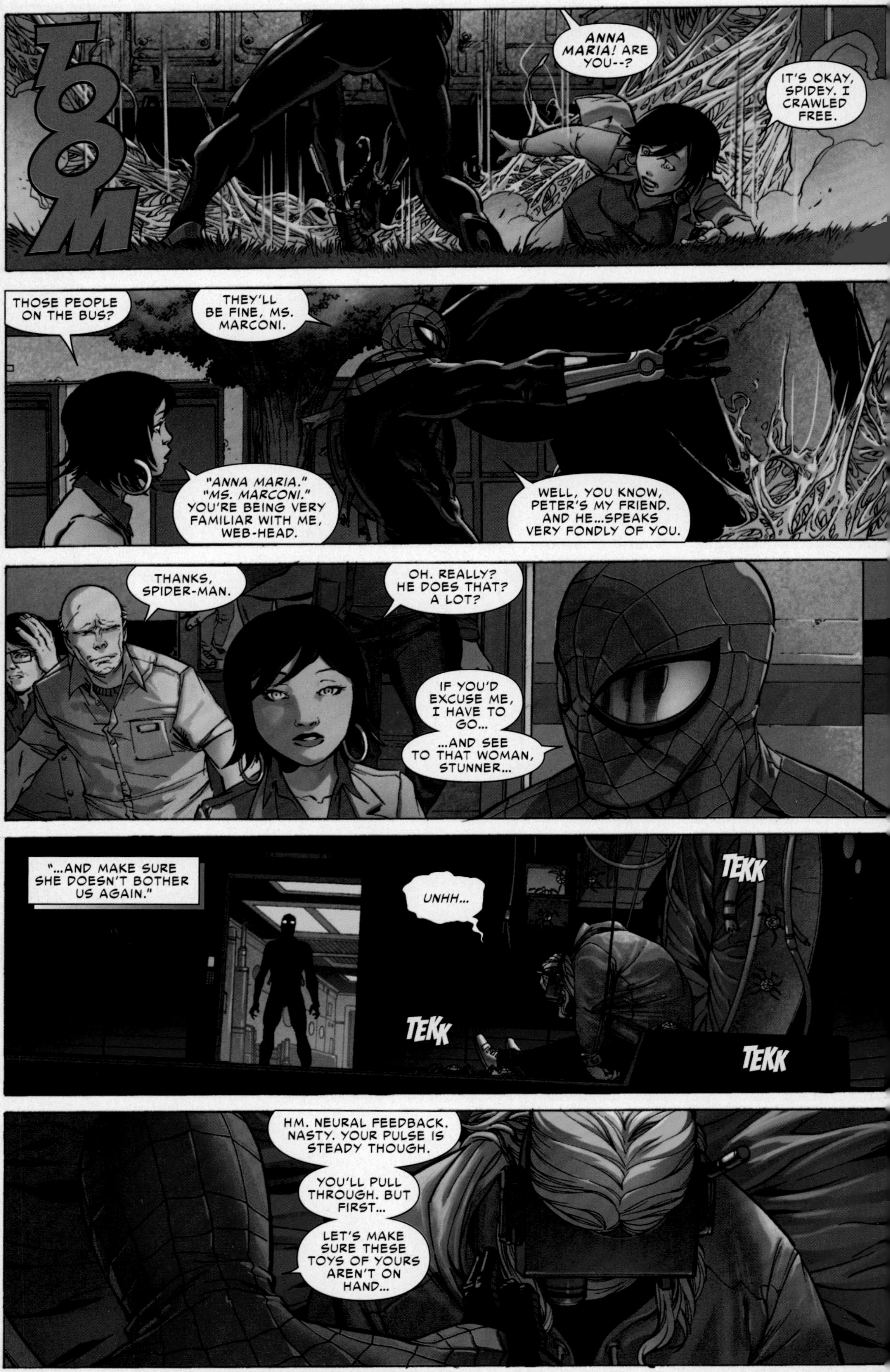
TOOM
ANNA MARIA! ARE YOU--?
IT'S OKAY, SPIDEY. I CRAWLED FREE.
THOSE PEOPLE ON THE BUS?
THEY'LL BE FINE, MS. MARCONI.
"ANNA MARIA." "MS. MARCONI." YOU'RE BEING VERY FAMILIAR WITH ME, WEB-HEAD.
WELL, YOU KNOW, PETER'S MY FRIEND. AND HE...SPEAKS VERY FONDLY OF YOU.
THANKS, SPIDER-MAN.
OH. REALLY? HE DOES THAT? A LOT?
IF YOU'D EXCUSE ME, I HAVE TO GO...
...AND SEE TO THAT WOMAN, STUNNER...
"...AND MAKE SURE SHE DOESN'T BOTHER US AGAIN."
UNHH...
TEKK
TEKK
TEKK
HM. NEURAL FEEDBACK. NASTY. YOUR PULSE IS STEADY THOUGH.
YOU'LL PULL THROUGH. BUT FIRST...
LET'S MAKE SURE THESE TOYS OF YOURS AREN'T ON HAND...

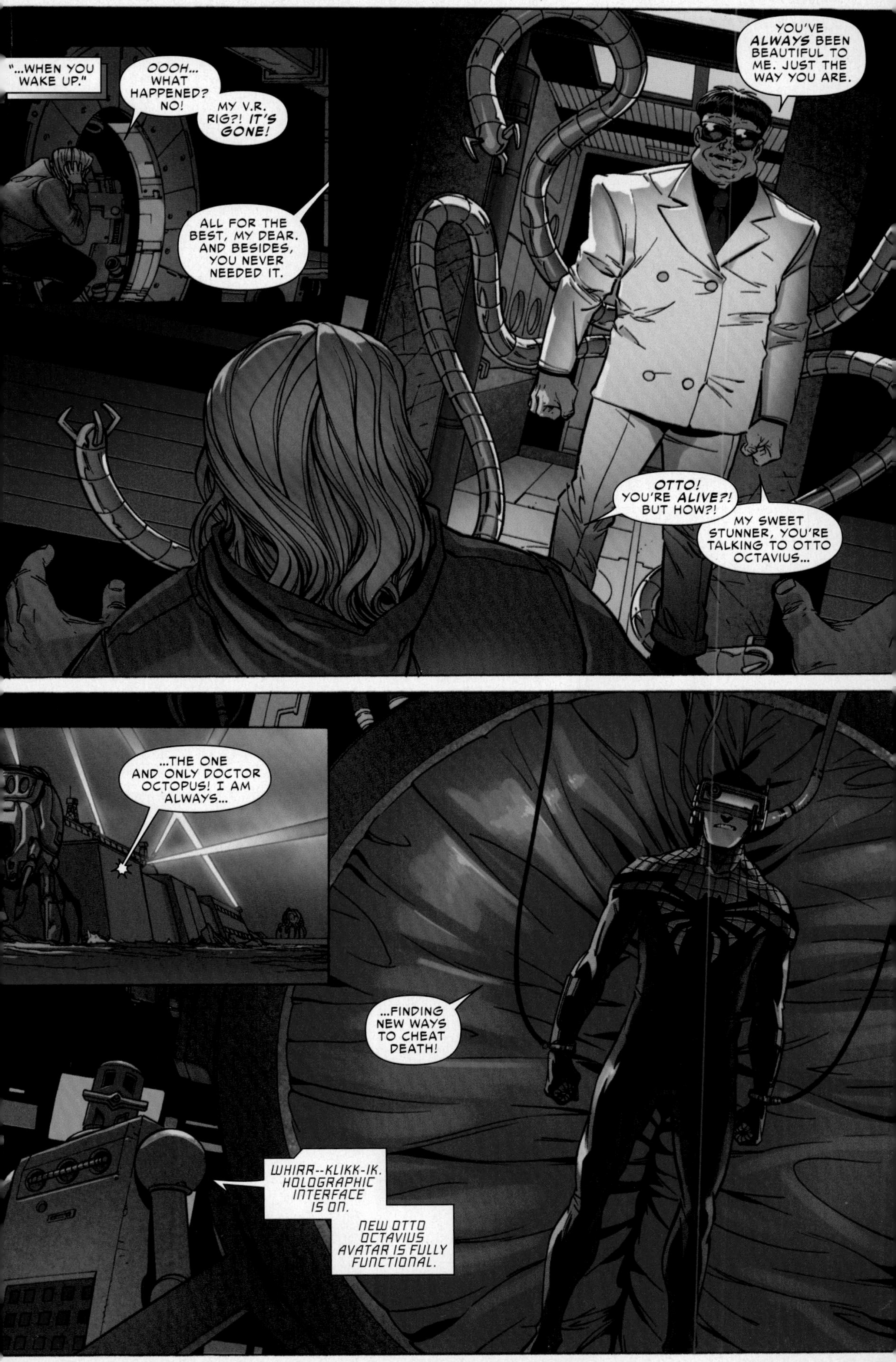

"...WHEN YOU WAKE UP."
OOOH... WHAT HAPPENED? NO!
MY V.R. RIG?! IT'S GONE!
ALL FOR THE BEST, MY DEAR. AND BESIDES, YOU NEVER NEEDED IT.
YOU'VE ALWAYS BEEN BEAUTIFUL TO ME. JUST THE WAY YOU ARE.
OTTO! YOU'RE ALIVE?! BUT HOW?!
MY SWEET STUNNER, YOU'RE TALKING TO OTTO OCTAVIUS...
...THE ONE AND ONLY DOCTOR OCTOPUS! I AM ALWAYS...
...FINDING NEW WAYS TO CHEAT DEATH!
WHIRR--KLIKK-IK. HOLOGRAPHIC INTERFACE IS ON.
NEW OTTO OCTAVIUS AVATAR IS FULLY FUNCTIONAL.

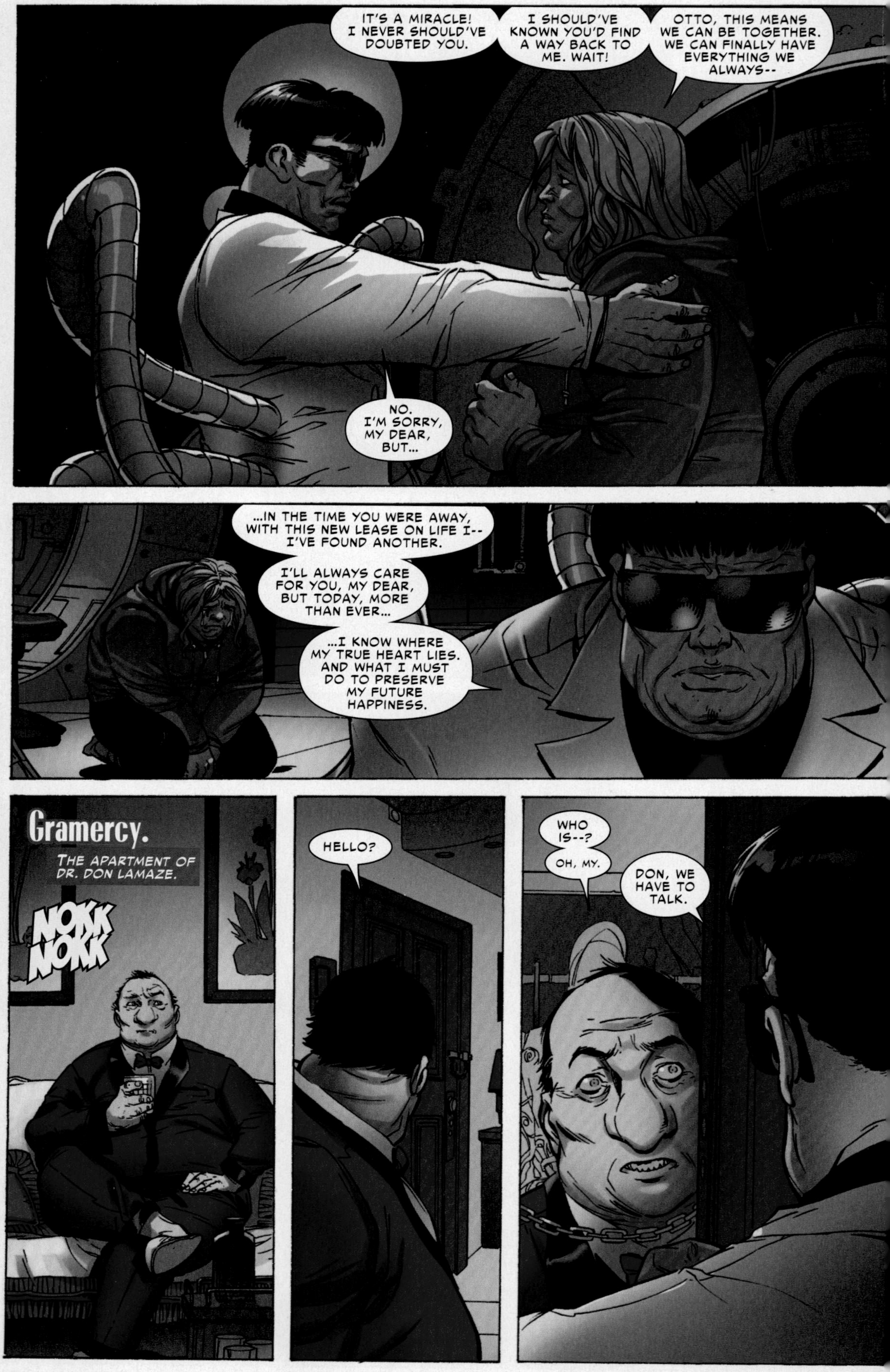
IT'S A MIRACLE! I NEVER SHOULD'VE DOUBTED YOU.
I SHOULD'VE KNOWN YOU'D FIND A WAY BACK TO ME. WAIT!
OTTO, THIS MEANS WE CAN BE TOGETHER. WE CAN FINALLY HAVE EVERYTHING WE ALWAYS--
NO. I'M SORRY, MY DEAR, BUT...
...IN THE TIME YOU WERE AWAY, WITH THIS NEW LEASE ON LIFE I-- I'VE FOUND ANOTHER.
I'LL ALWAYS CARE FOR YOU, MY DEAR, BUT TODAY, MORE THAN EVER...
...I KNOW WHERE MY TRUE HEART LIES. AND WHAT I MUST DO TO PRESERVE MY FUTURE HAPPINESS.
Gramercy.
THE APARTMENT OF DR. DON LAMAZE.
NOKK NOKK
HELLO?
WHO IS--?
OH, MY.
DON, WE HAVE TO TALK.

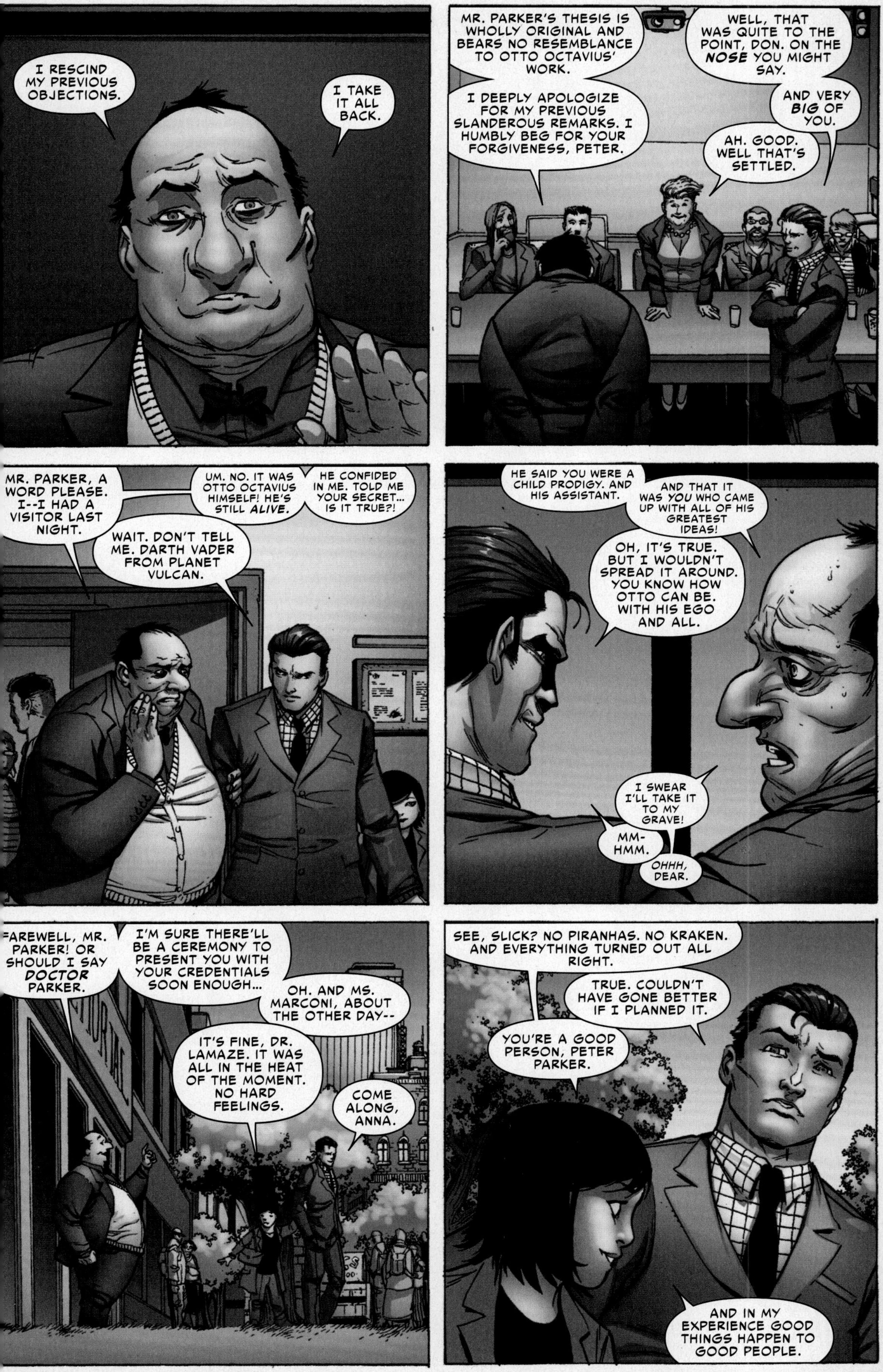
I RESCIND MY PREVIOUS OBJECTIONS.
I TAKE IT ALL BACK.
MR. PARKER'S THESIS IS WHOLLY ORIGINAL AND BEARS NO RESEMBLANCE TO OTTO OCTAVIUS' WORK.
I DEEPLY APOLOGIZE FOR MY PREVIOUS SLANDEROUS REMARKS. I HUMBLY BEG FOR YOUR FORGIVENESS, PETER.
WELL, THAT WAS QUITE TO THE POINT, DON. ON THE NOSE YOU MIGHT SAY.
AND VERY BIG OF YOU.
AH. GOOD. WELL THAT'S SETTLED.
MR. PARKER, A WORD PLEASE. I--I HAD A VISITOR LAST NIGHT.
WAIT. DON'T TELL ME. DARTH VADER FROM PLANET VULCAN.
UM. NO. IT WAS OTTO OCTAVIUS HIMSELF! HE'S STILL ALIVE.
HE CONFIDED IN ME. TOLD ME YOUR SECRET... IS IT TRUE?!
HE SAID YOU WERE A CHILD PRODIGY. AND HIS ASSISTANT.
AND THAT IT WAS YOU WHO CAME UP WITH ALL OF HIS GREATEST IDEAS!
OH, IT'S TRUE. BUT I WOULDN'T SPREAD IT AROUND. YOU KNOW HOW OTTO CAN BE. WITH HIS EGO AND ALL.
I SWEAR I'LL TAKE IT TO MY GRAVE!
MM-HMM.
OHHH, DEAR.
FAREWELL, MR. PARKER! OR SHOULD I SAY DOCTOR PARKER.
I'M SURE THERE'LL BE A CEREMONY TO PRESENT YOU WITH YOUR CREDENTIALS SOON ENOUGH...
OH. AND MS. MARCONI, ABOUT THE OTHER DAY--
IT'S FINE, DR. LAMAZE. IT WAS ALL IN THE HEAT OF THE MOMENT. NO HARD FEELINGS.
COME ALONG, ANNA.
SEE, SLICK? NO PIRANHAS. NO KRAKEN. AND EVERYTHING TURNED OUT ALL RIGHT.
TRUE. COULDN'T HAVE GONE BETTER IF I PLANNED IT.
YOU'RE A GOOD PERSON, PETER PARKER.
AND IN MY EXPERIENCE GOOD THINGS HAPPEN TO GOOD PEOPLE.

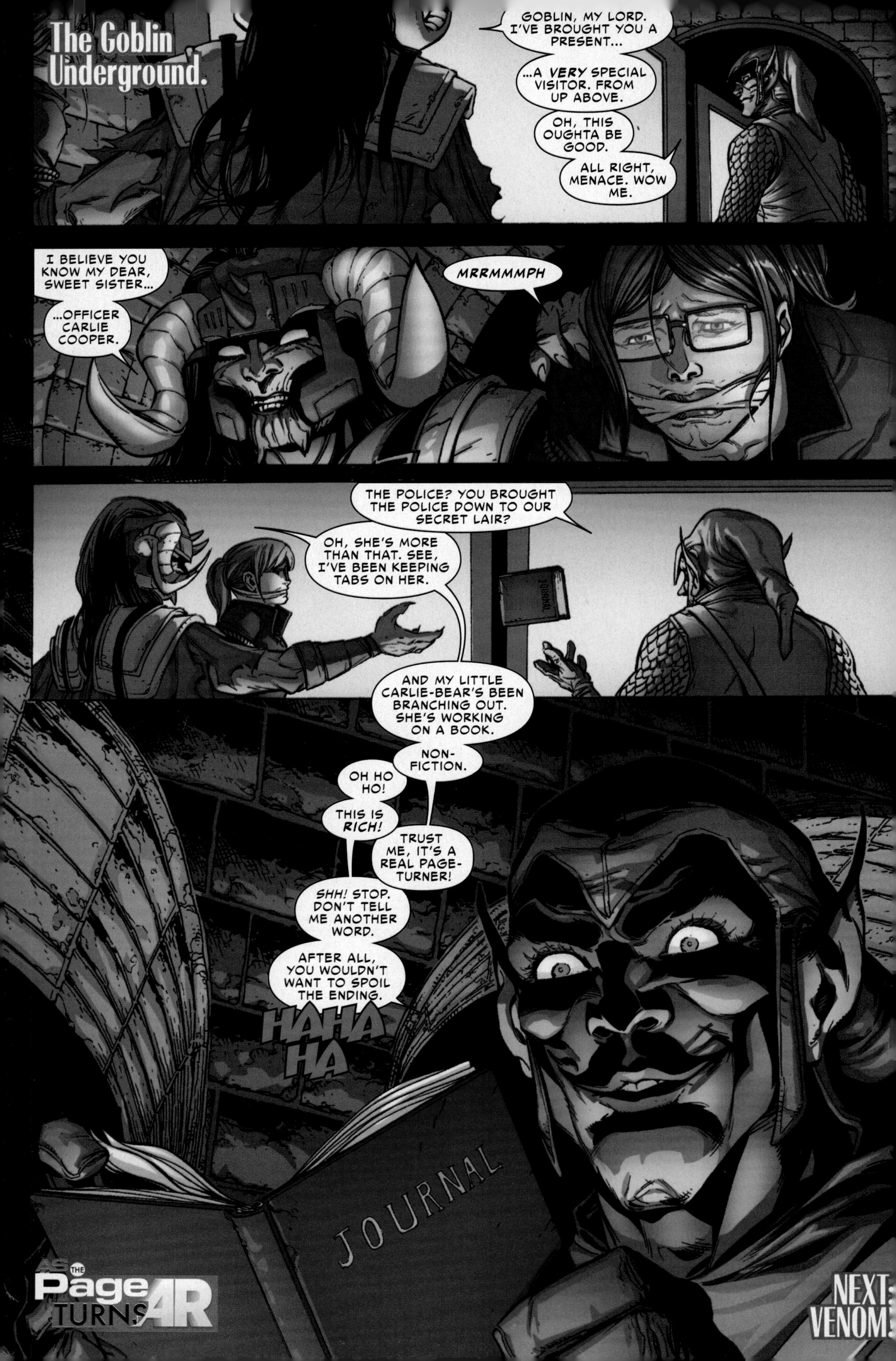The Goblin Underground.
GOBLIN, MY LORD. I'VE BROUGHT YOU A PRESENT...
...A VERY SPECIAL VISITOR. FROM UP ABOVE.
OH, THIS OUGHTA BE GOOD.
ALL RIGHT, MENACE. WOW ME.
I BELIEVE YOU KNOW MY DEAR, SWEET SISTER...
...OFFICER CARLIE COOPER.
MRRMMMPH
THE POLICE? YOU BROUGHT THE POLICE DOWN TO OUR SECRET LAIR?
OH, SHE'S MORE THAN THAT. SEE, I'VE BEEN KEEPING TABS ON HER.
AND MY LITTLE CARLIE-BEAR'S BEEN BRANCHING OUT. SHE'S WORKING ON A BOOK.
NON-FICTION.
OH HO HO!
THIS IS RICH!
TRUST ME, IT'S A REAL PAGE-TURNER!
SHH! STOP. DON'T TELL ME ANOTHER WORD.
AFTER ALL, YOU WOULDN'T WANT TO SPOIL THE ENDING.
HAHA HA
JOURNAL
AS THE Page TURNS AR
NEXT: VENOM!

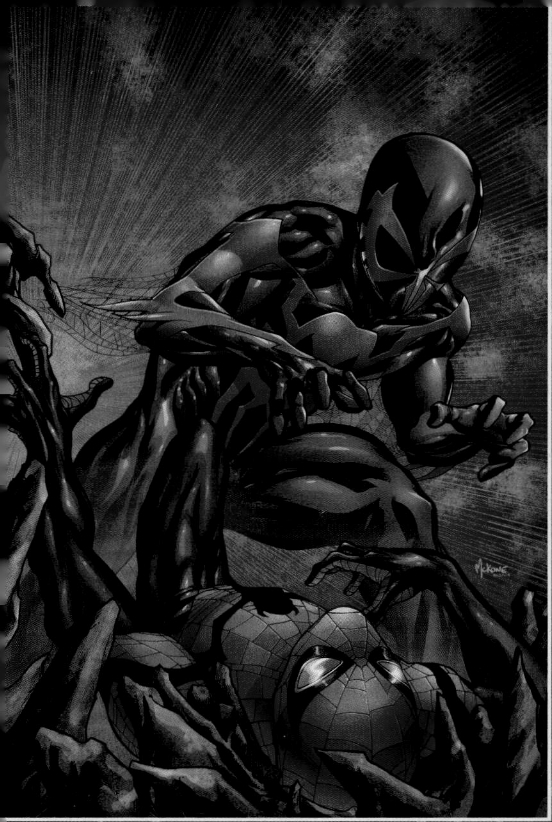

#17 HASTINGS VARIANT
Y MIKE MCKONE & PAUL MOUNTS

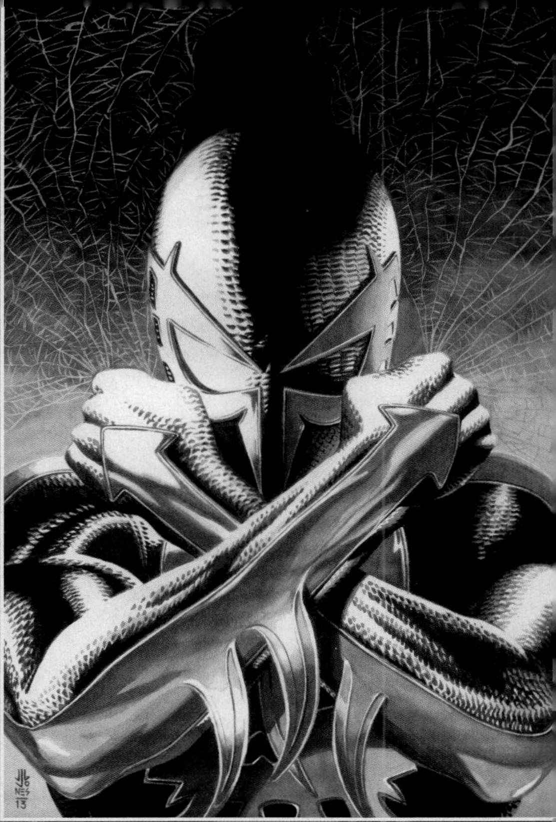

#17 VARIANT
BY J.G. JONES

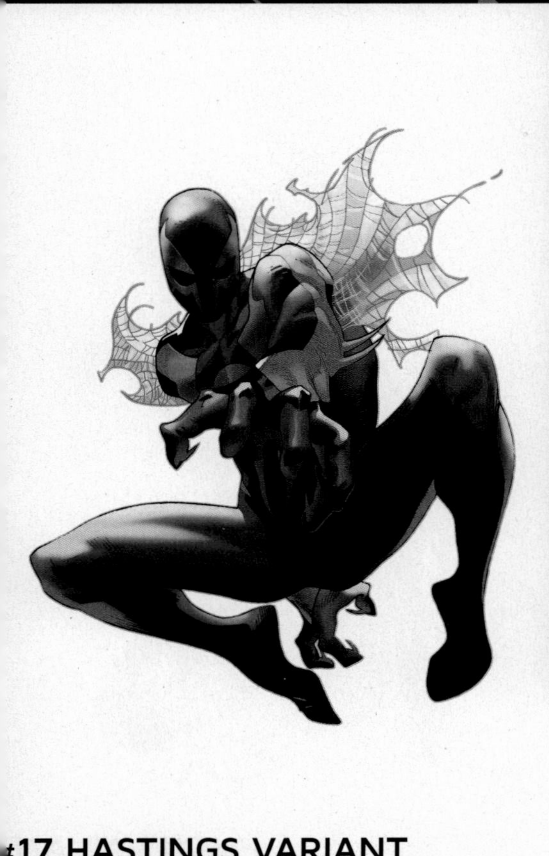

#17 HASTINGS VARIANT
Y OLIVIER COIPEL

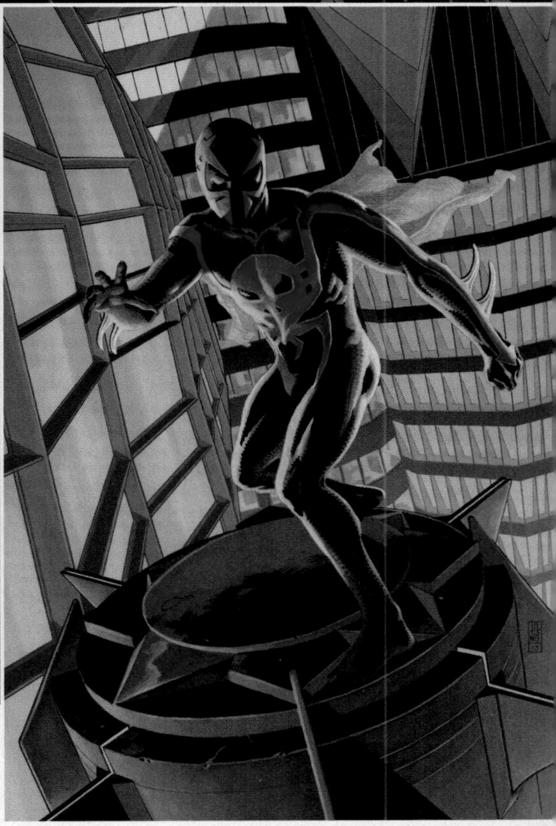

#18 VARIANT
BY J.G. JONES & DAVE STEWART

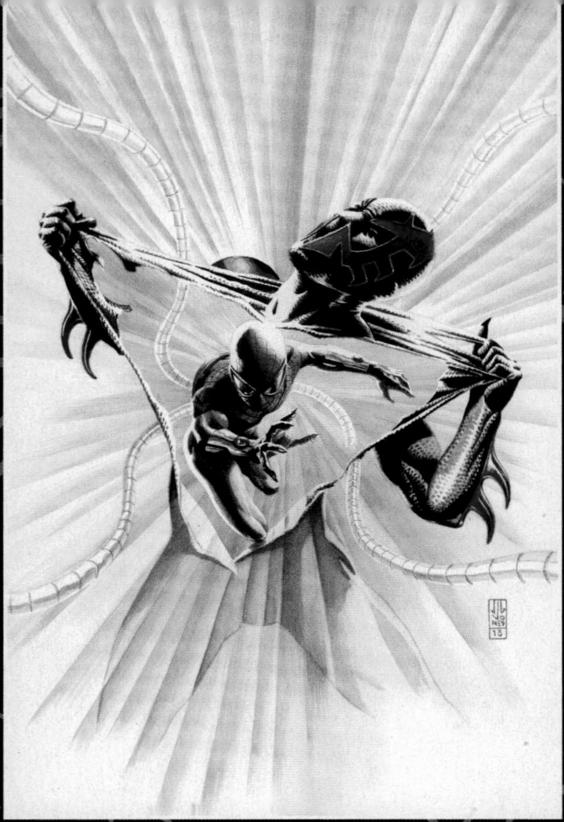

#19 VARIANT
BY J.G. JONES & DAVE STEWART

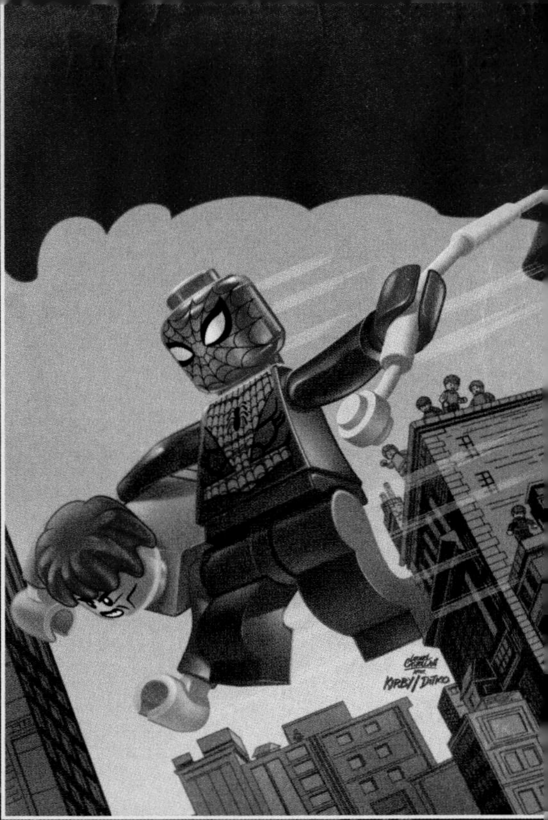

#19 LEGO VARIAN
BY LEONEL CASTELLAN

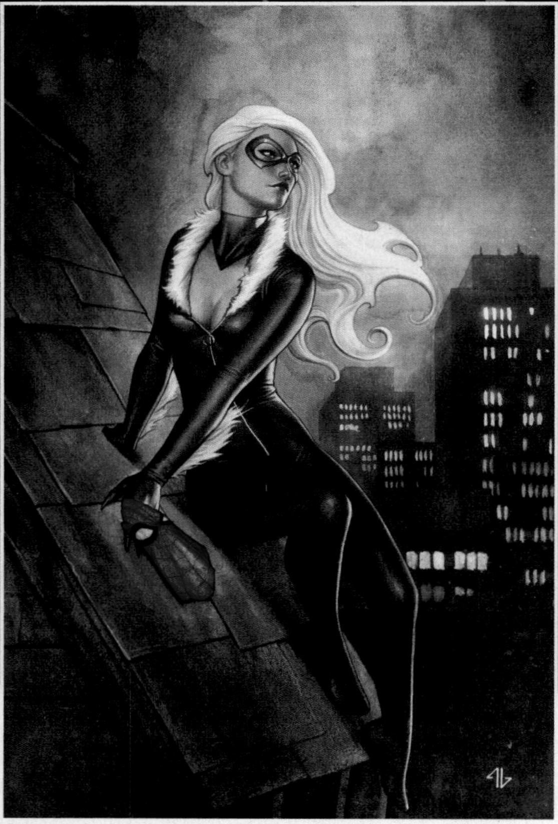

#20 VARIANT
BY ADI GRANOV

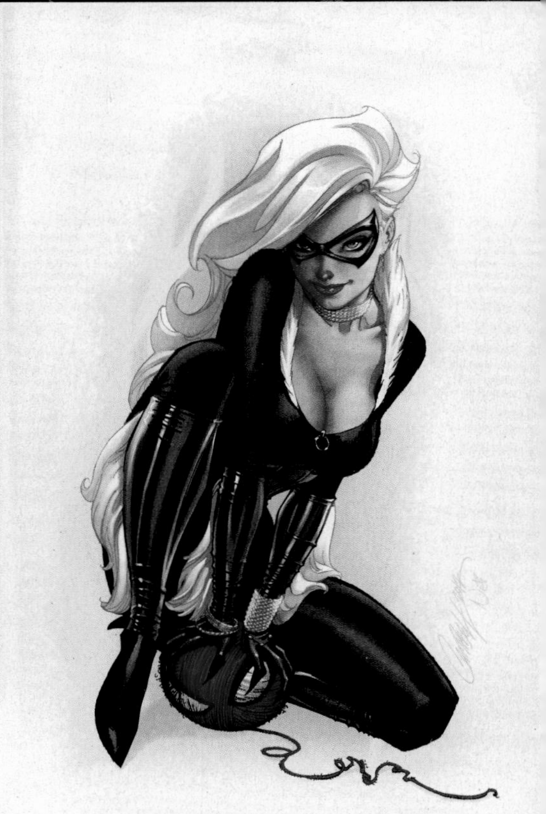

#20 VARIAN
BY J. SCOTT CAMPBELL & NEI RUFFIN

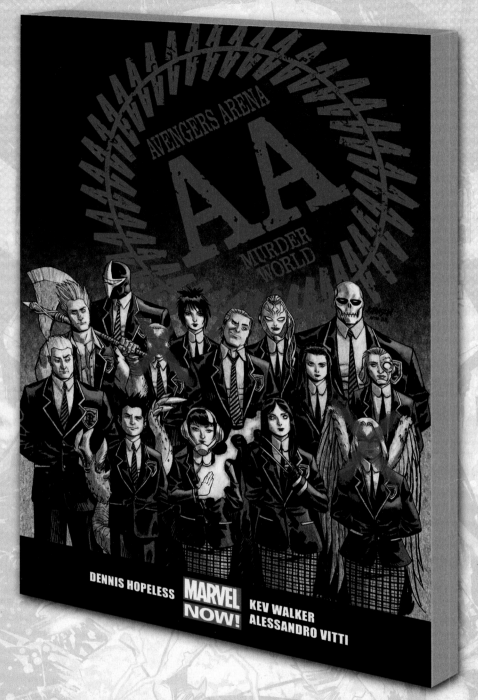

TO ACCESS THE FREE *MARVEL AUGMENTED REALITY APP* THAT ENHANCES AND CHANGES THE WAY YOU EXPERIENCE COMICS

1. Download the app for free via marvel.com/ARapp
2. Launch the app on your camera-enabled Apple iOS® or Android™ device*
3. Hold your mobile device's camera ove any cover or panel with the AR graph
4. Sit back and see the future of comics in action!

*Available on most camera-enabled Apple iOS® and Android™ devices. Content subject to change and availability.

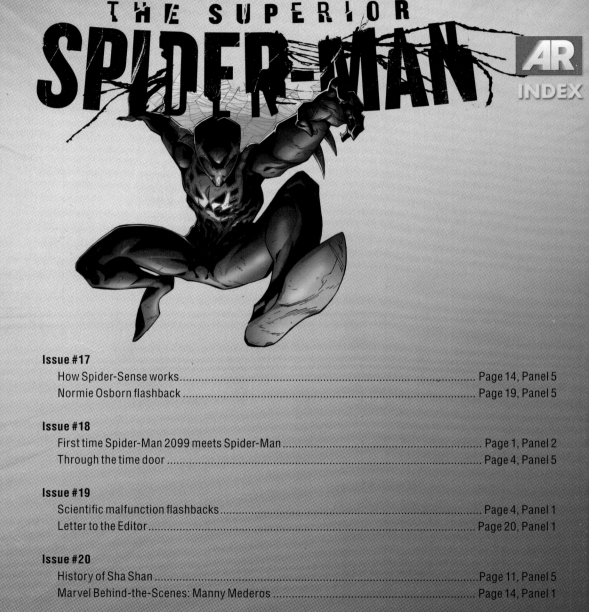

THE SUPERIOR SPIDER-MAN

AR INDEX